Literature and Catholicism in and 20th Centuries

Literature and Catholicism in the 19th and 20th Centuries

Edited by

David Torevell

Cambridge
Scholars
Publishing

Literature and Catholicism in the 19th and 20th Centuries

Edited by David Torevell

This book first published 2021. The present binding first published 2021.

Cambridge Scholars Publishing

Lady Stephenson Library, Newcastle upon Tyne, NE6 2PA, UK

British Library Cataloguing in Publication Data
A catalogue record for this book is available from the British Library

ISBN (10): 1-5275-7454-7
ISBN (13): 978-1-5275-7454-0

TABLE OF CONTENTS

FOREWORD

DAVID TOREVELL

If Nicholas Boyle is right, then literature is the employment of engaging language, free of instrumental purpose, which seeks to tell the truth. It shows us the significance and beauty of life and has an undeniable association with Being. In other words, it is revelatory. As Boyle (2004) writes, '*our* truth is being told to us and we look each other in the eyes and know that our truth is everyone else's' (2004, 130). The revelation communicated to us is that life *matters.* This insight is allied to a sense of vital enjoyment which comes about because all creation is important – even the sparrows on the window ledge. Such a recognition reflects a *Genesis* trope – 'God saw everything that he had made, and behold, it was very good' (1, 31). Literature sustains this endeavour by the memorable and innovative acts of representation of those things which are of worth to God. Whether low or high life, comic or serious, consoling or tragic, a Catholic approach to literature always conveys the worthwhileness of living and dying. Representation becomes another act of creation or, more precisely *recreation,* as it encourages those who receive it to be reformed in a shared response towards those things which are true and life-giving. There is a life embedded in literature which we recognise in conjunction with our own lives, primarily through our shared humanity and the relationships we form; there is also the wasting of it.

The Catholic literary revival in the late 19th and 20th centuries, discussed in this book, illustrates and celebrates this positive philosophy of life. It draws attention to how an impressive corpus of literature during this period reflects deeply Catholic themes and trajectories – for example, sacramentality, self-sacrifice, ritual, beauty and many others. Some of these writers were 'cradle Catholics', many were converts, and one, Thomas Mann, was neither, though you may be surprised to read about his Catholic sensibilities. Drawing from the autobiographical novelist Antonia White's observation that Catholicism exhibits a creative paradox of the supernatural and otherworldly with the human and ordinary, a large percentage of the book reflect this convergence. The contributors deal with how their chosen authors reveal a paradoxical truth about life, a claim which admits there is no significant division at all between human life and supernatural life as one cuts deeply into the other, so as to make them inseparable. Enjoyment of the things of God is made possible simply by being alive and remaining open to the wonder and sadness of everyday life and what they teach us about our universe, ourselves and others.

In his discussion of the modern Catholic literary landscape, Joseph Pearce (2014) suggests Catholicism - although no longer illegal as it was in Campion's and Southwell's Reformation days - is still considered 'illegitimate'. Perhaps 'irrelevant' is a better word, judging by those critics who airbrush out its significance and the role it plays in numerous artistic endeavours during (post)modernism. As the literary theorist, Terry Eagleton astutely puts it, the present western age regards religion, interiority and a stable self as nothing more than 'a clapped out metaphysics', but as he warns, 'to eradicate them is to abolish God by rooting out the underground places where He has been concealing himself' (2015, 186-7). More broadly, David Jasper argues that the discussion between literature and theology continues to be a crucial one, for it introduces us to the deep traditions by which we have been formed; we forget, to our peril, the nature of theology and 'the place of humanity within the span of its history and *sub specie aeternitatis*' (2016, 10).

My opening chapter discusses the way in which beauty and vocation are inextricably linked in the poetry and prose of the Victorian Jesuit poet, Gerard Manley Hopkins. Living a holy existence by means of a 'heart right' was the goal he sought, but he came to realize that this was always associated with his vocation as a poet and priest, along with his appreciation of Christ's beauty witnessed in humanity and in nature. *The Spiritual Exercises of Ignatius of Loyola.* in which he took part, reminded him of this association and the need to offer a 'sigh of consent', even if - and because - it entailed hardship and suffering. During the long retreat he made in December 1881 as part of his ongoing formation as a Jesuit, he took to heart the message of *Philippians, 2 5-11* about the sacrificial *kenosis* of his Saviour, something he sought to echo in his own life as a priest and as a poet.

The next discussion by Professor Adam Schwartz (Christendom College, USA) sets the scene for our journey into the Catholic literary imagination in the twentieth century. He suggests that in the face of a 'confident agnosticism' during modernism, it was hardly surprising that a group of leading literary intellectuals would challenge such bold positions and begin to articulate a spiritually based countercultural attack. This might be summarised as a rebellion against secularism, individualism, belief in Progress and cultural fragmentation, in favour of the supernatural, tradition, authority and what he refers to as 'civilizational integration.' If left unchecked, the very grain of Being would be trampled upon and the door pushed wide open to a flagrant and destructive will-to-power. In its place, Catholicism offered an anthropology rooted in the inalienable dignity of each person, a religious meaning to human existence and the stirrings of a moral imagination which would prevent people from collapsing too readily into avarice and the pursuit of selfish power. Catholic authors harnessed their literary skills and with their religious acumen and insight, formed a countervailing tradition in engaging and persuasive ways, a dynamic outlined throughout the book.

Two further contributions discuss Chesterton's vision of a Catholic life and what it might entail. His 1904 novel, *The Napoleon of Notting Hill* is drawn on by Dr. Daniel Frampton to demonstrate how the author offers a creative 'theology of participation', epitomised by the author's phrase 'gazing with rapt attention at the row of little shops', demonstrating how ordinary, localised things are more important than extraordinary, far off things, since they reflect divine creation. Adam Wayne is absorbed far more by Notting Hill than by world-shattering affairs. The streets themselves are starry and revelatory and point, like nothing else, to God and His wondrous work. The novel should not be seen primarily as Chesterton's treatise on anti-imperialism, but on a theological truth – the embeddedness of transcendence within immanence. In other words, it forms an imaginary account of where we are most likely to discover God while on earth.

Professor David Deavel (University of St. Thomas, USA) homes in on this theme too, suggesting that Chesterton's 1912 novel *Manalive*, through his portrait of Innocent Smith, captures a capacious and fully Catholic imagination. He relates this to the tradition of the *holy fool,* a trope identified within the broader Catholic intellectual tradition. This religious eccentric indulges in peculiar acts of poverty and charity, becomes an enigma to those closest to her and divorces herself from ordinary life. A biblical precedent for this is St. Paul's teaching about imitating the suffering Christ in our endeavours - 'we are fools for Christ, but you are wise in Christ … we are ill-clad and buffeted and homeless' (Cor 4 10-11).

The first world war writings of three soldiers – Thomas Kettle, Patrick MacGill and David Jones -- form the subject of a chapter by Dr. Terry Phillips (Honorary Research Fellow, Liverpool Hope University, UK). Her analysis situates their moving accounts within Christ's sacrifice and their identification with His saving mission. She contends that the figure of Christ provided a helpful parallel for those who believed the war was both 'holy' and 'just'. Kettle's writings show a strong feeling for the morality of war, coupled with a keen sense of national duty to fight; however, his view did not constitute an inclusive theology of redemption, since the children of Cain and the killers at the foot of the cross, were deemed unworthy of salvation. MacGill's work counters Kettle's theology by insisting that there is a shared Christianity between friend and foe, exhibited largely through the manner in which he emphasizes 'Christ as fellow-sufferer', rather than simply as redeemer. Jones' work might be said to be even more daring, as he emphasizes the sacredness of all human life and collapses all social divisions into one, witnessed most starkly in times of war, when pain and killing have no regard for rank. Published in 1937, *In Parenthesis,* highlights how the demonisation of the enemy was not shared by the ordinary soldier at all, and that all human beings, not just the allies, possessed a shared humanity with Christ.

Rev. Professor Dr. Michael Kirwan, S.J. (Loyola Institute, Trinity College, Dublin, Ireland) deals with how literary modernism in the novels of Thomas Mann, reflects distinctly religious and in particular, Catholic themes. However, he argues that a 'special pleading' is required with regard to this German author because he is sometimes thought to be not only non-Christian, but also anti-Christian. However, Kirwan argues strongly that there is a powerful religious sensibility in his publications drawing from two of his works to outline this strand – *The Magic Mountain* and *Joseph.* In Mann's portraits of Hans Castorp (*The Magic Mountain*) and Joseph, we see a 'seriousness of ethical but also religious purpose'. The way into understanding this dynamic is by exposing Mann's 'ironical' style and his search for '***bürgerliche*** (bourgeois) man'). Kirwan suggests that each of these themes has a theological ring to them, elucidating this claim with the assistance of Erich Heller who identifies a 'theology of irony' in the novelist and Johann Baptist Metz, who offers a critique of ***bürgerliche*** Christianity in light of the holocaust.

Dr. Emilio Castaño (Shandong University, China) examines the work of the early twentieth century poet and dramatist Manuel Benitez Carrasco, with particular reference to his play *Castillo de Dios* written in 1945. He argues this work was part of the revival of the *auto sacramentales* in Spanish theatre. The play is written in verse, has three acts and the plot traces salvation history from the Old to the New Testament. Reflecting the author's personal religious beliefs, the work was written only six years after the end of the Spanish civil war and during the year the second world war ended. Fittingly, the chapter shows how the text might be read as a reminder and critique of the devastating effects of tyrannical power.

The contribution by Rev. Dr. Mark Bosco, S.J. (Georgetown University, USA) centres on a comparison between the sixteenth century Italian artist Caravaggio and Flannery O'Connor to illuminate how the writer explores the crisis of meaning in the 20th century, while at the same time embracing a Catholic medieval vision of life. He claims that her success is partly due to her skill in showing how the human and divine collide. He defends the view that O'Connor and Caravaggio have something essential in common in their countering of the cultural norms of their times. For Caravaggio, this was the Protestant distrust of art and any possible alignment with the propagandist intentions of his Catholic patrons, while for O'Connor this entailed challenging the secular assumptions of her time and the pietistic leanings of a misplaced, proud American culture. In their shared exposition of the grotesque and sometimes violent epiphanies of life, both might be said to have excavated 'the contours of a Catholic baroque aesthetic'.

Dr Michael Murphy (Loyola University, Chicago, USA) offers a chapter on two writers with same surname: O'Connor. He pinpoints the theme of revelatory moments in the experiences of child characters, expressed in Flannery O'Connor's 1953 *A Temple of the Holy Ghost* and Frank O'Connor's *The Face of Evil* (1954.) Murphy shows that in both writers childhood is presented not so much as an era, but as a geographical place – 'a location with scents and sights' linked to the notion of nostalgia and humanity's embarking on a journey of *exitus* and *reditus*, the procession from and return to God; this is associated with the mystery of place and space. In more theological terms, it is a lived experience of the incarnational and the sacramental. Murphy extends these notions by suggesting that Flannery's aesthetics is largely epistemological, a distinctive way of coming to know things, best summarised as a mode of Christian realism. He notes that Frank O'Connor asks his readers what might constitute a good Catholic? One answer lies in the battle against pride and narcissism, as well as the rejection of what he calls 'bourgeois' prescriptions of sanctity. Murphy's final section explores the notion of community and solidarity, key constituents in both writers and central strands in any understanding of Catholic living.

An important African-American perspective is given by Professor Carolyn Medine (University of Georgia, USA) in her discussion of Toni Morrison's novel, *Beloved* (1987). The two central trajectories she explores are moments of revelation during the exigencies of ordinary life and key rites of passage that transform and re-create human beings and situations. The chapter begins by recalling how Morrison's confirmation name is Anthony, the patron saint of lost things. Medine relates this to our amnesia about African-American life, particularly the life of enslaved women. She reads her novel through the lens of the Catholic imagination and a distinctly Black Catholic perspective. The chapter exposes how Morrison's text reveals not only the inherent goodness of the world, but also how this is frequently shot through with moments of revelatory significance either through a radical insight by one of the characters, or by means of a divine power slicing into the drama of ordinary life – in other words, *Kairos* moments. Healing brought about by ritual also reveals something distinctive about a Catholic way of life and it is this feature which Medine discusses at some length.

I hope you enjoy reading this Catholic vision of life.

References

Boyle, Nicholas. 2004. *Sacred and Secular Scriptures. A Catholic Approach to Literature.* Cambridge: CUP.

Jasper, David. 2016. *Literature and Theology as a Grammar of Assent* London: Routledge.

Pearce, Joseph. 2014. *Catholic Literary Giants. A Field Guide to the Catholic Literary Landscape.* San Francisco: Ignatius Press.

ACKNOWLEDGEMENTS

When I was sixteen years old and in the lower sixth of my Catholic grammar school in Blackburn, I decided to read during the Christmas holidays my first big novel – Alexander Solzhenitsyn's *The First Circle*. It had such an impact on me that I decided I wanted to read English Literature at University. This decision was endorsed by my inspiring 'A' level English teacher, Brian Donaldson, who revealed to me the wonders of Shakespeare and much else in the literary canon. As it happened, I ended up completing a combined degree in Religion and English Literature and I'm glad I did; it was an enriching experience.

This interdisciplinary interest continued after graduation and is reflected now in this book. It includes contributors who, like me, have a passion for great writing which deals imaginatively and subtly with theological ideas. I am deeply grateful to all the American, Irish, Spanish and British academics for their time, efficiency, warmth and generosity of spirit as well as their undoubted competence, as I compiled this text during the global pandemic. I would also like to pay tribute to the following individuals who have sustained me both personally and professionally, over a number of years: Michael Ford, Patrice Haynes, Elizabeth Harris, Richard Hooper, Clive Palmer, David Phinnemore, Damian Norton, Mike Thompson, Paul Rowan and Gordon Abbs. And to my close family for their love and support.

THE CALL OF STRANGE BEAUTY
IN THE POETRY AND PROSE
OF GERARD MANLEY HOPKINS

DAVID TOREVELL

'Ah! There was a *heart right*!
There was a single eye!
Read the unshapeable shock night
And knew the who and the why'
(Hopkins: *The Wreck of the Deutschland* – st., 29).

Introduction

The poetry and prose of the English Jesuit priest, Gerard Manley Hopkins (1844-89), continue to inspire readers, academics and students alike, who regard him as one of the greatest of all late 19th century European poets (Brett, 1965; Ellsberg, 2017; Gardner, 1971; MacKenzie, 1970; Mariani, 2018; Robson, 2018).[1] In the light of western secularization and de-traditionalization, this is an intriguing phenomenon. This chapter focuses on two dimensions which assist appreciation of his work – *vocation and beauty*. While I expound these two categories as distinct facets of investigation, I

---

[1] It was not until 1918 that Hopkins' friend, Robert Bridges, sought to get Hopkins' poetry published. 750 copies of his work were made available, but it took ten years to sell that number. The Jesuits themselves were never fully convinced of the beauty and significance of his poetry, and it was not until the 1930s that a number of leading poets in Oxford, including W. H. Aden and Stephen Spender, recognised his genius (Mariani, 2018). The American poet, Robert Lowell, admired Hopkins for his 'heroic sanctity' and understood him as living an exemplary Jesuitical life - 'a soldier's life, close to the physical Incarnation, in some ways rather footloose; it seems to flower most in furious activity, as in the case of the Canadian martyrs' (1944, 583-84). Lowell converted to Catholicism largely due to Hopkins' influence. The American poets, John Berryman and Hart Crane, were also deeply affected by his work, as was Denise Levertov. His extraordinary appeal continues worldwide today.

present an argument which suggests their inseparability. The 'call' and corresponding 'sigh' that Hopkins felt to write poetry *and* to become a priest were never wrenched from his experience and appreciation of beauty. In particular, the beauty of Christ, as reflected in humanity and nature, was the overriding influence and driving force of his life, even though this became challenging for him on a daily basis. The 'great sacrifice' of Christ was to become so embedded in his consciousness that it became impossible for him to regulate his life without recourse to its theological dynamic. Despite feelings of 'strangeness', unrest, alienation, loneliness, ill-heath and depression during his relatively short life, his work and priesthood are testimony to this 'sacrifice', offered for the sake of others, for whom he wished his endeavours to be 'as the circling bird', bringing order, harmony and 'Love, O my God' (*Let me be to Thee as the circling bird*).

Vocation

Living a holy existence by means of a 'heart right' *(The Wreck of the Deutschland,* stanza 29), was always what Hopkins sought, but as his life progressed, he realised this would inevitably entail disappointment and suffering. During a retreat in Beaumont in September 1883, he wrote, 'In meditating on the Crucifixion, I saw how my asking to be raised to a higher degree of grace was asking also to be lifted on a higher cross' (Hopkins, 1959a, 254). Like Newman, he understood failure as success, epitomised by the paschal mystery of Christ and taught how the good cannot conquer, except by suffering (Nixon, 1989, Ker, 2007; Schlatter, 2008). The annihilation of the self was a necessary step to take before a higher stage of spiritual awareness could take place. *Carrion Comfort* relates how avoidance of such mortification *is* one possibility; he 'Can something hope, wish day come, not choose not to be'. On the surface, this act of free-will seems a defiant declaration of resilience in the face of depression, but for Hopkins it amounted to a selfish example of disobeying his Creator. As Wolfe comments, '… in not choosing not to be, he is pitting himself against the Almighty. Taking pride in the invincible human spirit, Hopkins is coming close to denying man's essential dependence on God' (1968, 91). This tension between Hopkins' own will and God's will is witnessed throughout his life and poetry, becoming a constant struggle for him as a Jesuit 'Soldier of Christ'. In *The Soldier*, he admires the one 'who served his soldiering through…' and he asks why do we look up to such a person? His answer: because his selfless calling and action are 'manly' and the reward is great, because Christ out of gratefulness and love for the soldier will 'lean forth' and 'kiss' his endeavours, crying 'O Christ-done deed!' The conflict is essentially about what one is called to do and whether one can answer that invitation. During his retreats, Hopkins reflected prayerfully on St Ignatius' *The Spiritual Exercises* and would have been familiar with the words '… if someone did not answer his call, he would be scorned and upbraided by everyone and accounted as an unworthy knight' (Ignatius of Loyola, 1991,146). In light of such quotations, he deliberated throughout his life on whether or not his vocation as a priest could be reconciled with his yearning to be a poet. At one stage, he burned all the poems he had written.

Hopkins sees in the figure of the martyr a supreme model of answering Christ's demanding call and refers to 'The Christ-ed beauty' of St Margaret Clitheroe's 'mind'. In his sermon at St Joseph's Church, Leigh, Lancashire, in December 1879, he tells the congregation that she was 'so marvellously cheerful and happy' (Hopkins, 1959a, 48) on her final journey to painful death in York in 1586 and suggests to parishioners that they should react in a similar spirit during their own tribulations. He also wrote a 'great ode' on the Jesuit St Edmund Campion who was hanged, drawn and quartered for treason at Tyburn in 1581, but this has not survived (Dubois, 2017, 114). In *The Wreck of the Deutschland,* he equates the death of the 'tall nun' due to her banishment, with Christ's passion; she becomes a 'martyr-master'(st. 21). Any such attainment of a Christ-like persona in relation to a divine call dominated Hopkins' thinking. In one of his *Sermons* he describes how St Joseph travelled to Bethlehem because of the Roman census, which was 'inconvenient and painful' but was necessary to serve the divine plan (1959a, 263). What makes a person who he really is - and free - is partly a decisive willingness to obey a transcendent call. As Sobolev comments, '… what matters is not only the deed, but the choice, the action of the free will (of the *arbitrium* in his scholastic terms), which is the direct continuation of the self in the realm of inner spiritual freedom' (2001, 308). The gradual perfection of a person comes about by the cumulative choices he makes and by committing himself to a sense of duty, even though Hopkins acknowledges this is testing when 'work goes on in a great system and machinery which even drags me on with collar round my neck though I could and do neglect my duty …' (1959a, 263).

For Hopkins, genuine 'self-consciousness' is about discovering the uniqueness of one's own personhood and destiny, without which human fulfilment and happiness are not possible. By reading Duns Scotus's lectures given in Oxford in 1298, he learnt the importance of God-given individuality and of appreciating that one is not like any other being. One of the medieval theologian's disputed questions is: '*Utrum substantia materialis per aliquid positivum intrinsecum sit de se individua'* - whether material substance is of itself individual through some positive intrinsic thing'- (Duns Scotus, 1987, *Ordinatio,* Distinction 3, Q.2.) In his *Comments on the Spiritual Exercises*, he echoes the theologian's claim: 'Nothing else in nature comes near to this unspeakable stress of pitch, distinctiveness, and selving, this selfbeing of my own' (Hopkins, 1989, 309). However, the 'self' cannot bestow 'self' upon 'oneself' alone - it must come from without: 'to be determined and distinctive is a perfection, either self-bestowed or bestowed from without' (McKenzie, 1989, 312). Like Jacob wrestling with the angel, Hopkins battled against any Pelagian self-determination, telling himself not 'to feast on thee' (*Carrion Comfort*). This is not to suggest that he does not see individuality as a good in itself, but it must be related to the grace-filled harmony of all things, exemplified in the beauty of the chestnut which is both original and part of a universal species. *Haecceitas* ('thisness') *is* the key to understanding *humanitas* but is only made sense of in relation to losing the self to something greater. Purcell's music 'is the rehearsal/Of abrupt self there so thrusts on, so throngs the ear' but is only so (as he adds in his introductory rubric to the poem) because 'he has uttered in notes the very make and species of man … and in all men generally' (*Henry Purcell*).

Perfecting the Self

Perfectionism was a driving motivation and incentive for Hopkins. As a workaholic, he strove to the point of obsession for the very best he could do, and this applied to his spiritual life too. Following a strong Ignatian lead, he knew that humanity was 'made to give to God glory and to mean to give it; to praise God freely, willingly to reverence him, gladly to serve him' (Hopkins, 1959a, 239). Deeply influenced by St Paul's 'hymn' in Philippians 2.1-11, Hopkins loved Christ because he 'annihilated himself, taking the form of servant … he emptied himself' (Hopkins, 1959, 108). He pledged to do likewise, even though he knew this would entail an intense struggle with the God he loved. In *Carrion Comfort* God is 'lion-limb' with 'devouring eyes' and that is why, at times, the poet is 'frantic to avoid' and 'flee'. He was frequently agonised with the question: 'Can I face and act on who Christ wishes me to become, as He Himself did?' As a Jesuit, he would have practised the *Particular Examen* in the *Spiritual Exercises,* which involved a daily self-scrutiny to encourage and sustain the desire to live like Christ. The text makes a distinction between 'consolation' and 'desolation' within the spiritual life, the former being characterised by joy when attracted to heavenly things and 'desolation' when there is loss of hope, a darkening of the soul and a troubling of mind, a movement to base and worldly things

(Ignatius, 1991). The struggle which Hopkins, like all Jesuits faced, was to align oneself to 'consolation' by relentlessly following God's directive of service, not one's own.

However, as von Balthasar notes, there is a more central question: 'What is the human self, the person, in the face of God's gracious election in Christ?' (1986, 377). It is to this matter that I now turn. Hopkins' attempt to address this dilemma is given primarily in three prose pieces: *Homo creatus est* (1880), *On Creation and Redemption: The Great Sacrifice* (November, 1881) and *On Personality, Grace and Free Will* (December, 1881), the latter two written during his nine month tertianship (his Long Retreat) at Roehampton. The first, written on 20th August in Liverpool when he was 36 years old, is his account of what he considers to be the foundational principles of the *Spiritual Exercises*. His understanding of personhood and vocation come into view here: 'I find myself both as man and as myself something most determined and distinctive, at pitch, more distinctive and higher pitched than anything else I see' (Hopkins, 1958, 122). He acknowledges that his life is exactly aimed at something, like an arrow that hits the bull's-eye, set on its course, marked out, harmonised, picked out, elected. The source of this pitch is the One who is Himself 'of finer and higher pitch' and who is able to 'force forward the starting and stubborn elements to the one pitch required' (notice here the trope of 'movement' and any possible resistance to this). This determination is felt in one's sensuousness, the feeling one has of oneself: 'that taste of myself, of *I* and *me,* above and in all things, which is more distinctive than the taste of ale or alum, more distinctive than the smell of walnut leaf or camphor, and is uncommunicable by any means to another man … to me there is no resemblance: searching nature I taste *self* but at one tankard, that of my own being' (Hopkins, 1959a, 123**).** However, clearly, Hopkins *did* try in poetry to transmit this inalienable 'taste' of self and individuality in both human beings and nature.

A person is able to choose from his 'freedom of field' what he wishes to achieve in his life. This becomes perfected over time, as the individual integrates himself with the distinctive taste and sound of his own being, preconceived and destined by God from eternity. St. Ignatius explains how God trains the human will to choose what God has *already* chosen for him from eternity (St. Ignatius, 1991, 135). It is necessary to 'ask in what kind of life or in what state his Divine Majesty wishes to make use of us?' (St. Ignatius, 1991, 35). This requires a disciplining of the mind, so that it can choose in keeping with the mind of Christ (de Mello, 2010). If there is no internalised personal philosophy in keeping with the Christ's way of seeing things, a person is unlikely to make the correct decision. Hopkins took seriously the *videre personas* and *videre locum* of Ignatian contemplation: 'As all places are at some point of the compass and we may face to them: so every real person living or dead or to come has his quarter in the round of being, is lodged somewhere and not anywhere, and the mind has a real direction toward him' (Hopkins, 1959a, 186). However, because there is a selfish reluctance to choose this direction as a result of sin, it can become a refusal to opt for the archetype of the self, conceived and chosen by God and, logically, for it to develop into the murder of God, from where sin 'receives its meaning and structure, and to which it is in fact related to the Cross of Christ' (von Balthasar, 1986, 378). Hopkins' understanding of grace is crucial to this estimation of personal choice (*arbitrium*), for this is how a person is able to determine himself in relation to the supernatural plan. Prevenient (forestalling) grace moves us naturally towards the good – 'it *rehearses* in us our consent beforehand' (Hopkins, 1959a, 150). As it penetrates, movement starts to occur, a new 'strain' for the exercise of freedom, a new 'cleave' associated with a 'shift' occurs. Then, an emerging consenting self starts to occur, and at this stage the personal *arbitrium* begins to travel along the road to a higher self, accompanied by grace 'in a decision that man can achieve only inchoately, only in a "sighing of consent"' (Balthasar, 1986, 379). Hopkins writes that this decision is 'found to be no more than the mere wish, discernible by God's eyes, that it might do as he wishes, might correspond, might say Yes to him… and this last sigh of desire, this one aspiration, is the life and spirit of a man …' (Hopkins, 1959a, 155). This 'sigh' is 'in fact prayer', an 'aspiration or stirring of the spirit toward God is a *forestall* of the thing to be done' and once this is acted upon, the decision made becomes 'the bridge across the gulf between humanity and God'. The future is open to change now since 'The sigh of correspondence links the present … to the future … it *begins* to link it, it is the first infinitesimal link in the chain or step of the road' (Hopkins, 1959a, 158). At the height of this free positive response to God's calling, one experiences 'God's finger touching the very vein of personality … and man can respond to... by bare acknowledgement only, the counter stress which God alone can feel…' (Hopkins, 1959a, 158). Humanity it still free to discard this future, as Hopkins was free to do throughout his life, and to abandon his priesthood and return to being a poet or another occupation as his primary calling.

Hopkins tries to gauge whether the emerging self can be compared to the self in other things. He rejects chance but offers that maybe some universal spirit of nature or the world (in the Hegelian sense), is 'enselfed in my self.' However, this does not seem to be the case, since 'self tastes different to him than to me' (Hopkins, 1959a, 129). It is God, says von Balthasar in his summary of Hopkins' position, who 'as the highest self may indwell all created persons in virtue of his uniqueness and transcendence, but only because he has singled out these selves ... and set them in being' (1986, 376). In one of his 1882 sermons, Hopkins takes up Bonaventure's theology of 'utterance' carried forward by Scotus: 'God's utterance of himself in himself is God the Word, outside of himself in this world. The world, then, is word, expression, news of God. Therefore, its end, its purport, its meaning, is God and its life or work to name and praise him' (Hopkins, 1959a, 129). His laudatory poem about nature *Pied Beauty* starts with 'Glory be to God for dappled things' and ends with the exhortation 'Praise him'. And *Harry Ploughman* tells of the dignity of manual labour out of a sense of 'selving' and service to others: 'And features, in flesh, what deed he each must do -/His sinew-service where do'.

Hopkins developed his ideas about the person during a Long Retreat he undertook in December 1881 and it centres around the 'great sacrifice' of Christ. Following Philippians 2:5-11, he writes that Christ 'annihilated himself... taking the form of servant; that is, he could not but see what he was, God, but he would see it as if he did not see it ... he emptied or exhausted himself so far as that was possible.... It is this holding back of himself ... seems to me the root of all his holiness and the imitation of this is the root of all moral good in other men' (Hopkins, 1959a, 108). The eternal, universal, temporal and spatial instantiation of God in Christ is seen in the emptying and sacrifice of Himself in the created order. Hopkins realised how this theme was the key to unlocking the Christological history of the universe and his own life. He did not believe that Christ became incarnate due to humanity's sinfulness but saw creation as dependent upon the incarnation. He believed it as an act of love which would have taken place in one form or another, even if there had not been any sin. Again, influenced by Scotus, he saw that the world of angels and humanity were fields for Christ where He was able to offer his joyful adoration of the Father. He became increasingly interested not only in how Christ is the 'inscape' of creation, but also how humanity could work out God's design for themselves and the world, through their own sacrificial choices and actions. After reading Marie Lataste's work in 1878, he began to formulate how there were two 'strains' or intentions by which God acts on the world. There is the creative strain which moves things according to their nature and there is the sacrificial strain which depends upon the personal choices of free agents. The latter is rooted in the sacrifice of Christ, and 'is a consequence and shadow of the procession of the Trinity, from which mystery sacrifice takes its rise. ... It is as if the blissful agony or stress of selving in God had forced out drops of sweat or blood, which drops were the world' (Hopkins, 1959a, 110). Both as a priest and poet, he wished to imitate the 'Great Sacrifice' and believed that Lucifer's sin was an excessive, narcissistic dwelling on his own nature as likeness to God, so much so that when newer images of God presented themselves, he averted his will from them. The exemplar to be imitated is Christ at Gethsemane, who kept his own free will balanced as he learnt to follow the divine will. Hopkins derives the distinction between the elective will (*voluntas ut arbitrium*) and the 'affective will' (*voluntas ut natura*) from St Ignatius and sought to live out the non-separation of desire and choice, epitomised in the marriage union. In *'As kingfishers catch fire'*, he writes that 'Each mortal thing does one thing … Crying *What I do is me: for that I came'*, showing how doing and being are interconnected and, as in St Augustine of Hippo's writings, demonstrating how humanity is free to choose the objects of their love which, in turn, may lead to a flight to the divine. As he sets forth in *Love preparing to fly:* 'He play'd his wings as though for flight … In eddies of the wind he went/At last up the blue element'.

There are times when Hopkins clearly cannot keep desire and choice in union, when the recalcitrant will struggles against all that is most attractive to its higher nature. What becomes clear in Hopkins' life, poems and prose, is that this 'natural' tendency to choose the desirable was a fraught one for him to sustain. His own struggles with his sexual feelings and his constant sense of alienation, made the inseparability difficult at times. In *Carrion Comfort*, he experiences the divine as 'terrible' and questions why God would 'rude on me /Thy wring-world right foot rock? 'Is it to bring about 'joy' within God or within himself or both? Whichever it is, like Jacob, the poet lay 'wrestling with (my God!) my God'. The sheer number of heart-felt questions in the poem is testimony to Hopkins' inability to answer them definitively in his own life. [2]

---

[2] Sobolev puts forward the thesis that there is a severe split in Hopkins between faith and human existence. He refers to how during a retreat in 1988 he indicates how the earthly life can be compared to a person who is dazzled by a spark or star in the darkness. Sobolev argues that there is an ontological dichotomy between human existence and faith. Unlike Aquinas who sees this division is metaphysically overcome by recognising the goodness of the world, Hopkins acknowledges a real discrepancy between the natural world and human living, although he does see the possibility of redemption when the two realms come side by side. But he suggests that this remains only a possibility – it is part of a *colloquy,* a wish, a summons. Even in *God's Grandeur,* which is regarded as one of Hopkins' most positive poems, the discrepancy between nature and human existence is great. Although the *volta* marks

A Christic Form

Hopkins believes that the creation of the world is an implication of the Incarnation; thus, it follows, that the cosmos manifests as a whole, a Christological form, if seen with a spiritual eye. Even in the most challenging occurrences, Christ is witnessed and 'admired'. In the storm and devastation of *The Wreck of the Deutschland,* he is able to 'admire thee, master of the tides/Of the yore-flood, of the year's fall; The recurb and recovery of the gulf's sides/' (st. 32). Through Christ's descent into hell and a person's imitative spiritual death of himself, a victory will occur. Conversely, those who live simply for themselves, can never ascend through descent, just as the murderer in *St. Winefred's Well* only has 'thoughts sour as blood' and in refusing to yield to Christ, no longer hopes or prays and ends in 'despair'. Hopkins wishes for the brother and sister in his 1886 unfinished poem, *On the Portrait of Two Beautiful, Young People,* a life of 'selfless self of self' which is 'most strange, most still', in other words, one devoted to following Christ's ways. And in *'As kingfishers catch fire',* he records that Christ is able to be 'enselved' in each person, if he works with God's grace, to the extent that He '…plays in ten thousand places,/Lovely in limbs, and lovely in eyes not his', a metaphor reiterated in *On Personality, Grace and Free Will* : 'That is Christ playing at me and me playing at Christ, only that it is no play but truth; That is Christ *being me* and me being Christ' (Hopkins, 1959a,154).

---

a dividing line allowing the poet to return to nature once again in the sestet, the theodicean question at the end of the first quatrain remains unanswered. The sonnet implies that human existence does not correspond to nature, not only due to sin but 'gives birth to metaphysical questions that the poem has to leave unanswered' (2011, 119). However, he does concede that for Hopkins the poetic space can become both the mirror and the symbolic alternative to his existential situation.
I am in part agreement with Sobolev's thesis and while I acknowledge Hopkins is disappointed with humanity's failures and sin and gives no easy answers to the apparent meaninglessness of human existence, his poetry as a whole, gives testimony to the redemptive power of human suffering and alienation and there is a strong sense in some of Hopkin's poetry that once the beauty of Christ's theophany is recognised, human life itself becomes transformed. The fact that Hopkins felt alienation, anxiety and depression for some of his life, does not mean he experienced a severe split between nature and life in the manner in which Sobelov suggests. Christian living does not give surety, but, as Hopkins discovered throughout his life, the possibility of aligning oneself to Trinitarian life and sensing that all will not end in despair.

Hopkins' understanding of the *theosis* of the self drew partly on Aristotle's metaphysics, in particular his writings on potentiality and actuality. In his 1867 undergraduate essay 'The Probable Future of Metaphysics', he outlines how from Heraclitus to Hegel, Not-Being, Being and Becoming have been set forth as the three most important stages in any understanding of Reality and correspond to notions of the potential, the actual and the passing over of one to the other (Hopkins, 1974). This attention given to 'becoming' assists us in understanding Hopkins' attitude to spiritual growth. For example, he uses the word 'hollow' to indicate the receptivity and ongoing development of humanity to receive the divine presence. In 1881 he claimed 'God rests in human 'as in a place, a *locus*, bed, vessel, expressly made to receive him as a jewel in a case hollowed to fit it, as the hand in the glove or the milk in the breast' (Hopkins, 1959a, 195). As Dau comments in her fine analysis of love in Hopkins' poetry, 'his 'synecdoches signal our capacity to receive and contain God; the bed suggests the intimacy of that reception' (2013, 70). He uses the simile of lettering on a sail which 'are best seen when it fills' and compares humanity's reception of Christ into its heart, to Mary's carrying of Christ in her womb. The undated Latin hymn to Mary, *Ad Matrem Virginem* contains the following lines: 'He creeps in, O Mary/In the Eucharist. He Himself wishes to enter: I cannot deny myself to Him'. A person's true nature is only realised when it becomes filled with Christ.

Persuaded by his reading of Parmenides (Brown, 1997, 168-191), Hopkins shows that his metaphysics rests on a distinctive notion of Being and Becoming. All inscapes are grounded in Being and this is why difference does not hold any difficulty for the poet, since any individuality is part of a larger whole and rooted in God's Being. The words of his 1877 poem *Pied Beauty* echoes this philosophy: 'All things counter, original, spare, strange' are a reflection of God whose 'beauty is past change'. Every person has the potential to be immortal, because he holds the inner capacity to be one with Christ: 'I am all at once what Christ is, since he was what I am' he writes in *That Nature is a Heraclitean Fire and of the comfort of the Resurrection*. As Brown notes, this belief is shown in the language and metre of the poem: 'Change and its fluctuous word patterns are finally banished by this tautology (and pedantically perfect rhyme), which pivots about the copula, the simple assertion of *being*: 'immortal diamond,/Is immortal diamond' (2004, 77). The 'aspiration' to change and become Christ-like depends upon a person being inspired to respond to the Holy Spirit: 'Even the sigh or aspiration itself is in answer to an inspiration of God's spirit and is followed by the continuance and expiration of that same breath which lifts it ...to do or be what God wishes his creature to do or be' (Hopkins, 1959a, 156).

Poetry itself is a reply, a giving back to God, an utterance He helps us to give by his incarnational 'utterance'. Between May 1868 and December 1875, he found a growing reconciliation between his dual vocations as priest and poet which is why he had no qualms about writing *The Wreck of the Deutschland* when invited to compose a piece by his superior at St. Beuno's in honour of nuns drowned in the mouth of the Thames. His sprung rhythm, with its carefully placed stresses and emphases, was to become in Hopkins' mind another method of ministry, a creative way of acknowledging and proclaiming Being: 'each word is one way of acknowledging Being' he wrote (Hopkins, 1959b, 129). He also began insisting that his poetry was to be read out loud, a spiritual exercise of inhaling and exhaling, as the reader negotiates his breath throughout the delivery of a poem. Any such 'utterance' is exhalation, a natural response to the inspiration of the Holy Spirit. This is why Hopkins uses the expression 'ah!' numerous times in his poetry to signal, on the one hand, the breath of God and humanity and, on the other, to express astonishment that poetry is able to be an 'aspiration' to God's 'inspiration' (Hopkins, 1959a, 158).

Conversely, a refusal to answer the call and 'pitch' results in a person becoming 'To his own self-bent so bound...' (*Ribblesdale)*. This is diametrically opposite to St Margaret Clitheroe's calling whose 'will was bent at God's (*Margaret Clitheroe*). Paradoxically, by her silent submission to death, she was able to echo the divine voice of the Trinity - Father, Son and Holy Spirit: 'The Utterer, Uttered, Uttering.' The martyr 'caught' (a word Hopkins uses frequently to indicate a brief, sensate glimpse of beauty) the Trinitarian 'eternal ring' when she heard the 'crying of those Three', as God mourned for her death. Akin to a bell tolling, she tells 'His name times-over three', just as in *As Kingfishers Catch Fire,* stones 'ring' out 'broad' God's 'name'. The Word becomes 'uttered', in poetry, bringing about the fleshing of God, as in the incarnation.

Beauty

In 1865 as an Oxford University undergraduate, Hopkins wrote his essay *On the Origins of Beauty. A Platonic Dialogue* where he imagines a conversation on the nature of beauty between a newly appointed Professor of Aesthetics and a student. The core of the dialogue concerns how beauty is characterised by irregularity, variety and strangeness, as much as by conformity, unity and harmony; regularity and irregularity co-exist. The chestnut-fan with six leaves illustrates this idea well because it is similar to and yet different from one with seven leaves. Such an emphasis on uniqueness within uniformity is fundamental to Hopkins' metaphysics, upon which much of his life, poetry and prose rests. In his 1881 letter to his friend, Bridges, eight years before his death, he admitted that 'You give me a long jobation about eccentricities. Alas I have heard so much about and suffered so much for and in fact been so completely ruined for life by my alleged singularities that they are a sore subject' (Hopkins, 1935, 126).

His final years in Dublin were characterised by an acute sense of isolation and alienation which became the springboard for his 'dark' or 'terrible' sonnets. In 1885, he was able to combine his own sense of difference with that in nature as a whole: *To seem the stranger lies my lot, my life* epitomises this feeling which pervaded his entire life. And yet, paradoxically, the creation of beauty emerges from difference, for God 'fathers-forth' … 'All things counter, original, spare, strange' (*Pied Beauty*). As early as 1863 in a letter to Baillie from the Isle of Wight (a location he liked visiting for its beauty), he recorded: 'I think I have told you that I have particular periods of admiration for particular things. … The present fury is the ash, and perhaps barley and two shapes of growth in leaves and one on tree boughs and also a conformation of fine-weather cloud' (Hopkins, 1970, 202). Hopkins' early drawings, which he hoped would be seen from a 'Ruskinese point of view', capture both the peculiarities of a scene, as well as its organic unity (Ward, 2002, 56-75). About his sketch of waves from Freshwater Bay on the Isle of Wight in 1863, he said he was able to 'catch' both the individuality and the form of the sea - that 'network' which he tried to 'law out'. The skilled eye and other senses, are capable of discovering the 'inscape' in things – the distinctive quality of 'the dearest freshness deep down things' as he puts it in *God's Grandeur,* besides the overall pattern and symmetry of the scene. This passage indicates why he moved from painting to poetry as his preferred art. Enraptured by the touch 'huddle', sound 'clocked' and movement 'the backwater runs over' more than the mere sight 'network', of the waves, Gardner's observation that 'painting's very stillness and dumbness would have oppressed him… and 'he would have been plagued by all the nightingales of nature and art', is a judicious one I think (1948, 15). What really captivated Hopkins was the beauty of the sound, of words, carefully spaced to maximise their rhythmic patterns and hues, which he often compared to music. Like colours in nature, he was fascinated with the sound of nature and he refers to 'the chord of colour' of a lily (Hopkins, 1959b, 237, Brown 29). While Professor of Rhetoric at Manresa House between September 1873 and July, 1874, he wrote *Poetry and Verse* in which he comments: 'Verse is speech having a marked figure, order of sounds independent of meaning' (1959b, 276). The visceral, Anglo-Saxon intensity and 'primitive', guttural, tone of his verse compels a democratic audience of listeners primarily through their rhythm and sound. The uneducated can be drawn into Hopkins' verse, just as much as the educated, akin to the plays of Shakespeare, which draw all kinds of audiences into their musical folds.

The 'heart right'

Hopkins' poetry is characterised by how the heart is lifted in admiration for the wonder and beauty of Being. In *The Windhover* dedicated 'To Christ our Lord', the poet discloses: 'My heart in hiding/Stirred for a bird …' as he becomes caught up by its 'Brute beauty', 'the mastery of the thing', the kestrel's surging flight and speed of movement, its individuality, its self-confident 'pride', its uniqueness. Such language reflects an intimate reciprocity between the *looker* and the *looked at*: 'When you look hard at a thing, it seems to look hard at you' he observes in 1863. (Hopkins, 1989, 140).

Like a great painter, Hopkins was able to see things which other eyes could not, and his love of Van Gogh's work influenced his own contemplative ability to see the unique beauty of things, such as 'skies of couple-colour as a brinded cow' or 'Fresh-firecoal chestnut-falls'(*Pied Beauty*). While he lived at Stonyhurst College, Lancashire, a gardener was amazed to notice how he kept looking intently at stones; and, in May 1870, Hopkins exclaims: 'I do not think I have ever seen anything more beautiful than the bluebell I have been looking at. I know the beauty of our Lord by it' (Hopkins, 1989, 134). This attention to the natural world is due to his capacity to appreciate, like Whistler (one of his favourite painters), 'what I call inscape (the very soul of art…)'. His own joyful engagement with the particularity in nature is, he believed, available to everyone. But in 1872 he reflects: 'I thought how sadly beauty of inscape was unknown and buried away from simple people and yet how near at hand it was if they had eyes to see it and it could be called out everywhere again' (Hopkins, 1959a, 221;1989, 161).

Hopkins' own confident ability to discern the beauty of Christ in everything was derived from his reading of Scotus. On the subject of encountering him in the Baddeley library on the Isle of Man in 1872, he reflected: 'At this time I had first begun to get hold of the copy of Scotus on the *Sentences* … and was flush with a new stroke of enthusiasm. It may come to nothing or it may be a mercy of God. But just then when I took in inscape of the sky or sea I thought of Scotus' (Hopkins, 1989, 161). The word *haecceitas* or 'thisness' in Scotus is often linked to Hopkins' use of the word 'inscape', although his use of this word is contested. Persuasively, Sobolev rejects this association because he believes he uses the word as a general guiding principle for his work; Ward, too, is sceptical and suggests that Scotus' concept of *formalitates* is a far better way to describe Hopkins' use of the word 'inscape', since it involves how the imagination is able to be shaped and moulded by the senses, organising these by a method of *formaltates,* a strategy for separating out the particularities of a thing, without destroying its inseparability from the whole (Ward, 2002, 187-191; 194-197). As Baker (undated) contends in her phenomenological reading of Hopkins, his enthusiasm for Scotus was likely due to the fact that he saw in him an avenue for epistemology, a basis for knowledge through *feeling and sensing* the divine within nature and humanity which all people could experience. This analysis resonates with the poet's reading of and correspondence with John Henry Newman, in particular his notion of the illative sense which encourages a confidence in the 'felt sense' of truth. Hopkins read *Grammar of Assent* in 1873, three years after its publication and referred to the work as 'heavy reading' but 'The justice and candour and gravity and rightness of mind is what is so *beautiful* in all he writes …' (Hopkins, 1970, 58).

In some of Hopkin's poems a sense of beauty and inscape is associated with the movement and extension of the human body, as it goes about its work *Harry Ploughman* records how he 'leans to it, Harry bends, look. Back, elbow, and liquid waist/In him, all quail to the wallowing o' the plough' suggesting a mouldable aspect to his form, looked at from a distance by the poet, who shares a common, if different corporeality. In *Felix Randall*, there is again an emphasis on physicality, movement and employment, 'When thus…/Didst fettle for the great grey horse his bright and battering sandal!' But there is a closeness between them both here, since as priest he comes near to him with the last sacramental rites. Felix's sickness and mortality draws him beside the poet who regrets the decaying of the once strong body, as he approaches death. In *Epithalamion,* written in 1888, he conjures up the beauty of a pastoral scene, as healthy boys with 'bellbright bodies' swim 'waterworld thorough hurled' in a river while a 'listless stranger' does the same in a nearby pool.

However, without doubt, the central dynamic in Hopkins' estimation of beauty is the figure of Christ. Beauty is Christ's own gift to humanity and nature, and what becomes possible by this, is a mutual act of exchange. He encourages readers of *The Leaden Echo and the Golden Echo* to 'Give beauty back, beauty, beauty, beauty, back to God, beauty's self and beauty's giver'. And in *To What Serves Mortal Beauty?* Hopkins is keen to acknowledge the Source of beauty, as well as a warning against its ability to entrap by its sensual power. It can be 'dangerous', because it has the potential to lead to lust; keeping 'warm' and alive 'Men's wits' to 'the things that are' is not the full story. The priest gave up looking at things closely for six months of his life due to this 'danger'. However, Hopkins does want to emphasize that beauty can often lead to Christian action and refers to how Pope Gregory caught a sight of beautiful English boys in the slave market in Rome which encouraged him to act and send out missionaries to that country. Human beauty, too, is to be cherished, because it prevents us from worshipping 'block or barren stone' and has the potential to lead to a higher spiritual beauty, 'God's better beauty, grace'. Hopkins makes an important distinction between a 'glance' which signals a response of *ascesis* and a 'gaze' which effects lust. Saville suggests that the sestet presents the most difficult conundrum which faced Hopkins during his entire life - 'if we are to love the "selves" of men, their pitch, *haecceitas,* or thisness, and if stalling on the inscape or patterns of physical form leads us to appreciate that *haecceitas,* are we not justified in gazing on the body of the beautiful … through which we may glimpse the beauty of the soul?' (2000, 180). The Hopkinsian response is clear: one may look only long enough to catch the divine sublimity of such beauty: 'Merely meet it; own/Home at heart, heaven's sweet gift; then leave, let that alone'. Thus, it is beneficial to remember that times of renunciation and brief moments of pleasure, give way to the experience of more lasting spiritual grace. The beauty captured in the transient flying of a bird, for example, is also able to be at the same time, an experience of Christ's beauty.

During his years of pastoral activity Hopkins came to see human beings as sacramental forms of God. He 'could hardly bear the pollution of innocent souls. … and on the other, men and women, in their homecoming, as sinners, to God…' (1989, 398) suggests von Balthasar. In a letter to E. H. Coleridge on January 22, 1866, he writes 'It is one adorable point of the incredible condescension of the Incarnation (the greatness of which no saint can ever have hoped to realize) that out Lord submitted not only to the pains of life …but also to the mean and trivial accidents of humanity …it is not surprising that our reception or non-reception of its benefits shd. be also amidst trivialities' (1970, 19). As Mariani comments in his analysis of *Felix Randall,* 'Hopkins' 'vision is to have seen in the daily shoeing of horses by a common blacksmith, without "forethought of" its special significance, the abiding presence of Christ' (1970, 172). 'The metamorphosis of the "great grey drayhores" into light, supple, Pegasean steed with "bright and battering sandal" is an exact parallel of Felix Randall's spiritual transformation' (1970, 171). Hopkins sees himself as an agent of change secured by the dying man's receiving of the viaticum, assisting his soul's final journey to death, just as the horse on its ongoing life's journey is made strong by the 'sandal' (Mariani, 1970, 171- 40).

The beauty of Christ has the ability to 'capture' Hopkins' imagination and spiritual aspirations. Although in one of his letters to Bridges in February 1879 he regrets that his love for Christ is only occasionally felt: 'the only person that I am in love with seldom, especially now, stirs my heart sensibly' (1935, 66), some of his best poems illustrate his passionate love for Christ. In *The Windhover,* the poet flies upwards like the bird, just as in Plato's *Pheadrus* the soul in love, regenerates its wings and returns to its original home. In relation to the description of *eros* in Plato and the dove in the *Song of Songs* (both texts known well by Hopkins), we read in *The Wreck of the Deutschland* that the 'heart in flight embodies the heart of the one who has fallen in love with Christ' (Duc, 2013, 65; Saville, 2000, 3). However, this movement of expansiveness, and the freeing of the heart, in a sudden outburst of emotion is often in tension with Hopkins' Jesuitical ascetic training which encouraged self-denial and obscurity; the phrase 'my heart in hiding' reflecting this disciplined ideal. As Dubois suggests: ''The Windhover' tussles across its *volta* with how much admiration for nature's vigour can be reconciled with the seclusion demanded by religious vocation' (2017, 104). And Saville notes that Hopkins 'draws from a long-standing devotional rhetoric that uses erotic imagery to convey spiritual thoughts' (2000, 22). Even though he is disappointed that much of God's creation has been 'wrecked', he longs, in compensation, for the day 'with eager desire to seeing the matchless beauty of Christ's body in the heavenly light' (Hopkins, 1959, 36). He is also reassured that God knows the deeply felt tension in humanity between the temporary and the eternal. Indeed, God looks on the beauty of His own creation and hears its yearning cries, or as von Balthasar puts it: 'He hears 'man's inchoate sigh of assent...' (1989, 386). God sees behind the surface a person's struggles and assists him with grace to start again when he falls: 'Complete thy creature dear O where it fails,/Being mighty a master, being a father and fond' *(In the Valley of the Elwy).* It is Christ who is the 'instress' which is felt within all created things and grace operates as 'mouthed to flesh-burst/Gush! – flush the man, the being with it, sour or sweet/Brim, in a flash, full! –' (st. 8, *The Wreck of the Deutschland).* Due to the consoling, beautiful cross which is imprinted on humanity in all their endeavours, Hopkins is able to say, in a sermon at Leigh on December 14th 1879 to his working-class congregation: 'We must put a stress on ourselves and make ourselves find comfort where we know the comfort is to be found. It *is* a comfort that in spite of all, God loves us … We have only to force ourselves to see it, to dwell on it and at last to feel that it is so' (Hopkins, 1959a, 47-48). It was such comfort which allowed him to say as his last words, 'I am so happy. I am so happy' (Mariani, 2019, 71).

Conclusion

As I have suggested throughout, Hopkins learnt to read the forms of nature and personhood in relation to Christ's sacrifice and expressed them in poetic and prosaic language so he might utter God's Word and encourage others to do the same. Summing up Hopkins' ambition, von Balthasar writes: 'Together with the man, the language must reach out beyond its immanence because the mystery of God does not hold sway as something incomprehensible *behind* the forms of the world; rather, the Divine Word was made flesh' (393). His genius lies in his use of language, rhythm and sound to communicate such a fleshed-out metaphysics, which a 'heart right' (*cor rectum)* is able to capture. I believe Hopkins would have been content and be able to rest peacefully in his grave, if he thought he had succeeded in this.

Bibliography

Baker, Carole, undated. "Taste and See: A Phenomenological Reading of Gerard Manley Hopkins". https://www.academia.edu/10573985/Taste_and_See_A_Phenomenolo gical_Reading_of_Gerard_Manley_Hopkins (Accessed 24.5. 20) .

Brett, R.L. 1965. *Poems of Faith and Doubt.* London: Edward Arnold Pub. Ltd.

Brown, Daniel. 1997. *Hopkins' Idealism. Philosophy. Physics, Poetry.* Oxford: Clarendon Press Oxford.

Brown, 2004. *Gerard Manley Hopkins.* Tavistock: Northcote House.

Dau, Duc. 2013. *Touching God. Hopkins and Love.* London: Anthem Press.

De Mello, Anthony. 2010. *Seek God Everywhere. Reflections on the Spiritual Exercises of St. Ignatius,* London: Penguin Random Books.

Dubois, Martin. 2017. *Gerard Manley Hopkins and the Poetry of Experience.* Cambridge: CUP

Duns Scotus. 1987. *Duns Scotus. Philosophical Writings.* Indianapolis: Hackett Pub. Co.

Ellsberg, Margaret. 2017. (ed). *The Gospel in Gerard Manley Hopkins.* New York: Plough Publishing House.

Gardner, Helen. 1971 Religion and Literature. London: Faber and Faber.

Gardner, William. 1948. *Gerard Manley Hopkins. A Study Poetic Idiosyncrasy in Relation to Poetic Tradition.* London: Martin Secker and Warburg Ltd.

Gardner, William and MacKenzie, Norman. 1948. (ed). *The Poems of Gerard Manley Hopkins* 4th edition. Oxford: OUP.

Hopkins, 1935. *The Letters of Gerard Manley Hopkins to Robert Bridges.* London: OUP.

Hopkins, 1959. Devlin, C. (ed). *The Sermons and Devotional Writings of Gerard Manley Hopkins.* London: OUP.

Hopkins, 1959. House, H & Storey, G. (ed). *Journals and Papers of Gerard Manley Hopkins.* London: OUP.

Hopkins, 1970. Abbott, Claude. (ed). *Further Letters of Gerald Manley Hopkins.* London: OUP.

Hopkins, 1989. MacKenzie, Norman (ed). *The Early Poetic Manuscripts and Note-books of Gerard Manley Hopkins,* New York: Garland.

Ignatius of Loyola, 1991. *The Spiritual Exercises and Selected Works.* New York: Paulist Press.

Hart, Kevin. 2018. *Poetry and Revelation. For a Phenomenology of Religious Poetry.* London: Bloomsbury Academic

Jasper, David. 2009 *The Sacred Body. Asceticism in Religion Literature, Art and Culture.* Texas: Baylor.

Kearney, Richard. 2011. *Anatheism {Returning to God after God}.* New York: Columbia University Press.

Kearney, Richard and Zimmermann, Jens. 2016. (ed). *Reimagining the Sacred Richard Kearney Debates God.* New York Columbia University Press.

Ker, Ian. 2007. "John Henry Newman and Hopkins" http://gerardmanleyhopkins.org/Lectures_hopkins-and-newman (accessed 28.5.20).

Lowell, Robert. 1944. "Hopkins' Sanctity". *Kenyon Review.* 6: 583-86.

MacKenzie, Norman. 1970. "Hopkins". In *The Victorians,* edited by Arthur Pollard, 312-333. London: Sphere Books Ltd.

Mariani, Paul. 1970. *A Commentary on the Complete Poems of Gerard Manley Hopkins.* Cornell: Cornell University Press.

Mariani. 1989. "The Consoling, Terrifying Presence of Hopkins". *Renascence.* 42(1/2):13-20: 583-86.

Mariani. 2008. *Gerard Manley Hopkins. A Life.* New York: Viking.

Mariani, 2018. U-tube interview, Boston College. 'Gerard Manley Hopkins. A Life'. https://www.youtube.com/watch?v=so0dDJwLOBo (accessed 1.6.20)

Mariani, 2019. *The Mystery of it All. The Vocation of Poetry in the Twilight of Modernity.* Massachusetts: Paraclete Press.

Martin, Robert. 1991.*Gerard Manley Hopkins. A Very Private Life.* London: Harper Collins.

Nixon, Jude.1989. "The Kindly Light: A Reappraisal of the Influence of Newman on Hopkins". *Texas Studies in Literature and Language.* 31(1): 105-142.

Robson, Catherine. 2018. "Gerard Manley Hopkins", In *The Norton Anthology of English Literature. The Victorian Age* edited by Stephen Greenblatt, 592-605.New York: W.W. Norton.

Saville, Julia. 2000. *A Queer Chivalry. The Homoerotic Asceticism of Gerard Manley Hopkins.* Charlottesville: University Press of Virginia.

Schlatter, Fredric. 2008. "Hopkins and Newman: Two Disagreements". *Christianity and Literature.* 57(3): 401-18.

Sobolev, Dennis. 2001. "Hopkins' Portraits of the Artist: Between the Biographical and the Ideological". *Connotations.* 10 (2-3): 304-28.

Sobolev. 2011. *The Split World of Gerard Manley Hopkins. An Essay in Semiotic Phenomenology.* Washington: The Catholic University of America Press.

von Balthasar, Hans Urs. 1986. *The Glory of the Lord. A Theological Aesthetics Volume III: Studies in Theological Style: Lay Styles.* Edinburgh: T&T Clark.

Waterman Ward, Bernadette. 2002. *World as Word. Philosophical Theology in Gerard Manley Hopkins.* Washington: Catholic University of America Press.

Wolfe, Patricia. 1968. "The Paradox of the Self: A Study of Hopkins' Spiritual Conflict in the "Terrible" Sonnets". *Victorian Poetry.*6(2):85-103.

"A STANDING TEMPTATION
TO THE INTELLIGENTSIA":
THE CATHOLIC LITERARY REVIVAL
IN TWENTIETH-CENTURY BRITAIN[1]

ADAM SCHWARTZ

Upon learning in 1928 of T. S. Eliot's conversion to Christianity, Virginia Woolf wrote to her sister:

> I have had a most shameful and distressing interview with poor dear Tom Eliot, who may be called dead to us all from this day forward. He has become an Anglo-Catholic, believes in God and immortality, and goes to church. I was really shocked. A corpse would seem to me more credible than he is. I mean, there's something obscene in a living person sitting by the fire and believing in God.[2]

Woolf's dismissal of belief in traditional Christianity as a distressing obscenity was typical of British intellectuals' attitudes during her era. From G. B. Shaw to H. G. Wells, from Bertrand Russell to Arnold Bennett, a common supposition among the day's cultural leaders was that dogmatic religion was so much shameful hidebound superstition that people must be liberated from for the sake of their own well-being and society's progress. Although such sentiments had been growing steadily among the *literati* throughout the nineteenth century, several trends converged in the late Victorian and Edwardian ages to accelerate this secularization of British high culture. Evolutionism had already destroyed the idea of providential design for many thinkers; and these epochs' greater attention to the dark side of Darwinism, with its stress on struggle and randomness, weakened further whatever hold the notion of nature's ultimate benevolence still had on modern minds. Moreover, biblical Higher Criticism simultaneously posed a radical challenge to received

---

[1] An earlier version of this essay appeared in *Logos* 4 (Winter 2001): 11-33.
[2] *The Letters of Virginia Woolf*, ed. Nigel Nicholson and Joanne Trautmann (New York: Harcourt Brace Jovanovich, 1977), 457-58.

understandings of Christianity and the authorities behind them, even as scholarship in comparative religions questioned customary conceptions of Christian uniqueness. Finally, certain orthodox teachings—particularly the Atonement and Hell—were increasingly judged immoral. Hence, as Adrian Hastings notes, by the late 1910s and 1920s, "the overturning of Christianity effectively achieved by the previous generation could be, and was, openly accepted as a fact of modern life," making this period's predominant mindset an unprecedented "confident agnosticism." In short, "Modernity simply had no place for religion in general or Christianity in particular."[3]

Yet Eliot's action was not as anomalous as it may appear initially. Despite this hostile cultural atmosphere, a substantial segment of prominent thinkers reared in the late-Victorian and Edwardian epochs still chose to become Christians—and Catholic Christians—as adults, especially during the century's unpropitious early decades. Even more strikingly, in view of its longstanding minority, persecuted, and oppositional status in British society, a disproportionate number of these converts migrated to the Roman Catholic Church: those eventually so drawn included G. K. Chesterton, Christopher Dawson, Eric Gill, Ronald Knox, Edith Sitwell, Siegfried Sassoon, David Jones, Graham Greene, Evelyn Waugh, Muriel Spark, Maurice Baring, Frederick Copleston, Malcolm Muggeridge, and E. F. Schumacher. Add to this muster "cradle Catholics" Hilaire Belloc and Barbara Ward, "cradle convert" J. R. R. Tolkien, and the Anglo-Catholics Eliot, C. S. Lewis, Charles Williams, W. H. Auden, and Dorothy L. Sayers, and one has a roster of some of the age's most accomplished public intellectuals. Orthodox Christianity's ability to attract such a large portion of these generations' leading writers into its ranks at a time when antithetical attitudes were at their apex is thus a central phenomenon of twentieth-century British culture.

In fact, it was precisely traditional Christianity's dissent from modern, post-Christian norms that rendered it appealing to this network of minds, making the Catholic literary revival an "articulate counterculture."[4] Despite coming from widely different backgrounds, working in diverse genres, and being driven by highly individual feelings and experiences, these seekers' spiritual journeys shared common landmarks: they sensed that dominant cultural trends were imperiling cherished beliefs that arose from decisive personal, often youthful, episodes; that orthodox

---

[3] Adrian Hastings, *A History of English Christianity, 1920-1985* (London: Collins, 1986), 221-24.
[4] James Lothian, *The Making and Unmaking of the English Catholic Intellectual Community, 1910-1950* (Notre Dame: U of Notre Dame P, 2009), xi.

Christianity offered an intellectual and spiritual framework for upholding these ostensibly threatened ideals; and that this faith would resist modern movements unwaveringly on behalf of its ancient doctrines and mores that seemed a truer, more resonant explanation of life and thought. They were persuaded both by rational arguments in favor of orthodoxy and by the ethical example of Christian acquaintances and mentors. Similarly, adherence to Christianity shaped not only their theologies, but also their views of human nature, society, and politics. Anchored in what they considered the truth about God and man, these authors faced confidently a culture governed by contrary convictions and the frequently angry and astonished reactions of their friends and families.[5] Specifically, they countered modern secularism, subjectivism, individualism, belief in Progress, and cultural fragmentation with a Christian stress on supernaturalism, objectivity, authority, tradition, a tragic view of life, and civilizational integration.

First, the literary Christians contravened their secularist peers' understanding of religion and its effect on thought and art. Against the prevalent assumption that traditional faith was a superstitious relic that diminishes human dignity, the Christians claimed that recognition of life's supernatural element was necessary for a genuine humanism and vital art. Greene argued that "human beings are more important to believers than they are to atheists. If one tells oneself that man is no more than a superior animal, that each individual has before him a maximum of eighty years of life, then man is indeed of little importance."[6] To Greene, however, such "unimportance in the world of the senses is only matched by his enormous importance in another world," making characters with "the solidity and importance of men with souls to save or lose" the stuff of lasting literature. He therefore chided the likes of Woolf and E. M. Forster for creating characters who "wandered like cardboard symbols through a world that was paper-thin," due to these novelists' loss of "the religious sense," as "with the religious sense went the sense of the importance of the human act."[7] Waugh echoed this assessment, holding that "you can only leave God out by making your characters pure abstractions," a perspective he conceded was "unpopular." Yet (like Greene) he regarded this repudiation of modernist principles as an affirmation of a deeper appreciation of

---

[5] Joseph Pearce, *Literary Converts* (London: HarperCollins, 1999); Adam Schwartz, *The Third Spring* (Washington, D.C.: The Catholic U of America P, 2005).
[6] Marie-Francoise Allain, *The Other Man: Conversations With Graham Greene* (New York: Simon & Schuster, 1983), 152.
[7] Graham Greene, *Collected Essays* (New York: Penguin, 1966), 91-92.

human destiny: to represent "man in his relation to God" was to "represent man more fully."[8]

The orthodox Christians also rebutted what they saw as another central facet of both literary and theological modernism: subjectivism. They maintained that truth is not the product of particular minds that varies from thinker to thinker but is an objective reality that exists apart from individual inquirers and is meant to be discovered by them. Arnold Lunn felt that "personal experience...has no validity as an argument for those who do not share this experience,"[9] and Knox contended that if something is true, "it would be true if every human mind denied it, or if there were no human minds in existence to recognize it."[10] Such authors were drawn to orthodoxy because it appeared to possess this objective validity. Religion as "an objective reality far transcending one's private experience"[11] had stirred Dawson from childhood, and was fulfilled for him in the Catholic Church, "a society which possesses no less objective reality and juridical form than a state, while at the same time its action extends to the very depths of the individual human soul."[12] Belloc likewise cast Catholicism as "the exponent of *Reality*. It is true. Its doctrines in matters large and small are statements of what is" at the temporal and spiritual levels alike.[13]

But the Christians realized that these doctrines could be misapprehended or misapplied by imperfect minds and wills. They thus determined that some definitive means of preserving and promulgating these truths about reality was required. In search of what Chesterton called a "truth-telling thing," the Roman Catholics were impressed by the Church's *magisterium* and its claims to binding authority in matters of faith and morals. As Greene put it during his instruction, "It's quite possible after all to believe it at this early stage, because the acceptance and belief in the Church as a guide includes faith in everything I've still got to be taught."[14] Even those,

---

[8] *The Essays, Articles, and Reviews of Evelyn Waugh,* ed. Donat Gallagher (London: Penguin, 1986), 302.

[9] Arnold Lunn, *Come What May* (London: Eyre & Spottiswoode, 1940), 201.

[10] Quoted in Evelyn Waugh, *Ronald Knox* (Boston: Little, Brown, 1959), 334.

[11] Christopher Dawson, *Education and the Crisis of Christian Culture* (New York: Henry Regnery Co., 1949), 12.

[12] Christopher Dawson, *Christianity in East & West*, ed. John Mulloy (1959; reprint, Peru, Illinois: Sherwood Sugden & Co., 1981), 217.

[13] Quoted in Maisie Ward, *Gilbert Keith Chesterton* (London: Sheed & Ward, 1943), 474. Emphasis in original.

[14] Greene quoted in Norman Sherry, *The Life of Graham Greene, Vol. I: 1904-1939* (New York: Viking, 1989), 259, who estimates the letter's date as early December, 1925. Even as Greene later questioned numerous authoritative Church teachings, he continued to insist on the importance of dogma, affirming as late as

like Eliot, Lewis, and Sayers, who were troubled by this Roman Catholic assertion of authority still found orthodox Christianity a compelling ordering principle for the mind, soul, and polity, and they defended staunchly the normative force of the ancient creeds and the teachings of the Four Ecumenical Councils.

Similarly, it was in part because they foresaw disorder resulting from defiance of those traditional truths and their teachers that these writers opposed modern individualism. To abjure Christian standards in the name of personal freedom, they remonstrated, was to go against the very grain of Being and to leave the will-to-power as the sole arbiter of meaning and value. In such a scenario, Lewis declared, "we thus advance towards a state of society in which not only each man but every impulse in each man claims *carte blanche*." The end result would be either chaos issuing ultimately in tyranny or a nihilistic cultural suicide, "the abolition of man."[15] To prevent this decay of liberty into license, the Christians averred, freedom needed to be governed by dogma. Sayers mused that "If I am free from *all* bonds, even the right to bind myself, I am not free to believe in anything definite, to make any definite decision...because there is no paramount claim to bind the will to a single course."[16] But binding the will to the fixed course of the perennially valid body of verities provided by Christianity gives one the grounding in reality necessary to explore it positively and profitably. As Chesterton put it, "Catholics know the two or three transcendental truths on which they do agree; and take rather a pleasure in disagreeing on everything else," making dogmatic Catholicism the foundation of "an active, fruitful, progressive and even adventurous life" of the intellect and spirit.[17] In allowing Christian convictions to set the lines of excellence in lieu of drafting them themselves, people are enabled to exercise their vital powers in ways that ennoble human nature rather than degrade it, because their behavior is in conformity with reality instead of in discord with it.

1979: "I believe in the necessity of a minimum of dogmas, and I certainly believe in heresy...If one considers oneself a Catholic there are a certain number of facts which have to be accepted...So long as differences between the churches exist, these differences ought to be upheld." Allain, *Other Man*, 158-59.

[15] C. S. Lewis, *God in the Dock*, ed. Walter Hooper (Grand Rapids: Eerdmans, 1970), 322.

[16] *The Letters of Dorothy L. Sayers, vol. 2: 1937-1943*, ed. Barbara Reynolds (Cambridge: The Dorothy L. Sayers Society/Carole Green Publishing, 1997), 425. Emphasis in original.

[17] *The Collected Works of G. K. Chesterton*, vol. 3, *The Thing* (San Francisco: Ignatius Press, 1990), 265, 299.

The Christian intellectuals' belief in the prescriptive wisdom of their religious heritage and their sense of the perils that befall those who disregard it combined to forge a deep disquiet with the modern ideal of Progress. Against those (like Wells and Russell) who asseverated that men could be like gods if they let the new winds of science and social change sweep away orthodoxy's outdated implausible teachings and stifling morality, the literary Christians contended, with Eliot, that the way forward is the way back. The Christians decried equating sequential advance with substantial improvement as what Lewis called "chronological snobbery," charging that such a cosmology closed one's mind to all but the ascendant prejudices of his own day. To them, the Christian assertion of a longstanding, persistently vital, legacy of worship, thought, and art supplied a permanent standard for, and fundamental alternative to, any temporarily ruling outlook; and they regarded the content of this inheritance as truer, richer, and deeper than what they deemed the radically truncated vision of anthropocentric materialism prevalent in their time. As Eliot noted, this stress on tradition was a key attraction of Catholicism to writers who chose it, in either Anglo or Roman form, as adults:

> It is always the main religious body which is the guardian of more of the remains of the higher developments of culture preserved from a past time before the division took place...Hence it is that the convert...of the intellectual or sensitive type is drawn towards the more Catholic type of worship and doctrine.[18]

Although they disputed which church had the most direct succession from the Apostles and was therefore the purest legate of the Catholic tradition, both groups saw Catholic Christianity as the best conservator of Christendom's religious and cultural patrimony.

The Christians further reproved Progressivism on anthropological grounds. They alleged that this worldview presupposed the temporal perfectibility of human nature, an assumption they felt both the doctrine of original sin and historical experience refuted abundantly. Yet they found this mistake about man not only false but dangerous. To premise plans for social reengineering on it, they warned, was to invite great cruelty, as such programs would demand more of fallen humans than they were capable of and their ensuing failure would precipitate mistreatment of people as incorrigible sub-humans or malicious traitors for their inability to become the ideologues' dreamt of demigods. Attempts to build New Jerusalems

---

[18] T. S. Eliot, *Christianity and Culture* (New York: Harcourt, Brace, Jovanovich, 1988), 155.

out of the crooked timber of humanity could only end in the Babylon of Belsen. Sayers voiced the tragic view of life shared by her compatriots cogently in 1943:

> For the last two hundred years or so we have been trying to persuade ourselves that there was no such thing as sinfulness—that there was nothing intrinsically unsatisfactory about man as such. But isn't there? I am sorry for the Humanists—they trusted in man so blindly, and now they are bewildered by the present condition of the world. All this science and education and toleration of opinions, and enlightenment and so forth, issuing, not in peace and progress, but in frustration and reactionary violence. But it isn't surprising if one recognizes that the inner division is still there, and that increased knowledge and science and power have only enlarged the scope and opportunity for both good and evil, not altered man's nature, which remains what it was—capable of choice because its will is free; capable of and indeed inclined to make, the wrong choice, because it centers itself on man and the relative rather than on God and the absolute.[19]

These theological and philosophical objections to modern thought helped mold the literary Christians' perception of their day's political ideas and systems. For example, although some (like Chesterton and Dawson) applauded political liberalism's stress on limited government, they and their associates saw its philosophical basis as a merger of the progressive disdain for tradition and belief in historical perfectibility with an atomic individualism and a lack of teleology that affronted basic human needs for community and a meaningful order and purpose in life. Liberalism's economic counterpart, industrial capitalism, was nearly universally condemned, most plangently in Tolkien's indictment of "the cursed disease of the internal combustion engine of which all the world is dying."[20] The Christians considered the "machine age" lethal because it rested on a mechanistic metaphysic, exploited labor by commodifying it, and despoiled the natural world rather than kindling human creativity that mirrors that of the Creator in whose image and likeness men are made and promoting stewardship of His other creatures. This critique situates the Christian critics within a broader British heritage of religious and romantic rebellion against industrial modernity, one they made a distinct

---

[19] *Letters of Sayers*, 2: 402-3.
[20] Quoted in Philip and Carol Zaleski, *The Fellowship* (New York: Farrar, Straus & Giroux, 2015), 411.

contribution to by articulating their dissent in an orthodox Christian idiom.[21]

Yet the chief twentieth-century nemeses of liberalism and industrialism were no more satisfactory to these Christian protesters. As their judgments of industrialism suggest, many were sympathetic to Marxist criticisms of capitalism, and they respected communism for being teleological, but (unlike myriad secularist sages) they felt it offered an inadequate diagnosis of and prescription for modern ills. Because of its atheistic and materialistic premises, they deduced, communism posited the immanent perfectibility of mankind, and was hence insufficiently sensitive to the human capacity for evil; they also inferred that its progressive dynamic made it a participant in the modern denigration of tradition. Even Greene, who yearned for a rapprochement between Catholicism and communism, deemed traditional Christian humanism a more realistic and compassionate response to suffering than Marxist pledges of qualitative temporal transformation. Postulating that "it is not possible to create a New Man, so all we can expect is a change in conditions so that the poor are less poor and the rich are less rich,"[22] Greene concluded in 1988 that "as the Church becomes more concerned with poverty and human rights the Marxists become less concerned with poverty and there's nothing to show they are concerned with human rights."[23] To him, and to his Christian brethren, the Marxists' certain trumpet blew a siren's song.

Many of Greene's peers had an analogous attractive-repulsive relationship with fascism. Of the viable political systems of their time, this one seemed initially the most patient of Christian baptism due to its abhorrence of materialism, and its ostensible respect for tradition and Christianity's role in cultural life. The likes of Chesterton, Dawson, and Jones were thus willing to explore a *modus vivendi* between it and their faith. But their enquiries soon convinced them that there was no sound common ground for fascism and Christianity to stand on, judging this ideology to be an ersatz religion of race-hatred that professed a neo-pagan morality and promised a tribalist utopia. As Chesterton put it, far from being opposed to

---

[21] The best treatment of this tradition's tenets for scholars of modern British Christianity is Meredith Veldman, *Fantasy, the Bomb, and the Greening of Britain: Romantic Protest, 1945-1980* (Cambridge: Cambridge UP, 1994), as she devotes extensive attention to Lewis, Tolkien, and Schumacher, and also discusses Chesterton and Belloc.

[22] Greene quoted in Dinesh D'Souza, "Beyond Marx and Jesus," *Crisis* 2 (May 1988): 21.

[23] Quoted in Maria Cuoto, *Graham Greene: On the Frontier* (New York: St. Martin's, 1988), 213-14.

modernity, this "wild worship of Race" actually was stamped by "heresy, license, undefined creed, unlimited claim, mutability, and all that marks Modernism."[24] Even most of the numerous controversialists who supported Franco in the Spanish civil war did so not from sympathy for fascist principles. Rather, they calculated that the Nationalists alone could prevent a communist take-over and would safeguard Catholics' cultural and religious rights, which the Republicans had been quick to violate. If some minor members of the Catholic literary revival had deeper fascist affinities, then, most of its leading lights had, at worst, a temporary or tactical attraction to this ideology and its representatives. The not uncommon labeling of, amongst others, Chesterton, Dawson, Eliot, Jones, and Waugh as fascist fellow travelers is therefore calumnious.[25]

Indeed, these thinkers generally regarded fascism and communism as species of the more fundamental evil of totalitarianism. To them, this form of government was unique and qualitatively different, for it sought to manufacture a normative political teleology, and to make its presence in the polity pervasive, so as to control not merely people's behavior, but also their thoughts and feelings. Dawson (the most precocious and thorough Christian analyst of totalitarianism) voiced the fears of many of his peers when he argued that totalitarianism's assertion of an all-encompassing, politicized teleology establishes it as a necessary rival of organized religion: "the moment that a society claims the complete allegiance of its members, it assumes a quasi-religious authority,"[26] and hence becomes "a competitor with the Church on its own ground."[27] Consequently, he warned, proponents of these "exclusive dogmatic anti-religions" desired not to imitate past persecutions of Christianity, but to extirpate it, along with the ancestral mores of Western culture, so as to foster undivided devotion to the new secularist Caesars of race, class, or simply the will-to-power.[28] Nor did Dawson and his counterparts consider this threat confined to Italy, Germany, and the Soviet Union. They worried that Britain's gradual adoption of a welfare state heralded the possible advent

---

[24] G. K. Chesterton, "The Heresy of Race," *G.K. 's Weekly*, 20 April 1933, 104.

[25] See, e.g., Kevin Morris, et. al., "Fascism and British Catholic Writers, 1924-1939," *The Chesterton Review* 25 (February & May 1999): passim. Tom Villis, *British Catholics and Fascism* (London: Palgrave Macmillan, 2013) presents an admirably fair-minded account that is "neither apologetic nor accusatory" (183), if not entirely accurate.

[26] Christopher Dawson, *The Modern Dilemma* (London: Sheed & Ward, 1932), 95.

[27] Christopher Dawson, *Religion and the Modern State* (New York: Sheed & Ward, 1935), 44.

[28] Christopher Dawson, "English Catholicism and Victorian Liberalism," *The Tablet*, 1950; reprinted in *The Dawson Newsletter* 11 (Fall 1993): 9.

of a more benign-sounding, though ultimately equally dangerous, strain of totalitarianism in their post-Christian homeland, as they saw power being steadily centralized and liberty being increasingly abridged in the name of social security, even as secular norms became more omnipresent and animated these policies. Belloc and Chesterton sounded this alarm about "the servile state" in the century's early years, and their successors echoed their admonitions consistently, particularly after World War II, as the likes of Dawson, Greene, Sayers, and Lewis grew more and more concerned that Britons were becoming (in Lewis's phrase) "willing slaves of the welfare state." Such anxieties set them apart from the postwar "consensus" endorsing an expanded welfare state, but were consistent with their overall conclusion that all modern political systems are potentially totalitarian.

Yet the Christian writers were not nay-sayers. With varying degrees of interest, participation, and sophistication, they subscribed to certain core canons of a positive alternative to modern social and political regimes. For instance, they typically upheld the distributist desideratum of decentralized government and widespread, small-scale ownership of productive property that was crafted and elucidated by Belloc, Chesterton, Gill, and (most famously) Schumacher's *Small is Beautiful*. Moreover, these authors largely favored the corporatist vision of society as an organic community directed by belief in God, in spiritual solidarity, and in work as a vocation, with a resultant accent on promoting human creativity, that Dawson (and to some extent Eliot and Sayers) advocated most trenchantly. But within this broad range of sociological agreement, significant differences nonetheless existed.

For example, although (with the exceptions of Waugh and Eliot) these figures tended to espouse populist stances in defense of the common sense and common things of common people against the scorn and schemes of secularist mandarins, few shared Chesterton's wholehearted, almost mystical, faith in the demos and popular culture. Instead, several (such as Lewis, Sayers, Jones, and Muggeridge) concurrently expressed grave reservations about democracy's potentially leveling effects on culture, the rise of mass-society, and the pernicious influence of media like tabloid journalism, advertisements, and, later, television. Moreover, while Dawson and Tolkien avoided populism's darkest side in their resolute eschewal of antisemitic bromides, the record of manifold counterparts (including Belloc, Chesterton, Greene, Eliot, Muggeridge, and Sayers) is more chequered; this topic demands a clear-eyed treatment that neither accusers nor defenders usually supply.[29] Additionally, whereas some

---

[29] Adam Schwartz, "G. K. Chesterton's Jewish Problem," *Seven* 34 (2017): 1-8,

distributists (like Gill and Vincent McNabb) had a neo-Luddite foreboding of technology, most of the Christians were less cassandric. If it had been unquestionably abused by modern men devoted to *scientia* and controlling nature (as epitomized for many of the Christians by the development of nuclear weapons), these intellectuals deduced that an order dedicated to *sapientia* and understanding nature could make humane and fruitful use of applied science. As Chesterton wrote, virtue or vice are "in a man's soul and not in his tools."[30] Furthermore, while the bulk of these commentators were persistently skeptical of the United States as the supreme avatar of dechristianized materialism, a minority (notably, Chesterton, Dawson, and Waugh) felt that American culture could be baptized by Catholicism, and that assumption of this orthodox ethos would enable America to use its global power to revitalize the Western heritage and protect it against the gathering storm of ideological tyrannies.[31] Yet, notwithstanding these important divergences on specific issues, the literary Christians' overall approach toward modernity is nevertheless clear: if they were conservatives for wanting to re-root their culture in orthodox Christianity and customary morality, they were simultaneously radicals for wanting to uproot modern mores utterly.

The variety in unity displayed in the Christians' social criticism suggests their final challenge to modern thought. To these authors, the diversity present in their community of discourse was permissible and productive because it was integrated by a common commitment to orthodoxy. Post-Christian culture, though, appeared hopelessly fragmented to them, as it no longer had the centrifugal force of faith—or an adequate replacement—to make the centripetal pressures of diverse ideals, ethics, politics, and aesthetics cohere, a condition bemoaned by Auden: "Ashamed civilians come to grief/In brotherhoods without belief."[32] Even as modernist art seemed to portray this splintering as desirable, or at least inevitable, Sayers articulated the darker, yet more hopeful, appraisal of the Christian writers: "If the whole fabric of society is not to collapse into chaos, we must either submit to an artificial uniformity imposed by brute force, or learn to bridge for ourselves these perilous gaps which sunder our behavior from reality."[33] For Sayers and her colleagues, assent to

---

www.wheaton.edu/media/wade-center/files/publications/vii/Vol_34_VII-Online_Edition_2017.pdf

[30] G. K. Chesterton, *Illustrated London News*, 5 June 1920.

[31] Adam Schwartz, "What They Saw in America: G. K. Chesterton's and Christopher Dawson's Views of the United States," *Faith & Reason* 28 (Spring 2003): 23-52.

[32] *The Collected Poetry of W. H. Auden* (New York: Random House, 1945), 313.

[33] Quoted in Pearce, *Literary Converts*, 225.

orthodoxy was the bridge to reality, for it spawned both spiritual and cultural unity grounded in transcendent truth. But so seeing traditional Christianity as sparking cultural, as well as religious, harmony also bred wariness of prepotent irreligion as a civilizational solvent.

For instance, one of Dawson's signature themes was that religion is the basis of culture and, consequently, that a society that loses its religion eventually loses its culture. He, and most Christian intellectuals, feared that the post-Christian West was so imperiled. If they largely rejected a crude Bellocian identification of Europe and the Faith, they did maintain that Christianity had been a crucial shaping influence on Western culture, and hence that forsaking that formative faith would eviscerate their society. As Waugh counseled in 1930, "It is no longer possible…to accept the benefits of civilization and at the same time deny the supernatural basis upon which it rests."[34] Dawson delineated what many Christians considered the implications of this denial five years later. He held that "the new social ideals and secular forms of cultures themselves represent partial and one-sided survivals of the Christian social tradition," as ideologies and institutions like democracy, nationalism, liberalism, socialism, humanitarianism, and Progress were all surrogates for Christianity that had been fostered by it and were rooted in it. But since secularism "did not create these moral ideals, so, too, it cannot preserve them. It lives on the spiritual capital that it has inherited from Christian civilization, and as this is exhausted something else must come to take its place." As Christianity disappeared, he cautioned, so would the virtues celebrated in their secular substitutes. Instead of having greater liberty, equality, fraternity, democracy, and social advance without Christianity, Europe would decay into some type of "'totalitarian' secularism."[35]

Dawson and his like-minded contemporaries therefore concluded that only a recovery of orthodoxy could give Western culture the cohesion and spiritual depth and energy it required to resist the hegemony of the worldly ideologies emanating from East and West. They insisted that plans for European unity must satisfy the soul's needs as well as the body's, and thus that political and economic unity were insufficient without accord on the underlying cultural mores that mold public policy, what Eliot called the "pre-political" sphere. They stipulated further that overarching adherence to a catholic faith would alone provide a suitably broad and transcendent source of unity to allow distinct Western nations to balance their legitimate desires for political and cultural autonomy with their

---

[34] *Essays, Articles, and Reviews of Waugh*, 104.
[35] Dawson, *Religion and the Modern State*, xxi, 64-65.

membership in this integrating European order and culture-heritage. As Eliot (who was heavily influenced by Dawson's views on religion and culture) summarized, "no political and economic organization, however much goodwill it commands, can supply what this culture unity gives," and "the dominant force in creating a common culture between peoples each of which has its own distinct culture, is religion…without a common faith, all efforts towards drawing nations closer together in culture can produce only an illusion of unity." And, Eliot stressed, the common faith that would be the foundation of this desired common European home with many mansions must be the traditional Christianity that was currently unfashionable: "I am talking about the common tradition of Christianity which has made Europe what it is…It is in Christianity that our arts have developed; it is in Christianity that the laws of Europe have—until recently—been rooted. It is against a background of Christianity that all our thought has significance."[36] The stone rejected by the builders of post-Christian Europe was hence the cornerstone of the Christian humanists' hopes for a renewed Christendom.

What, then, is the legacy of these thinkers who sought to make what they deemed the ever-ancient wisdom of the Christian patrimony ever-new? Some (especially Lewis, Tolkien, Greene, Waugh, and Eliot) continue to be both widely popular and seriously studied, while others (particularly Dawson, Jones, and Sayers) are emerging gradually from neglect of their achievement; yet even in 2012 the *TLS* opined that "the notion of the 'Catholic novelist' seems quaint now."[37] Although their vision of a restored Christian faith and culture was persistently unpopular and remains far from realization presently, this pragmatic measure misses the intellectual and historical significance of the twentieth century Catholic literary revival. Indeed, it was these authors' very willingness to swim against the secularist mainstream that defines their contribution to British and Christian letters. In contesting modernity's core principles, and in doing so from an identifiably orthodox Christian perspective, these writers used their considerable skills to obtain a hearing for ideals that were increasingly at odds with the tenor of their time. In fields ranging from

---

[36] Eliot, *Christianity and Culture*, 157, 200-201. Dawson marked portions of these passages in his copy.

[37] J.C., "Order, Order," *TLS*, 9 November 2012, 32. In a 1997 survey of readers by Waterstone's Booksellers, for instance, Tolkien's *The Lord of the Rings* was named the premier book of the twentieth century. *The Hobbit* also made this ranking of one hundred titles, as did volumes by Lewis, Waugh, and Greene. The *TLS* similarly listed *Small is Beautiful* among the most influential hundred postwar books. Lewis was enshrined in Poets' Corner in 2013, and scholarly collected works of Auden, Dawson, Eliot, and Waugh are underway.

journalism to fiction to poetry to history to social criticism, they offered a radical counterstatement to their era's ascendant precepts, and made their interpretations of a supposedly superseded creed a constituent element of their age's climate of opinion. Even if the modernist (and post-modernist) mythos remains dominant, posterity will be incalculably impoverished if it ignores a substantial proportion of the literary Christians, for they pose a challenge to that mentalité that its defenders disregard at the price of a truncated understanding of their own standpoint and of the genres in which they work. Surely Chesterton, Dawson, Eliot, Jones, Auden, Greene, Waugh, Lewis, Tolkien, and Sayers have a permanent claim on the attention of serious minds.

Whatever the future holds, though, students of the past will record a movement that confronted modernity at its roots, one that blossomed in an atmosphere more inimical to traditional religious growth than at any prior point in British history, and one that hence made orthodox Christianity part of twentieth-century culture to an extent that could scarcely have been predicted when this revival germinated. Eliot's eulogy of Chesterton thus also suits himself and all these authors: Eliot argued that even if Chesterton's ideas:

> appear to be totally without effect, even if they should be demonstrated to be wrong—which would perhaps only mean that men have not the good will to carry them out—they were *the* ideas that for his time were fundamentally Christian and Catholic. He did more, I think, than any man of his time...to maintain the existence of the important minority in the modern world.[38]

A character in George Orwell's *Keep the Aspidistra Flying* (1936) dubs the Catholic Church "a standing temptation to the intelligentsia." Although hostile himself to orthodoxy, Orwell was an astute observer of its extensive appeal to other authors, and his insight highlights that understanding why so many twentieth-century British thinkers could not resist what they deemed this good temptation is necessary for comprehending that epoch's intellectual milieu fully. In embracing a religion radically unlike the ideologies predominant in their time, these men and women discovered what they regarded as an authoritative source of personal religious meaning and moral imagination; this faith further provided a transcendent, tragic, traditional teleology that they proposed as an alternative public doctrine when opposing their era's regnant norms. To them, orthodox Christianity was a more holistic and realistic explanation

---

[38] *G. K. Chesterton: The Critical Judgments*, ed. D. J. Conlon (Antwerp: Universitaire Faculteiten Sint-Ignatius, 1976), 531-32. Emphasis in original.

of life, one promising order, respect for human dignity, cultural coherence and vitality, and the assurance that however foolish their own age was, the species is wise. The dreams of avarice and power propounded by irreligious ideologues that enchanted sundry other intellectuals seemed passing flights of fancy by comparison with the permanent sense of reality that the Christians felt they had found in orthodoxy. Believing (with Yeats) that their days were dragon-ridden, these self-styled guerrillas of grace sharpened the swords of the spirit and of imagination, many of them on the rock of Peter, hoping that what they considered their contemporary crusades would make them swords of honor.

"THE STARRY STREETS THAT POINT TO GOD": G. K. CHESTERTON'S "THEOLOGY OF PARTICIPATION" IN *THE NAPOLEON OF NOTTING HILL*

DANIEL FRAMPTON

"Nobody can say I am a novelist; nobody, at least, who has tried to read my novels", claimed G. K. Chesterton, the noted Catholic apologist, in a 1926 article for *The Illustrated London News*.[1] Later, in his *Autobiography*, published in 1937, the year he died, Chesterton similarly underrated these works:

> I have spoilt a number of jolly good ideas in my time. There is a reason for this; and it is really rather a piece of autobiography than of literary criticism.
> I think The Napoleon of Notting Hill was a book very well worth writing; but I am not sure that it was ever written.

"Considered as novels", such works as *The Napoleon of Notting Hill* (1904), Chesterton believed, "were not only not as good as a real novelist would have made them, but they were not as good as I might have made them myself, if I had really even been trying to be a real novelist". The reason for this, he supposed, was "the fact that I always have been and presumably always shall be a journalist".[2] And as a writer whose chief mode of expression was the essay, Chesterton was not wrong when he labelled himself a journalist. And generally, there has been little, if any, dispute on this matter; that, as Ian Ker has stated, Chesterton wrote "for the fun of the thing", and more importantly, because, as a "sage [...] who only 'pretended' to be a minor poet or novelist", Ker asserts, "he was ready to use any

---

[1] G. K. Chesterton, "The Silliness of Theodore Dreiser", in *The Collected Works of G. K. Chesterton*, Volume 34 (San Francisco: Ignatius Press, 1991), 88.
[2] G. K. Chesterton, *Autobiography* (London: Hutchinson & Co., 1937), 288-289

platform to spread ideas he considered both true and important".[3] And Chesterton appears to have confirmed this view himself, when, in his *Autobiography*, he claimed that "I have never taken my books seriously; but I take my opinions seriously".

It is the intention of this essay, however, to suggest that we should take Chesterton's novels seriously, especially *The Napoleon of Notting Hill*, his first attempt at a novel, taking into account one of the few positive remarks he made about his novels: that they were "more or less fresh and personal".[4] Indeed, I contend that *The Napoleon of Notting Hill* was the first major work by Chesterton that anticipated his conversion to Catholicism in 1922. Accordingly, I want to confirm and underscore William Oddie's own study *Chesterton and the Romance of Orthodoxy: The Making of GKC 1874-1908* (2008), in which he argued that there was already "the profession of belief in a specifically 'Catholic theology'" in Chesterton's journalistic output from at least 1903, in articles for *The Commonwealth* and *The Daily News*; also contending that, as early as the 1890s, Chesterton's work was "rooted in identifiable theological perspectives", which, Oddie asserts, "anticipated" his later reception into the Catholic Church.

Following up on Oddie's scholarship, I seek to examine in greater detail exactly what Chesterton's early "theological perspectives" were, as well as how they anticipated his later career as England's foremost Catholic apologist in the twentieth century. In particular, I want to forward the idea that Chesterton had expressed a vital "theology of participation" in *The Napoleon of Notting Hill*, four years before his great, arguably career-defining, work *Orthodoxy* (1908), by which time, as Oddie has shown, "politically and theologically, Chesterton's vision of life was essentially complete".[5] And in addition to this, it is also worth responding to recent resistance to Chesterton's classification as an apologist for the Catholic faith, specifically in *G. K. Chesterton, London and Modernity* (2013), where Matthew Ingleby, for instance, in his introduction to the work, stated that "the matter of his faith […] implicitly overrides or underwrites much that is said about him", and as a result, Chesterton risks "becoming reified, through

---

[3] Ian Ker, *G. K. Chesterton: A Biography* (2011; Oxford: Oxford University Press, 2012), 127.
[4] Chesterton, *Autobiography*, 110, 288.
[5] William Oddie, *Chesterton and the Romance of Orthodoxy: The Making of GKC 1874-1908* (Oxford: Oxford University Press, 2008), 64, 237, 382.

discursive reductionism, into little more than an emblematic concept".[6] However, one of the central points of this essay is that we should not underrate the importance of Chesterton's faith, especially since, as early as 1904, he expressed a conviction that was essentially Catholic. Although *The Napoleon of Notting Hill* cannot have been defined by Chesterton's Catholicism, which came later, of course, it may be said that it anticipated and even conditioned it. Indeed, such a consideration, far from being reductive, is to understand the fundamental being and direction of the author, as Chesterton himself understood when he wrote of John Henry Newman, another famous English convert:

> A mere conviction that Catholic thought is the clearest as well as the best disciplined, will not make a man a writer like Newman. But without that conviction Newman would not be a writer like Newman; and probably not a writer at all.[7]

Accordingly, we may observe in Chesterton's earliest endeavors, but especially in his literary work, the development of the Catholic "conviction" without which Chesterton would not have been a writer like Chesterton.

Set in a future London, in 1984, when "London is almost exactly like what it is now", Chesterton's introductory piece of verse to *The Napoleon of Notting Hill* provides us with the first hint at a Catholic conviction, when, in a few brief lines, he conjures a romantic vision of the streets set within the dreamy confines of his native Kensington:

> Far from your uplands set / I saw the dream; the streets I trod / The lit straight streets shot out and met / The starry streets that point to God. / This legend of an epic hour / A child I dreamed, and dream it still, / Under the great grey water-tower / That strikes the stars on Campden Hill.[8]

From the start, then, the novel strikes a personal note; Campden Hill being the place of Chesterton's birth, where, we are told, he dreamed of "starry streets that point to God". Indeed, it is clear that, as we shall see, the novel is substantively autobiographical, in terms of place, in particular, combining

---

[6] Matthew Ingleby, "Introduction", in *G. K. Chesterton, London and Modernity*, eds. Matthew Beaumont and Matthew Ingleby (2013, London: Bloomsbury Academic, 2016), 7.

[7] G. K. Chesterton, *The Victorian Age in Literature* (London: William & Norgate, Ltd., 1913), 9.

[8] G. K. Chesterton, *The Napoleon of Notting Hill* (1904: Teddington: The Echo Library, 2007), 3.

matter and spirit, since Chesterton's "starry" vision is ultimately rooted in the real, in the "Fantastic Suburb".

In his *Autobiography*, in a chapter titled "The Fantastic Suburb", Chesterton explained that *The Napoleon of Notting Hill* was largely a response to a perplexed journalist at the *Daily News*, where Chesterton worked, who, living in the London suburb of Clapham, "could not find it creditable or conceivable that *any* remark about Clapham could be anything but a sneer at Clapham" – that is to say, he "was ashamed of Clapham". And it was against "the Clapham journalist", whom Chesterton dubbed "the problem of my life", that he "marshalled the silly pantomime halberdiers of Notting Hill and all the rest". In this sense, the novel was his answer to "the problem of how men could be made to realise the wonder and splendour of being alive, in environments which their own daily criticism treated as dead-alive, and which their imagination had left for dead". Significantly, Chesterton commented that "everything" that he had "thought and done grew originally out of that problem". And in another notable admission, Chesterton, who, as indicated previously, saw himself chiefly as a journalist, admitted that, "in the thoughts of most modern people [...] the great city" had "become a journalistic generalisation", a sort of empire that was so broad that it was ultimately cold and impersonal. Subsequently, in "The Fantastic Suburb", Chesterton likened his negative reaction to the Clapham journalist to "what was called my dislike of Imperialism", which was really "a dislike of making England an Empire, in the sense of something more like Clapham Junction".[9]

This "dislike" is evident very early on in *The Napoleon of Notting Hill*, when, in a conversation between a group of Londoners, including a man named Auberon Quin, and the exiled President of Nicaragua, Juan del Fuego, the president defends, and is indeed proud of, the relative insignificance of his fallen nation, conquered by an alliance of "modern" cosmopolitanism. Yet one Londoner, a man named Barker, a modern advocate of cosmopolitanism, rejects what he refers to as the president's "Nicaraguan enthusiasm [...] not because a nation or ten nations were against you", he explains, but "because civilization was against you. We moderns believe in a great cosmopolitan civilization, one which shall include all the talents of all the absorbed peoples." Hearing this, the president retorts: "That is what I complain of your cosmopolitanism. When you say you want all peoples to unite, you really mean that you want all

---

[9] Chesterton, *Autobiography*, 134, 135.

peoples to unite to learn the tricks of your people."[10] Here, I think, Chesterton was voicing what was to become, throughout his career as both a journalist and a Catholic apologist, his informing skepticism about the modern world: "[That] there has crept into our thoughts, through a thousand small openings, a curious and unnatural idea. I mean the idea that unity is itself a good thing." As he wrote later in 1910, rallying against such unity by raising, significantly, I think, the example of religious poetry:

> Maudlin, inferior love poetry does, indeed, talk of lovers being "one soul", just as maudlin, inferior religious poetry talks of being lost in God; but the best poetry does not. When Dante meets Beatrice, he feels his distance from her, not his proximity; and all the greatest saints have felt their lowness, not their highness, in the moment of ecstasy.[11]

Therefore, we must realise that Chesterton's point here, which he had previously attempted to establish in *The Napoleon of Notting Hill*, was essentially religious rather than merely political. In other words, Chesterton's expression of "Nicaraguan enthusiasm", in 1904, should not simply be viewed as a projection of his anti-imperialist views, which, in the early 1900s, had made his name, above all as a journalist condemning Britain's war against the Boers in South Africa between 1899 and 1902. "I was called a Pro-Boer and, unlike some Pro-Boers, I was very proud of the title", he later recalled.[12] However, as the story of *The Napoleon of Notting Hill* progresses, it will become clear that, if it was "Pro-Boer", it was because Chesterton's aversion to imperialism underscored his proto-Catholic response to the Clapham journalist whose imagination had left Clapham "left for dead".

After his conversation with the President of Nicaragua, Auberon Quinn, a jovial and humorous man, is presented with the opportunity to imitate the president's "Nicaraguan enthusiasm", if only as a joke, when he is elected king of England – in the novel, England is once again a monarchy, though its monarchs are appointed at random. Tickled by the idea of "Clapham with a city guard" and "West Hampstead going into battle with its own banner", King Auberon, in a fit of humour, declares every London borough independent. And it is this "revival of the arrogance of the old medieval cities applied to our glorious suburbs" that provides the impetus for Chesterton's story, leading to the introduction of Adam Wayne, the

---

[10] Chesterton, *The Napoleon of Notting Hill*, 14.
[11] G. K. Chesterton, "What is Right with the World", in *The Apostles and the Wild Ducks and other essays*, ed. Dorothy E. Collins (London: Paul Elek, 1975), 166.
[12] Chesterton, *Autobiography*, 115.

"Napoleon" of Notting Hill, who, to the king's astonishment, has the temerity to take Notting Hill seriously. Possessed with his equivalent of "Nicaraguan enthusiasm", it is Wayne's refusal, as Provost of Notting Hill, to allow the construction of a highway through Pump Street, an insignificant row of five seemingly paltry shops, which leads to war with the other London boroughs.

Wayne's patriotic, even militant, resistance to the imperialism of London's other boroughs is Chesterton's response to the Clapham journalist, of course – defending what the modern age, in his mind, believed to be indefensible. Indeed, "My God in Heaven! […] is it possible that there is within the four seas of Britain a man who takes Notting Hill seriously?" is Auberon's befuddled rejoinder to Wayne's mooted defence of the "sacred" peak that, addressing the young Wayne ten years before, he had jestingly dubbed "so unutterably Notting". Nevertheless, Wayne is unfaltering in his love of his native Notting Hill, declaring: "The sacred hill is ringed with the armies of Bayswater, and I am ready to die." And at the root of Wayne's patriotism, which many think "absurd", is the notion that Notting Hill, a seemingly insignificant plot of "common earth", is defensible exactly because it is common and small. As Chesterton writes of Wayne, he "knew the supreme psychological fact about patriotism", which is "the fact that the patriot never under any circumstances boasts of the largeness of his country, but always, and of necessity, boasts of the smallness of it". And it is this statement that holds the key to Chesterton's "theology of participation", as we shall see, which was expressed for the first time in his spirited defence of what he dubbed "Adam Wayne's atmosphere […] the atmosphere which you and I thought had vanished from an educated world for ever".[13] And it is worth examining this "atmosphere", or rather this theology; the Nicaraguan enthusiasm that suffuses Chesterton's first novel, since it does show, I think, that by 1904 the author was in possession of a proto-Catholic conviction and theological perspective that cannot be written off as a mere Edwardian "revival of the arrogance of the old medieval cities".

In an interview with W. R. Titterton, in the late 1930s, Chesterton underscored the significance of the "spirit" of Notting Hill. As he related to Titterton, it was in the 1890s and early 1900s that he became "uneasily conscious" that so-called "Progressives" wanted to destroy what he "wanted most to preserve. Little things. Neighborly things." Chesterton informed Titterton that this unease was confirmed to him "in a flash when I was walking down a certain street in Notting Hill". Observing a row of "shops

---

[13] Chesterton, *The Napoleon of Notting Hill*, 25, 40, 41, 48, 70.

supplying all the spiritual and bodily needs of man", he "realised how completely lost this bit of Notting Hill was in the modern world". While such intellectuals as George Bernard Shaw, H. G. Wells "and the rest of them were interested only in world-shaking and world-making events", and how things "every day [became] bigger and bigger – in every way", Chesterton could not stop "gazing with rapt admiration at the row of little shops", believing that they mattered more than any "world-shaking" event.[14] As Wayne says, these are the houses that men have built, "in which they are born, fall in love, pray, marry, and die". Indeed, a key constituent of the "atmosphere" of Wayne is exactly this love of – and, as I argue, too, this participation and exultation in – such monotony, as he explains to Auberon:

> I was born, like other men, in a spot of the earth which I loved because I had played boys' games there, and fallen in love, and talked with my friends through nights that were nights of the gods [...] Why should they be commonplace? Why should they be absurd? Why should it be grotesque to say that a pillar-box is poetic when for a year I could not see a red pillar-box against the yellow evening in a certain street without being wracked with something of which God keeps the secret, but which is stronger than sorrow or joy? Why should any one be able to raise a laugh by saying "the Cause of Notting Hill"? – Notting Hill where thousands of immortal spirits blaze with alternate hope and fear.

This was Chesterton's answer to the challenge of the Clapham journalist, an answer that was provided in a non-literary form, four years later, in his classic work *Orthodoxy*, specifically in the chapter "The Ethics of Elfland".

Chesterton was plainly describing himself when he labelled Wayne "a genuine natural mystic, one of those who live on the border of fairyland", but "perhaps the first to realise how often the boundary of fairyland runs through a crowded city".[15] And it was Chesterton's mission, not only in his first novel, but in his later works of fiction and apologetics as well, to understand and convey this vision of the streets, of "starry streets that point to God", to a modern audience and make it see romance even in a lamppost. And the chapter "The Ethics of Elfland", contained within *Orthodoxy*, lauding the fairy-story as a literary mode of expression reviving "the ancient instinct of astonishment", was in this way a manifesto that, in *The Napoleon of Notting Hill*, he had already put into action. Such "astonishing tales" as

---

[14] W. R. Titterton, *G. K. Chesterton: A Portrait* (1936; London: Douglas Organ, 1947), 43, 44.
[15] Chesterton, *The Napoleon of Notting Hill*, 41, 42, 47.

these, he explained in 1908, "say that apples were golden only to refresh the forgotten moment when we found that they were green. They make rivers run with wine only to make us remember, for one wild moment, that they run with water." Accordingly, fairy tales were really for adults, since, to a child's mind, "mere life is interesting enough. A child of seven is excited by being told that Tommy opened a door and saw a dragon. But a child of three is excited by being told that Tommy opened a door." And we should mark this understanding, since this manner of "return", to a state of childlike innocence and vision, is what underscored Chesterton's reception into the Catholic Church in 1922.

It may be argued, then, that *The Napoleon of Notting Hill* exhibited exactly that literary ethic expounded in *Orthodoxy,* in "The Ethics of Elfland" – reminding moderns of what they had, almost by definition, forgotten: that "the things common to all men are more important than the things peculiar to any men. Ordinary things are more valuable than extraordinary things; nay, they are more extraordinary."[16] Accordingly, we should not underestimate the importance of *The Napoleon of Notting Hill* as a signifier of the direction that Chesterton was heading in, even if, at the time, he was not aware of the final destination. Although it is likely true that, "lacking the patience to write the sort of novel in which spiritual experience could be delineated at length", Chesterton "tended to express his ideas most effectively in concerted form such as his newspaper columns", as Nick Freeman has argued, the writing of *The Napoleon of Notting Hill*, which began around 1897, might have been enough of an "intellectual (and spiritual) provocation" to allow Chesterton to work through some of the "implications of his insights".[17] Moreover, the writing of this first novel, as well as such early works as *Charles Dickens* (1906), allowed Chesterton to examine and exude for himself the implications of the one nineteenth-century author who, in his "buffoonery and bravery", possessed "the spirit of the Middle Ages", a spirit that Chesterton would later recognise as essentially Catholic.[18]

Writing some years later, in his work *The Catholic Church and Conversion* (1926), Chesterton fathomed that "the return of Catholic ideas to the

[16] G. K. Chesterton, *Orthodoxy* (1908; Cavalier Classics, 2015), 33, 38, 39.
[17] Nick Freeman, "Chesterton, Machen and the Invisible City", in *G. K. Chesterton, London and Modernity*, 86.
[18] G. K. Chesterton, *Charles Dickens* (1906; Kelly Bray: House of Stratus, 2001), 70.

separated parts of Christendom was often indeed indirect":

> It came through the Romantic Movement, a glimpse of the mere picturesqueness of medievalism; but it is something more than an accident that Romances, like Romance languages, are named after Rome. Or it came through the instinctive reaction of old-fashioned people like Johnson or Scott or Cobbett, wishing to save old elements that had originally been Catholic against a progress that was merely Capitalist. But it led them to denounce that Capitalist progress and become, like Cobbett, practical foes of Protestantism without being practicing followers of Catholicism. Or it came from the Pre-Raphaelites or the opening of continental art and culture by Matthew Arnold and Morris and Ruskin and the rest.[19]

Whether or not he drew a connection between "romance" and Rome in the early 1900s, Chesterton, I think, identified with this same "indirect" tradition, but especially with Charles Dickens, who "was much more medieval in his attacks on medievalism than [...] [the Pre-Raphaelites] were in their defences of it". Indeed, Chesterton praised Dickens at the expense of the so-called "admirers of the Middle Ages", who, he claimed in 1906, "had in their subtlety and sadness the spirit of the present day". So while Chesterton's own medievalism was not necessarily Catholic in 1904, he had by this time studied and imbibed the implications of Dickens' insights, which he believed to be a more accurate representation of the true "spirit" of the Middle Ages. And the effect of this process of "intellectual (and spiritual) provocation", regarding Chesterton's familiarity with, and championing of, Dickens, was that Chesterton applied that spirit and literary ethic to *The Napoleon of Notting Hill*. Indeed, two years later, Chesterton explained that, possessing this ethic, "Dickens himself had, in the most sacred and serious sense of the term, the key of the street", since he "could always vitalise some dark or dull corner of London [...] a window, or a railing, or the keyhole of a door". This talent for "exaggeration", which was "the definition of Dickens's art", was *participatory* just as much as it was perceptive, Chesterton claimed, meaning that the commonplace, the everyday object, the lamppost, and even the common man, was – but more importantly, could be *made* to be – indicative of a reality above and beyond the visible: an ethic that, I suggest, Chesterton employed in the forwarding of his vision of "starry streets that point to God". This is what Chesterton was getting at when in his 1906 study of Dickens he championed the author's "eerie realism", where "things seem more actual than things really are", being chiefly concerned with a branch of "unbearable realism" that

---

[19] G. K. Chesterton, *The Catholic Church and Conversion* (1926; San Francisco: Ignatius, 2006), 96-97.

"does not exist in reality" and can only be got at, epistemologically, not by "walking observantly", but instead, "by walking dreamily in a place", as Chesterton argues:

> [Dickens] did not look at Charing Cross to improve his mind or count the lamp-posts in Holborn to practise his arithmetic. But unconsciously he made all these places the scenes of the monstrous drama in his miserable little soul. He walked in darkness under the lamps of Holborn, and was crucified at Charing Cross. So for him ever afterwards these places had the beauty that only belongs to battlefields.

"Dickens did not stamp these places on his mind; he stamped his mind on these places", Chesterton affirmed, and consequently, "for him ever afterwards these streets were mortally romantic".[20]

This supposedly Dickensian investiture of romantic status on the streets, as Chesterton saw it, is apparent in the character Wayne as well, who acts as a sort of proxy for Chesterton in *The Napoleon of Notting Hill*, likening his sword to a "fairy wand" that has the power to make "mean landscapes magnificent, and hovels outlast cathedrals". Endowed with "a magic from outside the world", so that "whatever is touched with it is never again wholly common", Wayne sees no reason why it should "not make lamp-posts fairer than Greek lamps; and an omnibus-ride like a painted ship". The magic of this wand, which is an analogy of the supercharged efficacy of the fairy tale, evinced in *Orthodoxy*, is exactly as Wayne says it is: that "if I touch, with this fairy wand, the railways and the roads of Notting Hill, men will love them, and be afraid of them for ever".[21] And as the writer Titterton later wrote, elevating Chesterton's ability to make dull streets seem extraordinary: "He saw, what you have never seen – a London street."[22] However, Chesterton's literary vision of the streets was not simply perception, but a creative and participatory act, I believe; literary, indeed, in the sense that Chesterton sought to participate in God's creation, albeit as a novelist. Moreover, Chesterton, in *The Napoleon of Notting Hill*, was teaching others, and perhaps even tutoring himself, to love in a specifically Catholic way.

In an article titled "A Defence of Patriotism", published in *The Defendant* in 1902, Chesterton had expressed a "love of the city" that, anticipating *The Napoleon of Notting Hill*, he likened to "that high and ancient intellectual

---

[20] Chesterton, *Charles Dickens*, 20, 21.
[21] Chesterton, *The Napoleon of Notting Hill*, 42, 43.
[22] Titterton, *Chesterton*, 9.

passion [...] on the same table with the primal passions of our being".[23] This "love", or rather that "being", I want to suggest, was, in Chesterton's mind, participatory; participating, that is to say, in God's creation. Indeed, it is my contention that Chesterton was responding, if only on an instinctual level at first, to what the theologian David L. Schindler would later define as a "modern culture [that] marginalizes love [...] God-centred love", an "order of love" and "bearer of a 'word' or 'logic' (logos) that presupposes an ordering intelligence [...] that gives things their deepest and most proper order and meaning, always and everywhere". Schindler saw that such "love" was by definition participatory, since it involved a created being, a "constitutive *relation* [...] mediating the love between God and the rest of the cosmos".[24] As D. C. Schindler, his son, also writes, there is "an implicit atheism" at the centre of modernity that, "effectively separating God's being from the being of everything else", underrates and accordingly undermines "the significance of receptivity".[25] And the writing of *The Napoleon of Notting Hill* was the first work that really allowed Chesterton to explore that notion of receptivity; being receptive in the sense that Chesterton, who already possessed an innate love of his native plot, centred around Campden Hill, could understand "being". Accordingly, as early as the late 1890s, Chesterton was forging a pathway to conversion along which he could pass, first through Anglo-Catholicism, on his way to Catholicism, which, being expressly sacramental, constituted an authentic medievalism.

Certainly, it is worth underlining the point that Chesterton's neo-medievalist/proto-Catholic vision – relating it especially to his Dickensian vision of Notting Hill's streets and the notion of a "mortally romantic" cityscape akin to a "battlefield" – was at once beautiful and frightful; what David Torevell has described, similarly, as "the early medieval notion that the cosmos was a thing of symbolic and spiritual potency, a sacred arena for discovering knowledge and truth, another book like scripture, from which one could constantly and easily read off the things of God".[26] Indeed, this

---

[23] G. K. Chesterton, "A Defence of Patriotism", in *The Defendant* (1902; Mineola: Dover Publications, 2012), 78.
[24] David L. Schindler, *Ordering Love: Liberal Societies and the Memory of God* (Grand Rapids: William B. Eerdmans Publishing Company, 2011), ix, x, 4, 6.
[25] D. C. Schindler, "Beauty and the Holiness of Mind", in *Being Holy in the World: Theology and Culture in the Thought of David L. Schindler*, eds. Nicholas J. Healy Jr. and D. C. Schindler (Grand Rapids: William B. Eerdmans Publishing Company, 2011), 15.
[26] David Torevell, *Losing the Sacred: Ritual, Modernity and Liturgical Reform* (Edinburgh: T & T Clark, 2000), 73.

might explain why Chesterton emphasised Dicken's medieval "bravery", not just his "buffoonery", since such an "arena", viewed from a Catholic perspective, founded on an "embodied" sense of the sacred, entailed a fervid encounter with what Adrian J. Walker, for instance, relates to as "the More-Than-World from within the world".[27] And it appears that Chesterton's novel does conclude that the street really is dangerous, since the "fanatical" love that it inspires, and is indeed part of, does lead to war on the streets; and even Wayne refers to himself as "I, the fanatic".[28] And in this sense, Wayne, the soldier and leader of Notting Hill, exudes this "theology of participation", as Glenn W. Olsen phrases it, for instance – meaning "the act-of-being" – "of the creature in the life [...] of the Creator", which Wayne is part of.[29] Moreover, since the novel, as a literary device, is chiefly taken up with such an act, of the participation of its characters in a created world, albeit on the page, Chesterton's chosen mode of understanding and delivery is, in this sense, synonymous with the response to the Clapham journalist that he sought to deliver through *The Napoleon of Notting Hill*, which is why we should, I think, take his novel seriously; that is, to take seriously "the causality of the intrinsic purposiveness of things", as the theologian Aidan Nichol's has put it, "rooted in the doctrine of creation", which "Western thought has managed to reduce [...] to a philosophy of knowledge", giving up the medieval "notion of participation" that is "key to a sound ontology", he writes. Indeed, it was via this understanding – which was able to "surmount both the closed transcendence of Plato, and the closed immanence of Aristotle", most of all through the thought of Thomas Aquinas – that Chesterton conveyed his vision of the streets, "through the key concept of participation", upholding the "structure of transcendental causality held together by the primordial universal Origin of all forms, all activity", as Nichols has described it.[30]

It does make sense, then, that Chesterton should also later opt into the sacraments and liturgy of the Catholic Church, which were by definition participatory, "enabling the self to develop in relation to the sacred world the rite upholds", as Torevell writes, so that the participant "is invited into

---

[27] Adrian J. Walker, "'Constitutive Relations': Toward a Spiritual Reading of *Physis*", in *Being Holy in the World,* 124.
[28] Chesterton, *The Napoleon of Notting Hill*, 110.
[29] Glenn W. Olsen, *The Turn to Transcendence: The Role of Religion in the Twenty-First Century* (Washington D.C.: The Catholic University of America Press, 2010), 209, 210.
[30] Aidan Nichols, *Christendom Awake: On Re-energising the Church in Culture* (1999; Edinburgh: T&T Clark, 2000), 63, 65.

the story of redemptive Christianity".[31] As Gerard Loughlin explains as well:

> The biblical story is present not only in the readings of the lectionary but in the very language of the liturgy which, through penitence and acclamation, comes to focus on the life, death and resurrection of Jesus Christ. The participants' absorption into the story is made possible through their absorption of the story in and through its ritual enactment. They are not simply witnesses of the story, but characters within it.[32]

Therefore, we should mark the following statement by Chesterton, in *Orthodoxy*, that "poetry could be acted as well as composed". Indeed, it may be that Chesterton was attempting to revive "this heroic and monumental manner in ethics" that he claimed had "entirely vanished with supernatural religion".[33] The irony, of course, in writing such "poetry", was that *The Napoleon of Notting Hill* underscored that very absence, an irony that I think Chesterton was aware of as a writer, since he was not a man of action. This was recognised by the Polish poet and army officer Bolesław Wieniawa-Długoszowski, when, meeting Chesterton in Warsaw in 1927, he greeted him "not as a famous writer, not even as a friend of Poland, but as a born cavalry officer who had just missed his profession".[34]

As we have seen, *The Napoleon of Notting Hill*, through its message but also its literary ethic, may be seen to anticipate and even underwrite Chesterton's later conversion. However, despite possessing the rudiments of a Catholic "theology of participation" in 1904, it took Chesterton nearly two decades to finally become Catholic, which might be seen to contradict Titterton's assertion that Chesterton "was a Catholic as soon as he began to see, and in perception as soon as he began to think".[35] If this was true, then we may say, modifying Wieniawa-Długoszowski's statement, that Chesterton was a born Catholic who almost missed his faith; and that, had this happened, it was the same "Nicaraguan enthusiasm", essential to Chesterton's theology of participation, which would have been to blame.

Commenting in *The Thing: Why I Am a Catholic* (1929), Chesterton, who had been a Catholic for seven years by this point, took special care to

---

[31] Torevell, *Losing the Sacred*, 196.

[32] Gerard Loughlin, *Telling God's Story: Bible, Church and Narrative* (Cambridge: Cambridge University Press, 1996), 223.

[33] Chesterton, *Orthodoxy*, 75.

[34] "News and Comments," in *The Chesterton Review*, vol. 3, no. 2 (1977), 301.

[35] Titterton, *Chesterton*, 83.

rebut the accusation, forwarded by "most critics of Catholicism", that the Catholic Church was "destructive of patriotism" – one such rebuttal by Chesterton being that "the name of Chaucer is alone enough to show that English literature was English a long time before it was Protestant". And Chesterton was adamant that, while "English literature will always have been Protestant [...] it might have been Catholic; without ceasing to be English literature, and perhaps succeeding in producing a deeper literature and a happier England".[36] Whatever the veracity of such claims are, what is relevant to this chapter is that Chesterton was aware of the tension between the catholicity of his Church and the "Nicaraguan enthusiasm" that he preached in 1904, when he had declared that "Notting Hill is right; it has always been right".[37] And it might be that Chesterton was so keen to dispel this tension, later, because he had, as an Anglo-Catholic, believed it himself.

Titterton, who I think understood Chesterton's Catholic ethic well, claimed that, despite being a Catholic in all but name before 1922, Chesterton had "for a time [...] conceived the possibility of a Catholic accepting the authority of the Church without accepting the authority of Rome. Later on he was to see that there is, in fact, no other *authority*. But at the time he did not see it."[38] Indeed, it could be that the reason why it took Chesterton so long to be received into the Church was the apparent contradiction between the Nicaraguan enthusiasm, voiced in *The Napoleon of Notting Hill*, and the *supranational* "authority of Rome", a tension, between the particular and the universal, which would only be resolved by the conception of a *supernatural* commonwealth of the particular untied under a new universal: what, in 1919, Chesterton concluded was "the only league of nations that ever had a chance".[39] As he wrote in his *Autobiography*, about Clapham being swallowed by the empire of London: "I came to admit that *some* sort of universality, another sort of universality, would be needed before such places could really become shrines or sacred sites."[40]

It was during the First World War that Chesterton appears to have truly taken up the cause of Christendom, which, in *A Short History of England* (1917), he defined as "variation without antagonism". In this work we can see that, as follows, Chesterton had resolved the tension between the

---

[36] G. K. Chesterton, *The Thing: Why I Am a Catholic* (1929; Gloucester: Dodo Press, 2009), 72, 159, 163.

[37] Chesterton, *The Napoleon of Notting Hill*, 100.

[38] Titterton, *Chesterton*, 84.

[39] G. K. Chesterton, *The New Witness*, June 20, 1919.

[40] Chesterton, *Autobiography*, 135.

particular and the universal, between Clapham and the rest of London, indeed, by forwarding William Shakespeare's ethic as a literary example of this solution afforded by Christendom:

> Shakespeare died upon St. George's Day, and much of what St. George had meant died with him. I do not mean that the patriotism of Shakespeare or of England died; that remained and even rose steadily, to be the noblest pride of the coming times. But much more than patriotism had been involved in that image of St. George to whom the Lion Heart had dedicated England long ago in the deserts of Palestine. The conception of a patron saint had carried from the Middle Ages one very unique and as yet unreplaced idea. It was the idea of variation without antagonism. The Seven Champions of Christendom were multiplied by seventy times seven in the patrons of towns, trades and social types; but the very idea that they were all saints excluded the possibility of ultimate rivalry in the fact that they were all patrons. The Guild of the Shoemakers and the Guild of the Skinners, carrying the badges of St. Crispin and St. Bartholomew, might fight each other in the streets; but they did not believe that St. Crispin and St. Bartholomew were fighting each other in the skies. Similarly the English would cry in battle on St. George and the French on St. Denis; but they did not seriously believe that St. George hated St. Denis or even those who cried upon St. Denis.[41]

Accordingly, it was Christendom that, by means of its own universality, that allowed the nation, the particular, to exist righteous yet uncompromised within the broader Christian commonwealth. Here, and only here, could St. George comfortably take up his seat, emblazoned with the red cross, alongside St. Denis at the sacred roundtable of the saints.

This instinct for brotherhood was already present in *The Napoleon of Notting Hill*, it may be said; evident, for example, in Wayne's jubilant response to hearing his enemies cry "Bayswater forever!" towards the end of the third battle of the war of London's boroughs, declaring: "We have won! We have taught our enemies patriotism!"[42] Although Wayne has no wish to be incorporated into Bayswater and a broader London collective, what he does have in common with the men of Bayswater now is patriotism, which Notting Hill's resistance has gifted to them. Accordingly, though they "fight each other in the streets", their rivalry, at the conclusion of the battle for the waterworks atop Campden Hill, is not defined by anything other than a love for the "particular", implying a shared *participation* in a transcending

---

[41] G. K. Chesterton, *A Short History of England* (1917; Teddington: Echo Library, 2008), 74.
[42] Chesterton, *The Napoleon of Notting Hill*, 89.

brotherhood, "another sort of universality" – a freeing catholicity, in the form of Christendom, which in 1904, I think, Chesterton was on his way to discovering – that, far from traducing the particular, actually embraced it. And it may be said that, ultimately, this was Christianity's achievement; that, as Pope Benedict XVI writes, Jesus "sits there as the greater Moses, who broadens the Covenant to include all nations" – by allowing for the "variation without antagonism" that Chesterton sought, one might add.[43]

As Lynne Hapgood has observed, the "Chestertonian" depiction of the city "consistently privileges what is distinctively single within the plurality of the material world because such objects/images have the power to carry meaning *in* history as well as create meaning *outside* history".[44] Indeed, this privilege was allowed for, and indeed encouraged, because the city, or the particular, as Hapgood indicates, was indicative of eternity. This was the foundation of what Michael D. Hurley has referred to as "Chesterton's counter-cultural love for London", which, he writes, implied "a metaphysical appreciation of, and for, the physical".[45] And, as we have seen, a key constituent of this rejection of modern cosmopolitanism was what Chesterton would come to define, in "The Ethics of Elfland", as the "poetry of limits", which had been with him since childhood.[46] As he wrote *Autobiography*:

> All my life I have loved edges; and the boundary-line that brings one thing sharply against another. All my life I have loved frames and limits; and I will maintain that the largest wilderness looks larger seen through a window.[47]

---

[43] As Pope Benedict explains, the Torah, which brought with it "a very definite social order [...] juridical and social framework [...] for just politics and for daily life", was merely for a chosen few, while the early Christians, such as St Paul the Apostle, recognised that the "literal application of Israel's social order to the people of all nations would have been tantamount to a denial of the universality of the growing community of God", which, Pope Benedict XVI writes, St Paul and others transformed into Christendom. Joseph Ratzinger, *Jesus of Nazareth: From the Baptism in the Jordan to the Transfiguration*, trans. Adrian J. Walker (2007; London: Bloomsbury, 2008), 66, 114, 118.

[44] Lynne Hapgood, "The Chestertonian City: A Singularly Plural Approach", in *G. K. Chesterton, London and Modernity*, 38.

[45] Michael D. Hurley, "Why Chesterton Loved London", in *G. K. Chesterton, London and Modernity*, 18, 20.

[46] Chesterton, *Orthodoxy*, 47.

[47] Chesterton, *Autobiography*, 32.

This also explains Chesterton's rejection of imperialism and collectivism, because they entailed "unification and centralisation on a large scale". As he argued in *Orthodoxy*, the "modern universe is literally an empire". And it was this failure of "modern thought", going "against the fairy feeling about strict limits and conditions", which undermined the appreciation of the ordinary and the "poetry of limits".[48]

Returning, then, to the Clapham journalist and "the problem of how men could be made to realize the wonder and splendour of being alive, in environments which their own daily criticism treated as dead-alive, and which their imagination had left for dead", it was Chesterton's conclusion, already evident in 1904, that modern man should first learn to love his own locality, his own street, since it was clear to him that "the imagination deals with an image. And an image is in its a nature a thing that has an outline and therefore a limit."[49] And by the time of the publication of *Orthodoxy* in 1908, Chesterton had finally realised that, having "fancied that I stood alone", and "not even thought of Christian theology", he "was really in the ridiculous position of being backed up by all Christendom", by which he meant, in this case, Christian ethics. And for all the hopes of the "Progressives", hoping "every day" that the world became "bigger and bigger – in every way", Chesterton could not help but conclude that, though "the age gave me no encouragement to feel it", the world was quite extraordinary already.[50] As he would write two years later, in an essay titled "What is Right with the World", he did, even as "an agnostic [...] affirm, with the full weight of sincerity, that trees and flowers are good at the beginning, whatever happens to them at the end", and "that human lives were good at the beginning". This "positive theology", as Chesterton described it, already apparent in *The Napoleon of Notting Hill*, was what ultimately conditioned his later Catholicism, I believe.[51]

The declaration that "the aim of life is appreciation" was especially vital to Chesterton, then, especially since, as a young student at the Slade School of Art in the 1890s, he had only "hung on to the remains of religion by one thin thread of thanks [...] a sort of mystical minimum of gratitude". And Chesterton remembered later that, in order to escape the pessimism of the 1890s, he was obliged to turn to a "makeshift mystical theory [...] that even mere existence, reduced to its most primary limits, was extraordinary

[48] Chesterton, *Orthodoxy*, 45, 46.
[49] Chesterton, *Autobiography*, 107.
[50] Chesterton, *Orthodoxy*, 4, 48.
[51] Chesterton, "What is Right with the World", 165.

enough to be exciting. Anything was magnificent as compared with nothing."[52] And it would not be so fantastic to suppose that *The Napoleon of Notting Hill* was that "makeshift mystical theory". And it hardly seems a coincidence that Wayne's victory – successfully tutoring Notting Hill's enemies in such appreciation, primarily through their participation in three pitched battles that culminate in the battle for the waterworks atop Campden Hill – takes place in the vicinity of Chesterton's birthplace, where, in the story, Wayne rejoices at hearing his enemies declare "Bayswater forever!" The love, manifested in Wayne's patriotic defence of Notting Hill, himself being a "constitutive relation", was a projection of Chesterton's love for his native Kensington, where he was born and raised. And Chesterton speaks through Wayne when the Lord High Provost of Notting Hill explains that:

> I am doing now what I have done all my life, what is the only happiness, what is the only universality. I am clinging to something [...] Fools, you go about and see the kingdoms of the earth, and are liberal and wise, and cosmopolitan, which is all that the devil can give you – all that he could offer to Christ only to be spurned away. I am doing what the truly wise do [...] The joy I have is what the lover knows when a woman is everything [...] It is what I know when Notting Hill is everything. I have a city. Let it stand or fall.[53]

Born at 32 Sheffield Terrace on Campden Hill, Chesterton was christened at St. George's Church, opposite the site of Wayne's last victory in *The Napoleon of Notting Hill*. Significantly, it was on Campden Hill, too, that Chesterton as a child felt in a sense "more wideawake" than he ever did as an adult, "and moving in broader daylight". What he meant, he explained, was that "I have never lost the sense that this was my real life; the real beginning of what should have been a more real life" – and the this "beginning", in such "strange daylight", was founded in a specific place, Campden Hill:

> It seems to me that when I came out of the house and stood on that hill of houses, where the roads sank steeply towards Holland Park, and terraces of new red houses could look out across a vast hollow and see far away the sparkle of the Crystal Palace [...] I was subconsciously certain then, as I am consciously certain now, that there was the white and solid road and the worthy beginning of the life of man; and that it is man who afterwards darkens it with dreams or goes astray from it in self-deception.

---

[52] Chesterton, *Autobiography*, 93, 94, 333.
[53] Chesterton, *The Napoleon of Notting Hill*, 105.

What Chesterton was affirming in this passage, I think, was what he had written in "What is Right with the World" in 1910: "that human lives were good at the beginning." Accordingly, what Chesterton sought was a return "to those first years of innocence [that] were the beginning of something worthy, perhaps more worthy than any of the things that actually followed them". Indeed, towards the end of his life, recalling these "first years of innocence", Chesterton made a significant admission when – remembering "the strange daylight" of his earliest years on Campden Hill, which was "something more than the light of common day" – he likened it to "the Sacrament of Penance", when a Catholic "by definition, [does] step out again" on "those steep roads down from Campden Hill [...] into that dawn of his own beginning and look with new eyes across the world to a Crystal Palace that is really of crystal". When Chesterton was received into the Catholic Church in 1922, then, and received Confession, as part of a theology of participation, he was returned to that same state of "innocence" when, as he noted at the beginning of *The Napoleon of Notting Hill*, as "A child I dreamed, and dream it still, / Under the great grey water-tower / That strikes the stars on Campden Hill". As he later wrote, he had discovered the "one religion which dared to go down with me into the depths of myself", and which was, as we have seen, founded on the following Chestertonian principle:

> That is the idea of taking things with gratitude, and not taking things for granted. Thus, the Sacrament of Penance gives a new life, and reconciles a man to all living, but it does not do it as the optimists and the hedonists and the heathen preachers of happiness do it. The gift is given at a price, and is conditioned by a confession. In other words, the name of the price is Truth, which may also be called Reality; but it is facing the reality about oneself.[54]

Accordingly, when, in the early 1900s, Chesterton "saw the dream; the streets I trod / The lit straight streets shot out and met / The starry streets that point to God", indeed pointing to his acceptance of, and true participation in, Catholicism two decades later, he was already on his way back to "something more worthy".

---

[54] Chesterton, *Autobiography*, 52, 329, 330, 341.

Two Visions of the Holy Fool

David Deavel

Introduction: Holy Folly in Twentieth-Century Catholic Literature

The twentieth-century Catholic revival in literature, particularly in English, was filled with the revival and re-use of various themes and tropes taken from the broader Catholic intellectual and spiritual patrimony. One of these, found in a variety of different writers, is that of holy folly and the accompanying holy fools who practice or bear it. This essay will explore two examples of holy folly found in novels in the first half of the century. Both of them manifest the main lines of the tradition of the holy fool in Catholic (and Orthodox) spirituality but do so in complementary ways that both reflect and advance the conception of holy folly. The first is that of J. Blue, protagonist of the 1928 novel *Mr. Blue*, authored by the American screenwriter Myles Connolly. A great fan of Chesterton, Connolly's own writing manifests his debt to Chesterton thematically by making Blue a kind of Franciscan Thomist who loves the transcendent God in the very details and particularity of the creation in which he is both immanent and cozy. But his main character is also the kind of holy fool who is readily recognizable in the traditions of East and West—one who disdains ordinary life, practices extraordinary and sometimes useless and odd acts of voluntary poverty and charity, confuses even those closest to him, and flees from ordinary life permanently, literally imitating Christ in his refusal to have a place to lay his head.

The second example is that of Chesterton's own Innocent Smith, hero of the 1912 novel *Manalive*. Though written before Chesterton's formal reception into the Catholic Church in 1922, the novel nevertheless reflects a capacious and fully Catholic mind and imagination that had largely been realized already by the publication of *Orthodoxy* in 1908.[1] *Manalive*'s main character represents Chesterton's own holy worldliness insofar as Smith's folly is depicted not as leading permanently away from the structures of ordinary middle-class existence into radical and permanent poverty. Instead, Innocent Smith is a married man whose folly leads those around him out of their own ungrateful (un-eucharistic) and blind existence into one that reveals to them the glory of God present in hobbies, labels on wine bottles, and, most importantly, others.

Before examining the two works in depth, it is important, however, to understand with some more specificity what is meant by the tradition of holy folly.

Holy folly in Christian Tradition

While some scholars talk as if the tradition of "holy fools" is one that is peculiar to Eastern Christianity as seen in the *iurodivyi* of late-medieval Russian life, the origins of holy foolishness are seen first in the Old Testament prophets, whose own bizarre behavior was inspired in order to reveal to Israel what it was that God desired for them and wanted out of them. Though some of them may only have done discrete foolish actions commanded by the Lord, others acted in ways that prefigured the Christian taking up of a life of foolishness. Hosea's marriage to a prostitute to symbolize the infidelity of Israel, the bride of the Lord, was the kind of committed foolishness seen in the Desert Fathers, Francis of Assisi, and various Byzantine and Russian figures famous for their eccentricities and holiness.

The reason the Christian tradition has produced more 'full-time' fools than Israel did is because the entirety of the Christian tradition has proclaimed that divine wisdom does not appear so to a world that is beset by sin and ignorance, which render most people incapable of judging rightly. What this means is that those who follow divine wisdom most consistently will inevitably appear to others, including other Christians whose redemption is not yet complete, as fools. It is, significantly, in St. Paul's letters to the Corinthian Church that we see the spelling out of this teaching on holy foolishness, for it is in these letters that the Apostle is attempting to navigate an ecclesial environment that seems less like the post-Pentecost snapshot of

---

[1] The best account of Chesterton's development in this regard is William Oddie, *Chesterton and the Romance of Orthodoxy: The Making of GKC, 1874-1908* (Oxford: Oxford University Press, 2008).

an idyllic community holding material goods in common and spending their spare time alternating between worship in the Temple, Eucharistic assembly, and devotion to the Apostles' teaching (see Acts 2:42-47) and more like what we know of the Church from the rest of history. That is to say, the Church is a community of people who have been redeemed by Christ's action on the Cross and given the fruits of redemption in baptism, yet for whom redemption has not become full: fits of faithfulness alternate with grievous sins and jockeying for position that would, perhaps, make the heathen blush.

St. Paul's correspondence with the Corinthians is an extended argument with that particular community and with every particular Church throughout time to understand that Christian faith is ultimately based on the logic of the Incarnation and Passion of Christ. The imitation of Christ is itself foolishness to the world, both Jewish and Gentile, because it presents a God who himself seems foolishly unworldly. The infinite, all-glorious, and all-holy Creator takes on the finitude and ingloriousness of human creaturely existence in order to dwell with them, teach them, and ultimately make them holy. If this is not bad enough, he does so not by any marvelous use of power but by a life characterized by rejection by his own people and the powers-that-be culminating in a shameful death by public execution that, in form, noted not only political defeat but also spiritual cursedness. As St. Paul wrote in his epistle to the Galatians, quoting from Deuteronomy, 'Christ redeemed us from the curse of the law, having become a curse for us—for it is written, "Cursed be every one who hangs on a tree"' (3:13 RSV).

The glory of the redeemer was manifest in his appearance as the lowest of the unredeemed—one fit for condemnation by both the political and the spiritual communities. Thus it is that in one of his finest appeals to the Corinthian Church, he holds out neither his knowledge of Torah (and the way in which Christ fulfills it) nor the authority emanating from his own extraordinary encounter on the Damascus Road with the risen Christ. Instead, he appeals to the evidence of his own similarity to the one crucified on the tree of shame.

> We are fools for Christ's sake, but you are wise in Christ. We are weak, but you are strong. You are held in honor, but we in disrepute. To the present hour we hunger and thirst, we are ill-clad and buffeted and homeless, and we labor, working with our own hands. When reviled, we bless; when persecuted, we endure; when slandered, we try to conciliate; we have become, and are now, as the refuse of the world, the offscouring of all things. (I Corinthians 4:10-13)

Is it any wonder, then, that the tradition that brags about its foolishness has produced a tradition of those who 'specialize' in foolish behavior? Just as the entire Christian people is priestly and also contains a specific ministerial priesthood, so too does this intrinsically divinely foolish people also contain, though not in the same way, a kind of specific ministry of foolishness. In, John Saward's 1981 book on tradition of holy foolishness, he judges that the keys to this Pauline teaching and to the phenomenon of holy folly are found in Christ's renunciation of self-protection, subjection to mockery, and a childlike quality of trust in divine protection, 'above all trust in the Father in the face of suffering and death'.[2] He expands on this central core with a more expansive list of the elements of behavior and attitude that make up the common patrimony of the holy fools.

1) The holy fool is Christocentric and is inspired by "identity with Christ crucified, participation in the Lord's poverty, mockery, humiliation, nakedness, and self-emptying."

2) Holy folly is considered a gift or *charism* of God.

3) A holy fool simulates madness—he leads a 'double life: "on stage" (in the streets, by day) he is imbecile; "in private" (in church, at night) he is a man of prayer'.[3]

4) The folly is eschatological. The madness of the holy fool is meant to draw a contrast between the values that reign in the present world and those that will reign in the world to come—when the values of the crucified Lord are supreme.

5) The fool acts and is a stranger, outsider, and pilgrim, one who wanders in order to find 'a lost country, the Promised Land', the one to which he ultimately is at home.[4]

6) Because the fool represents the values and citizenship of the kingdom of God, he represents a different kind of political power. This is why the fool 'appears most commonly at a time of political tranquillity' in order to show an authority that goes beyond this world.[5]

7) Holy folly is based in a discernment of spirits. Because the fool represents the true values of the everlasting kingdom of Christ, the fool can judge the world's 'conventional respectability', hypocrisy, and self-deception.

8) The asceticism of holy folly is based on *apatheia*, the complete balance of the powers of the soul, and aimed at the highest levels of humility, namely 'loss of all reputation and esteem'. This accounts for the fool's sense of solidarity with those who are not esteemed by the world whether

---

[2] John Saward, *Perfect Fools: Folly for Christ's Sake in Catholic and Orthodox Spirituality* (New York: Oxford University Press, 1981), 6-8. Quotation at 8.
[3] Ibid., 25.
[4] Ibid., 27.
[5] Ibid., 28.

because of mental or moral defects. While the fool does not condone immoral action, he does not allow self-righteousness to separate himself from them.[6]

9) The fool is filled with and 'protected above all by his *childlikeness*, his purity and simplicity of heart'. While the holy fool may occasionally be 'ferocious' on the outside, what lurks beneath is 'the gentle, trusting heart of a child'.[7]

This analysis of the main lines of holy folly, East and West, can be used as tools for evaluating how J. Blue and Innocent Smith match up to and apply the tradition of holy foolery in a modern world that is far technologically and societally from the world of the Desert Fathers, Francis of Assisi, and sixteenth-century Russia, but nevertheless still identical with it in the most important senses. It is a world to whom the kingdom of God is coming and is yet to come—a world in which holy fools are needed to announce and to dramatise what the world will be like when time is no more and when political and personal life are governed by the person and the ways of the crucified one whose foolishness was revealed to be wisdom, power, and glory.

J. Blue's Jazz Age Traditional Folly

Attention to Myles Connolly's *Mr. Blue* has been intermittent but overall steady over the years. First published, to little acclaim, in 1928 by Macmillan, it later became an underground success on U. S. Catholic college campuses in the 1930s, continued to sell in greater numbers throughout the 1940s, was published in Brazil and England, and had sold over 500,000 copies by the time Image Books released a paperback edition in 1954. After Vatican II its popularity dropped dramatically, though it has always had a small coterie of fans. It has been republished several times since the 1970s, notably in an edition by Loyola Classics with an introduction by John Breslin, S.J., and periodic essays about it, largely from the point of view of older liberal Catholic writers looking back at it and

---

[6] Ibid., 29.

[7] Ibid., 30. Sergey Ivanov, *Holy Fools in Byzantium and Beyond.* Trans. Simon Franklin (Oxford: Oxford University Press, 2006), 9, observes that holy fools are always involved in 'aggression', by which he means actions designed to 'disrupt the *status quo* in personal relations and which is perceived as hostile by the person at whom it is directed'. His book, which is less broad than Saward's in covering most closely the origins of notable holy fools in Byzantium through the Russian period, nevertheless reflects broadly an agreement with Saward's analysis.

finding it wanting because of its doctrinal orthodoxy.[8] It has never attracted significant academic attention. The fullest account of its history and interpretation, from which I have taken the account above, is found in Stephen Mirarchi's 2015 edition of the book for Cluny Publishers, which includes a lengthy introduction before the text as well as a full set of notes to the text.[9]

Mirarchi argues that there is much evidence that Connolly, a screenwriter, wrote his novel not just to entertain but also as a riposte to F. Scott Fitzgerald's *The Great Gatsby*, which Fitzgerald wanted to title *Under the Red, White, and Blue* at one point.[10] J. Gatsby, Mirarchi argues, is afflicted with the blues at the beginning of the book, due to his loss of Daisy Buchanan. The middle of the book is about their affair, which turns their blues "into a kind of wedding white." The book ends with the blood of Gatsby floating in a pool. "From blue to white to red—the American dream inverted, ruined by the restlessness of the denizens of the Jazz Age, with Gatsby its false savior."[11]

The story of Blue, told episodically from the standpoint of an unnamed narrator, an ordinary Catholic friend of his who is alternately amazed, bemused, and occasionally horrified by Blue's behavior, is similarly structured as a journey from blue to white to red, but rather than an inversion of the American dream, it is depicted as the fulfillment of it by means of progress in the Christian spiritual life. Mirarchi argues that the Irish Catholic Connolly would have known this color of progression that had descended from at least the seventh-century *Cambrai Homily*, which includes "passages written in Old Irish that speak of a threefold martyrdom: white, blue, and red."[12] White represents the separation of a Christian from goods of a material or emotional kind even though this might mean fasting or hard work; blue represents the separation from the desires themselves and the suffering inherent in such ascetical work; and red is the suffering of the cross

---

[8] Myles Connolly, *Mr. Blue*, with introduction by John B. Breslin (Chicago, Illinois: Loyola Press, 2004). For articles of the reminiscence type, see: Joseph Romano, "*Mr. Blue* by Myles Connolly" (Review), *American Catholic Studies* 130: (Winter 2019): 70-74; also Chet Raymo, "Mr. Blue Redux," *Spiritus: A Journal of Christian Spirituality* 3:2 (Fall 2003): 231-33.
[9] Myles Connolly, *Mr. Blue*, introduction and notes by Stephen Mirarchi (Cluny Media, 2015), account taken from VIII and IX. Cluny also offers four other novels, much less successful, by Connolly.
[10] Mirarchi, Introduction to *Mr. Blue*, XVIII.
[11] Ibid., XIX-XX.
[12] Ibid., XX.

or death for the sake of Christ.[13] The story thus begins with the titular character and his separation from a large fortune and the attendant goods available with it (blue), sets out to live in poverty, separating himself even from the desires for a normal life (white), and ends with him deciding that his vocation is to bring Christ to the poorest of the poor in the lumberyards and slums of Boston, a decision that will bring him to death via accident and malnourishment (red). While Mirarchi argues that the narrator is also himself undergoing a journey through the Christian life, the focus is on the title character, whose dramatic living out of what he understands his vocation to be is much more dramatic.[14]

Mirarchi's case for the literary structure and intent of the novel is very strong. It seems to be indeed a journey into the heart of Christian martyrdom—not only the generic early sense of martyrdom as 'witness' to Christ but also to death suffered because of faithfulness to Christ. Is Blue a holy fool, however? Given the traits established by John Saward, I think we can say that he fits the situation very well.

Blue is Christocentric, following the footsteps of great saints such as St. Francis, who wed themselves to 'Lady Poverty'. He is focused concretely on Christ. During one period in the book, when Blue is living on top of a building in Manhattan—a clear nod to the holy fools known as Stylites, who dwelt on top of pillars—the narrator comes to visit him and is asked whether he is a Christian. After nodding in the affirmative, he hears Blue say that 'my heart would break with all this immensity if I did not know that God himself once stood beneath it, a young man, small as I'.[15] This theme is reminiscent of Chesterton's emphasis on the coziness of the universe and the connection between Creation and the Incarnation inherent. Blue's stylitism is for the purpose of the discovery of Christ in the world. His pursuit of a vocation of permanent poverty and living among the outcasts is similarly motivated by imitation of and obedience to Christ. The narrator's assessment of Blue at the end of the book, when he works in a rough lumberyard, is that 'He was getting, little by little, what he had wanted: the cross God gives his friends' (119). Given this last observation, it is clear that Blue considers the folly of his own vocation to be a gift, the second of Saward's traits.

---

[13] Ibid., XXI. Mirarchi quotes the Orthodox theologian Kallistos Ware as to the presence of these themes in Eastern thought as well.
[14] Ibid., XXIV.
[15] Connolly, *Mr. Blue*, 35. Future citations will be in parentheses within the text.

Does he feign madness? In one sense, yes, though the narrator tells us that though 'he had many of the marks of insanity' he 'somehow gave you the impression that we were all crazy and he alone was sane' (13). His throwing off a huge fortune is done by handing out money at random to the poor but also in absurd projects such as a factory to make toy balloons, which he then used for his own delight, often attaching one hundred dollar bills to a balloon and letting it fly off in the wind (9-10). One can see in such mad actions that not only is he attesting to his own childlike trust in God, he is clearly making a judgment of some kind on the behavior of the wealthy and the ways of the world of the Jazz Age and its excesses from the standpoint of the eschatological kingdom of God. The last letter from Blue to the narrator is a meditation on the nature of that kingdom, a place where the saints dwell among peasants and 'our dreams of unbroken love and good talk and laughter will have come true' (75).

Finally, one can see Saward's eighth category—a kind of balance that allows him to dwell with those who are low in the esteem of the world—in Blue's decision to forego living in any fixed abode (an imitation of Christ who had nowhere to lay his head) and sleep outside among the vagrants. 'Now, he said, he thought his novitiate was over. He was ready to go forth, with no name or with any name, to live with the derelicts of modern civilization and bring to them the story that they would never heed elsewhere. And that story? It was, of course, the story of Christ' (111-12).

Connolly's Blue fits in many ways the classic profile of the holy fool and was, appropriately enough, inspiring to college students and also unappealing to those older. The recent articles on Mr. Blue with their somewhat dismissive tone about the character (mentioned above) show how the true holy fool will indeed grate on those who wish for a faith that is more at ease with the world. Chet Raymo, in writing about the book after fifty years, rejects the idea that Catholic or Christian faith is true in any objective sense, but one can see a bit of guilt and defensiveness in his own reflections that he is now affluent and retired: 'Blue dies young, without a life partner or children; Lady Poverty makes a cold companion in old age'. And: 'As for Lady Poverty. She may be a fine mistress for J. Blue, who can charm a meal or a place to sleep off everyone he meets. But she is a cruel and ravenous villainess for a majority of the world's population. I would gladly see her confined, with her acolytes, to the pages of history'.[16] While Raymo thinks that the book is not as great literarily as he initially thought it to be, what really bothers him is the provocation given by a figure in modern life

---

[16] Raymo, 'Mr. Blue Redux,' 233.

who would live as a holy fool voluntarily and who would embrace a life
without the natural goods of wife, children, and a comfortable old age.
Mirarchi quotes historian James Fisher similarly, calling the novel a 'grim
and melancholy work. The hero is sexless, rootless, and ageless' (XI). The
holy fool in literature has the power to provoke, but those with tenure, a
pension, and an investment in the current world of marriage and giving in
marriage will be provoked negatively. Whatever the literary quality, and I
will admit with Raymo and others that Connolly's work is finely crafted but
not on the level of a Georges Bernanos, Sigrid Undset, or Francois Mauriac,
the power involved in the story and the character is one that brought and
brings to life the strange and grotesque ideal of following Christ no matter
the cost, with no attention to self-preservation, self-esteem, or material
comfort.

Innocent Smith and the Holy Fool as Married Suburbanite

Myles Connolly had been heavily influenced by Chesterton, and the
themes of joy and wonder in a cozy universe redeemed by Christ are all over
his own brief novel. Even as a college student, Connolly had already
immersed himself in the joyful vision of Chesterton. Ten years before Mr.
Blue's appearance, he wrote in 1918 in the Boston College literary
magazine of the spirit of St. Francis of Assisi and Chesterton as one to which
his fellow collegians should attain: "St. Francis of Assisi sang as he died.
Chesterton would have Christ smiling at our foibles. By all means let us
make a Spring resolution: When everything goes wrong we shall whistle'.[17]
The reason why I treat Chesterton's novel *Manalive* second is that this
novel, not usually credited with being among his best, is nevertheless an
instance of Chesterton's use of the holy fool motif. Though instead of the
more traditional figure of J. Blue, who leaves behind the ordinary ways of
society altogether to live a life of holy folly, Chesterton's Innocent Smith is
an ordinary man who leaves behind his ordinary society to become a
stranger in order to rediscover the joy that characterizes holy folly in
childlike trust, renunciation of self-protection, and subjection to mockery—
and live it out in ordinary life.

---

[17] Quoted in Mirarchi's introduction, XIII.

According to Ian Ker, *Manalive* is 'the most autobiographical of the novels he published'.[18] It is certainly representative of Chesterton's philosophy of life. The novel opens with a blast of wind that tears through a neighborhood in London that houses Beacon House, a boarding house on top of a hill that has as its denizens a group of young adults who are coasting through life. This wind can be seen as reminiscent of the rushing wind at the time of Pentecost (see Acts 2:2) or even 'an apocalypse in a private garden'.[19] With the wind comes a strange, large man in a green set of clothes hurtling over the fence in the back of the boarding house. When the hat of one of the people standing in the yard flies off and lands in a tree, the figure starts muttering what seems like nonsense: 'Tree of life. . .Tydrasil. . .climb for centuries perhaps . . .owls nesting in the hat . . remotest generation of owls . . . still usurpers . . . gone to heaven . . . man in the moon wears it . . . brigand . . not yours . . . belongs to depressed medical man . . . in garden . . . give it up . . . give it up!' (8).

As the figure, soon revealed to be Innocent Smith, an old friend of one of the boarding house inhabitants, moves in and behaves in ways that indicate folly and also childlike joy and wonder, he awakens the dormant sense of life and wonder in all of those present, from the woman who owns the boarding house to all of the figures who live in it, though Dr. Warner the 'depressed medical man' remains skeptical. Smith seems alternately childlike and aggressive. He buys wine for the decorative labels, something that provokes in Inglewood, the childhood friend, 'an almost creepy sense of the real childishness of this creature'. What Inglewood decides is that this figure is really 'innocent' (14). He also brandishes a pistol, explaining that he 'deals life' out of it (19).   He preaches a gospel of 'Swiss Family Robinson' asceticism that holds that when one limits oneself to what is present, either on a deserted island or in an old boarding house, 'you really do find what you want' (24). He teaches the inhabitants of the house that 'All is gold that glitter' and that their only task is to pay attention: 'Open your eyes and you will see the New Jerusalem' (25). He teaches them that

---

[18] Ian Ker, *G. K. Chesterton: A Biography* (Oxford: Oxford University Press, 2011), 300.

[19] G. K. Chesterton, *Manalive* (Mineola, New York: Dover, 2000 [originally published by John Lane in 1912]), 3. All further references will be given in the text in parentheses. Giulio Maspero, 'G. K. Chesterton's *Manalive*: Narrative, grace, and humanity,' *Church, Communication, and Culture* 5:1 (2020): 63-73, interprets the novel as an apocalypse that is meant to reveal the idols operating in life, an interpretation congruent with my interpretation of Smith as a holy fool.

madness consists in 'giving in' and 'not breaking out' (26). It is a gospel of wonder in a world that has lost its wonder.

When a new woman, named Mary, moves into the boarding house, Innocent engages in a whirlwind romance with her, proposing marriage and convincing two other couples in the house to get married. Before they are about to leave, however, the skeptical Dr. Warner appears at the house to reveal that Innocent Smith has been married many times before, has abandoned the women, and is wanted for murder and breaking and entering. Part II of the book is thus engaged in a 'trial' of Innocent Smith that is held at Beacon House, with different members of the house playing the part of the court.

It is in this half of the book that the philosophy of Innocent Smith is more fully fleshed out via epistolary recounting of his supposed misdeeds while Smith sits innocently in court not speaking. He does not speak but instead makes him subject to mockery and accusations of immorality, all the while maintaining the childlike behavior that symbolizes his childlike trust. What is revealed via the letters from various people connected to Smith is that all the accusations are based on real provocative actions that Smith committed.

The first accusation of attempted murder is based in Smith's university days when he acted aggressively, pointing his pistol at a Schopenhauer-quoting Cambridge professor named Emerson Eames who proclaimed that it is better to be dead. The letter, written jointly by Smith and Eames, recounts the origins of the vocation of Smith to a life holy foolery. The young Smith had pulled out his pistol and proposed acting on this judgment so that he could better the don's state. After driving the professor out the window, he gets the professor to beg to 'get back to life'. Smith demands that the professor sing a hymn. The hymn, Jane Taylor's 'A Child's Hymn of Praise' (not identified in the novel) is sung as Eames repeats after Smith. After declaring that Eames has 'now engaged in public worship' (71), Smith requires that Eames give thanks for ducks, drakes, 'sticks and rags and bones and blinds', immediately amending it to 'spotted blinds' (72). Before departing, Smith had told Eames that he did not want the truth of the even to be known. Smith had to be 'sent down', or expelled, from Cambridge and nobody should know what he was about because he would be confronting others with his pistol:

> I mean to keep those bullets for pessimists—pills for pale people. And in this way I want to walk the world like a wonderful surprise—to float as idly as the thistledown, and come as silently as the sunrise; not to be expected any more than the thunderbolt, not to be recalled any more than the dying

breeze I want both my gifts to come virgin and violent, the death and the
life after death. I am going to hold the pistol to the head of Modern Man.
But I shall not use it to kill him. Only to bring him to life. I begin to see a
new meaning to being the skeleton at the feast (73-4).

We can see already from this episode that Chesterton's account of the
beginnings of Innocent Smith's career marks him off as a holy fool in
Saward's terms. Smith is clearly Christocentric despite the name of Christ
not being mentioned in the scene. Smith wants to bring people to life
through death in the way that Christ does. He also counts his career as a
kind of charism to which he is called, one whose folly is geared toward the
end things, though Smith's focus is on helping people grasp them in the
present. His simulated madness is for the purposes of awakening 'Modern
Man' to the glory of life eternal that is revealed in time. Smith's glimpse of
the meaning of death that provoked him to point his pistol at Eames made
him realize that *memento mori* the remembrance of death, 'isn't only meant
to remind us of a future life, but to remind us of a present life too'. He
observes that 'Providence has cut immortality into lengths for us, as nurses
cut the bread and butter into fingers' (74).

Smith's appearance is as a stranger, one who is searching for a promised
land. One of the later parts of the trial, dealing with his supposed
abandonment of his wife, is about a year-long trip around the globe that took
Smith to Norway, Russia, China, and the American West.   While in
California, Smith reveals to one figure that he has 'become a pilgrim to cure
myself of exile' (108). He represents to those he visits, just as he does the
inhabitants of Beacon House, a repudiation of the world's conventional
respectability, two-facedness, and self-deception. Though Chesterton does
not have Smith dealing with the downtrodden or the immoral explicitly, this
is only because he is a kind of apostle to those who are trapped in their
conventionality and fail to see the glories of the New Jerusalem around
them. The other accusations of breaking and entering and polygamy are
revealed to be similar misunderstandings of Innocent Smith's actions. The
first is an attempt at rediscovering the joy of what he possesses by breaking
into his own house, while the second is an attempt to rediscover the glory
of his wife, Mary, by leaving the children every year for a week or two,
showing up in a different place (just as they have done at Beacon House),
and falling in love all over again. All of these acts of foolishness are
designed to discover again the lost country even in the midst of this life.
This is not an absolute discovery of the promised land, for Smith admits to
the Californian with whom he stays that the saying of the Californian's
mother—'that we were all in exile, and that no earthly house could cure the

holy homesickness that forbids us rest' (108)—is correct. Yet Smith affirms that the earthly homes, even if they are not capable of being fully and finally our dwelling, are meant to reaffirm for us the reality of 'Paradise is somewhere and not anywhere, is something and not anything' (109). Eschatological reality just as real and 'firm'—nay more so—as is this world of gates, gardens, and houses. It is through our embrace of them in the proper ascetical way that we can perceive both the glory of this world and that which it points to.

At the end of the book, Michael Moon, a journalist of Irish extraction who lives in Beacon House and has been the most open to the unconventional wisdom of Smith, explains what it was that Smith, who has now vanished, was really teaching, the difference between convention and morality:

> The idea that Smith is attacking is this. Living in an entangled civilization, we have come to think certain things wrong which are not wrong at all. We have come to think outbreak and exuberance, banging and barging, rotting and wrecking, wrong. In themselves they are not merely pardonable, they are impeachable. There is nothing wicked about firing off a pistol even at a friend; so long as you do not mean to hit him and know you won't. It is no more wrong than throwing a pebble at the sea—less; for you do occasionally hit the sea. There is nothing wrong in bashing down a chimney-pot and breaking through a roof, so long as you are not injuring the life or property of other men. It is no more wrong to choose to enter a house from the top, than to choose to open a packing-case from the bottom. There is nothing wicked about walking around the world and coming back to your own house; it is no more wicked than walking around the garden and coming back to your own house. And there is nothing wicked about picking up your wife here, there, and everywhere, if, forsaking all others, you keep only to her so long as you both shall live. It is as innocent as playing a game of hide-and-seek in the garden. You associate such acts with blackguardism by a mere snobbish association; as you think there is something vaguely vile about going (or being seen going) into a pawnbroker's or a public-house. You think there is something squalid and commonplace about such a connection. You are mistaken.

Moon continues, giving the secret to Smith's 'spiritual power': 'that he has distinguished between custom and creed. He has broken the conventions, but he has kept the commandments' (122). While the language of *Manalive* is much less directly theological and religious, the power of the book is stronger in many ways for it since it is less susceptible to modern criticisms of being preachy.

Conclusion: Holy Fools in and Out of Society

What makes *Manalive* different from *Mr. Blue* is not just that the writing is better and the lines more memorable, but also the way in which Chesterton's Innocent Smith depicts a new and more worldly holy fool, one who embodies the call to be outside of the mainstream society mentally and spiritually while remaining in it. Innocent Smith has children and presumably works at an ordinary job when he is neither on his yearly nor his year-long pilgrimages to keep himself from internal exile. He is not married to anybody odd but instead the quintessentially normal and balanced Mary. His holy foolery is something that coexists with a kind of largely suburban and domestic life. Insofar as it does so, the novel provides a different kind of model of the holy fool than does Myles Connolly's novel or almost all of the examples of folly East and West in the literature. While both Blue and Smith might be perceived as unrealistic fictional figures, Smith is simultaneously more unrealistic and yet in certain ways capable of emulation than Blue is or perhaps should be for most readers, perhaps because Smith resembles Chesterton in so many ways.

WAR AND THE CROSS:
THREE CATHOLIC COMBATANTS AND THEIR
EXPERIENCE OF WORLD WAR ONE

TERRY PHILLIPS

The First World War challenged the people of the many nations involved, and particularly those who were actively engaged in the conflict, to find meaning in the apparently senseless slaughter.[1] In an era when church going was still widespread and even for most non-church goers, Christian belief was at least nominally professed, some abandoned Christian belief in the face of the reality of the conflict, while others turned to traditional Christianity in an attempt to endow the apparently meaningless with meaning.

The most obvious way of giving meaning to what was an increasingly meaningless experience for many people was in a simple comparison of the soldier's sacrifice to the saving act of Christ. This quotation from a poet of the time gives a typical example of such an approach:

> Who said 'No man hath greater love than this,
>   To die to serve his friend'?
> [...]
> The soldier dying dies upon a kiss,
>   The very kiss of Christ.[2]

This particular poem, 'Summer in England, 1914' does not make explicit any view about the justice or injustice of the conflict, its main theme being the contrast between the fate of soldiers and the beauty of the summer, so

---

[1] The figure of between 722,785 and 772,000 deaths among those fighting in the British forces estimated by Jay Winter in 1986 is still accepted, Jay Winter, *The Great War and the British People* (Cambridge: Cambridge University Press, 1986), 66–72.

[2] Alice Meynell, 'Summer in England, 1914' in Catherine Reilly, *Scars Upon My Heart* (London: Virago, 1981)

that it could simply be read as meaning that the sacrifice compared to that of Christ, is made to save the life of a fellow soldier, although Meynell, herself a Catholic, does seem to have believed that the war was just. War memorials constructed in the years following the conflict convey, much more explicitly, a belief that the deaths of the soldiers in the war were to be compared to the sacrifice of Christ, made in the service of justice. This inscription on the memorial outside the City Hall in Belfast includes a typical example of inscriptions to be found on many such memorials: 'erected by the City of Belfast in memory of her heroic sons who made the supreme sacrifice in the Great War 1914-18 pro deo et patria'.

To speak of sacrifice, in the cultural context of Western Europe in the years of the First World War, inevitably brought to mind the sacrifice of Christ. The figure of Christ provided a useful parallel for those who believed that the war was in some sense a 'holy' war and, provided at least some kind of rationalisation for large scale slaughter in a just cause, drawing either on the Doctrine of Atonement, a commonly accepted view at the time, or the idea that the crucifixion was the unavoidable culmination of an act of political resistance, inevitably driving Christ to conflict with both political and civil authorities and resulted in his death.[3] An emphasis on the crucifixion as a saving act, allows the comparison of the soldier to Christ, but is of cause, as suggested above, predicated on the view that the war is in some sense just, that the soldier lays down his life on behalf of others, while of course ignoring the fact that Christ offered no resistance to those who crucified him.

The Catholic Church's teaching on a just war is linked strongly to its developing recognition of civic authority, in which St Augustine of Hippo was highly influential. Augustine argued that 'Christians should heed these "counsels of perfection" in their personal affairs, but they should apply a different calculus when translating them to the complex arena of public governance. To kill selflessly for the common good may be the highest form of self-denial and love.'[4] The right of the civic authority to conduct war in self defence was further developed by St Thomas Aquinas and Francisco De Vitoria (1480-1546) who added two further ideas: the principle of

---

[3] For a discussion of theological explanations for the crucifixion of Christ see S. Mark Heim, *Saved From Sacrifice* and Sebastian Moore, *No Exit*, Darton Longman and Todd, 1968 and *The Contagion of Jesus*
[4] R.Scott Appleby, 'How Christians Went to War', *U.S.Catholic*, May 1999, 41.

proportionality and the avoidance of harm to the whole world.[5] Prior to Augustine, the predominant position in the church had been opposition to all war. Although Pope Benedict XV had expressed opposition to the war and a desire for the opposing parties to work for peace,[6] the predominant view of the Catholic Church in England, notably expressed by Cardinal Bourne was of support for the war.

However, regardless of whether they believed the war was just, or were gradually beginning to lose faith in its justice, there was for Christians, and, for present purposes, members of the Catholic Church, another way in which the cross of Christ was relevant to them. Many Christians have found spiritual inspiration and consolation in the contemplation of the cross- as a sign of vulnerability, brokenness and pain, a view which expresses the humanness of Christ. This was true for many of those who endured the horrors of the First World War, as active participants.

In this chapter I intend to examine the writings of three First World War soldiers, who all served on the Western Front, and who, in different ways, were strongly influenced by the beliefs of the Catholic church: the Irish Nationalist politician and writer, Thomas Kettle, the Irish writer Patrick MacGill and the Anglo-Welsh painter and writer, David Jones. Their relationships to the church as well as their views about the war in which they fought were varied and, in some cases, shifting, as will be seen.

Thomas Kettle, a lifelong Catholic from Ireland who had served as an Irish Nationalist MP, did not swerve from his conviction of the justice of the war, even after the British response to the Easter Rising, in 1916. This view was informed by his experiences in Belgium where he had been 'running arms for the National Volunteers' at the time of the German invasion.[7] His account of his experiences there includes an account of the destruction of Tremonde, a town of 12,000 people, and the destruction of the cathedrals of Malines and Louvain and the University and Library at Louvain.[8]

---

[5] William H Shannon, 'Christian Conscience and Modern Warfare', *America* 166, no. 5 (15 February 1992): 108–12.
[6] See Pope Benedict XV, 'Apostolic Exhortation To the Peoples Now at War and to Their Rulers', 1915, http://w2.vatican.va/content/benedict-xv/en/apost_exhortations/documents/hf_ben-xv_exh_19150728_fummo-chiamati.html.
[7] Thomas Kettle, *The Ways of War* (New York: Charles Scribner's Sons, 1917), 73.
[8] Thomas Kettle, 'Under the Heel of the Hun', in *The Ways of War* (New York: Charles Scribner's Sons, 1917), 125–38.

Kettle was first and foremost a politician and a somewhat indifferent poet, but his writing provides interesting evidence of his feelings, providing an example of views formed out of religion, nationality, politics and direct experience. The small number of poems he wrote about the war are included in *Poems and Parodies* which was published posthumously in December 2016 [9] and which includes poems first published in a volume authored jointly with Stephen Gwynn, entitled, *Battle Songs of the Irish Brigades,*[10] which had been explicitly designed, by its appeal to the memory of the 'Wild Geese', the Irishmen who had fought in the armies of the Catholic monarchs of Europe since the seventeenth century, to encourage recruitment to the army, somewhat controversial in the Ireland of 1915, which saw a split in the National Volunteer movement over the issue.[11]

Biblical, mainly New Testament references abound in both Kettle's prose and poetry, often presented without any self-consciousness, indicating a mind whose ideological framework was primarily Christian. For example, in *The Ways of War*, he describes Belgium's resistance to the German overtures before the invasion which would have compromised her neutrality: 'she lost the world in order to gain her own soul.'[12] This is, of course, a clear reference to Jesus's words in St Matthew's gospel, 'For what, then will anyone gain by winning the whole world and forfeiting his life.'[13] It is a very familiar quotation but it has a very particular relevance here, since the words were uttered in the context of Peter trying to persuade Jesus not to go to Jerusalem and face inevitable death. Belgium, in Kettle's view, like Jesus, has faced suffering, rather than compromise with what Kettle sees as evil.

Kettle's experiences in Belgium convinced him that the war was just. In 'Why Ireland Fought', he argues:

> Who then was the criminal? There is an invertebrate view according to which everybody is equally blameable and blameless for everything. The

---

[9] Thomas Kettle, *Poems and Parodies* (London: Duckworth, 1916).

[10] Stephen Gwynn and Thomas Kettle, *Battle Songs of the Irish Brigades* (Dublin: Maunsel, 1915).

[11] See Keith Jeffery, *Ireland and the Great War* (Cambridge: Cambridge University Press, 2000), 13–14., and Fearghal McGarry, *The Rising* (Oxford: Oxford University Press, 2010), 8–43.

[12] Kettle, *The Ways of War*, 94.

[13] *New Jerusalem Bible*, n.d., Matthew 16.26, www.catholic.org.

holders of this view have never gone quite so far as to take up the New Testament story and argue that Judas Iscariot was a misunderstood man.[14]

It is a caustic attack on modern social tolerance. So far, the argument is clear- the allies are to be equated with Christ and Germany and Austria-Hungary with Judas Iscariot, representing 'the gospel of force, and the sacrament of cruelty.'[15] At this point of course, Kettle's argument takes what might be argued an illogical step. For Christ's resistance was of course passive. Nowhere in Kettle's writing do we find a reference to the High Priest's servant's ear.[16] Christ's saving act for humanity- his submission to ignominious death on the cross, becomes for certain of his followers, including Kettle, a taking up arms and refusal to submit, rather than passive submission. Kettle and those who agreed with him could appeal to the Church's teaching on a just war, and its recognition of civil authority.

The comparison of the soldier to Christ referred to above, is based on the idea that the soldier is prepared to sacrifice his life as Christ sacrificed his. It should be pointed out, that in his political career Kettle's first instinct was a recourse to the pragmatic and he did not ignore the Gospel's message of reconciliation. Nevertheless, he was no pacifist. He wrote only a handful of poems about the War and I want to focus on two. The first of these, in *Songs for the Irish Brigades* entitled 'The Last Crusade', with the subtitle, 'A Song of the Irish Armies', is reproduced in *Poems and Parodies* as 'A Song of the Irish Armies'.[17] I have been unable to find an explanation for this- whether it was a change made by Kettle himself or posthumously by his editors. What can be stated with certainty is that the original title is freighted with implications, recalling a time when Christians, preposterous though it may seem to the modern believer, thought that a conquest of the Holy Land in the name of Christ, by military force was right. In 'Why Ireland Fought', Kettle declares, 'The sort of religion that tortures its enemies and puts them to death no longer flourishes under the standard of the Cross.'[18] For this reason, the title may seem surprising but the epithet 'Last' carries the implication of comparison, that this crusade, like the earlier ones, is religious in motivation but is different in that it is in defence of Christian values rather than the forcible imposition of Christianity. Furthermore, the

---

[14] Kettle, *The Ways of War*, 67.

[15] Kettle, 71.

[16] See Jesus' reprimand to Peter who has just cut off the high priest's servant's ear, *New Jerusalem Bible*, John 18.10.

[17] Kettle, *Poems and Parodies*, 84–86.

[18] Thomas Kettle, 'Why Ireland Fought', in *The Ways of War* (New York: Charles Scribner's Sons, 1917), 63.

hope may be that this will indeed be the final battle in defence of right, 'the war that will end all wars.'[19]

The introductory stanza is a description of evil. With its reference to Cain and devils, it is suggestive of a world seen very much through a binary lens arguing that both the 'Old Soldiers' (those already in the army when war broke out in August 1914), and the 'New Soldiers' are fighting against evil, implicitly on the side of its opposite, good. The 'Old Soldiers' Song', which follows, initially emphasises something more than a Manichean Old Testament opposition to evil and expresses the values which Kettle clearly sees as being represented by the allies:

> Not for this did our fathers fall;
> That truth, and pity, and love, and all
> Should break in dust at a trumpet's call

Nevertheless, the defence of these values, in the poet's view, necessitates a clear distinction between good and evil and so the stanza ends on a subtly different note:

> Not to this had we sacrificed:
> To sit at the last where the slayers diced,
> With blood-hot hands, for the robes of Christ,
>   And snatch at the Devil's Gold[20]

Again there is the return to scapegoating- there is little of 'forgive them, for they know not what they do' in the portrayal of those responsible for Christ's death casting lots for his garments, but the passage does nevertheless suggest the New Testament idea that the treatment of one's fellow humans is to be judged as treatment of Christ.

The New Soldiers call on the familiar words of the prophet Isaiah about turning swords into ploughshares to explain their actions. However, significantly, they in fact reverse the words of Isaiah as they declare confidently: 'Time for the plough when the sword has won;'[21] This use of Isaiah in reverse, so to speak, expresses something of an unresolved and not always apparent contradiction in Kettle's use of biblical sources, and

---

[19] This much quoted comment originated with H.G. Wells and is the title of a book he published in October 1914, H.G. Wells, *The War That Will End War* (London: F.&C.Palmer, 1914).
[20] Kettle, *Poems and Parodies*, 85.
[21] Kettle, 86.

particularly the story of the crucifixion to justify his advocacy of war. In fact, the whole of the Song of the Old Soldiers draws attention to the difficult theological question faced by Christians who believed, like Kettle, in the justice of the conflict based on the wrongs of the enemy. Does one make peace with the sinner, and at what cost?

In 'A Nation's Freedom' the focus is more exclusively on the New Testament and the saving act of Christ.[22] The poem puts side by side the fact of Russsia's retreat from Poland and the possible future freedom of Ireland. In the first two stanzas, what Kettle see as the liberation of Poland is compared to the Resurrection: 'The stone is rolled from the tomb, and Poland free[...]Have you not met her, my lords, a-walk in the garden,/Ranging the dawn, even she, the three times dead', a reference to the partitions of Poland and a comparison to Mary Magdalen's meeting with the risen Christ which demonstrates an easy familiarity with the New Testament[23]. The New Testament reference is extended by an allusion to the marriage feast at Cana, 'But now the water is wine, and the marriage read', suggesting the beginning of Jesus's work of salvation.[24] Thus, the liberation from sin brought about by Christ is linked to the liberation of a nation, a position which is tenable if that nation is seen as having suffered, which is suggested by the phrase 'in bondage, sundered from light and pardon.' Nevertheless, this does reflect a view which sees the salvation brought by Christ as more than a purely spiritual salvation. After three stanzas outlining the parallel to Poland in the searching for freedom by Ireland, the reader is challenged by the liturgical language of the opening of the next stanza, 'The altar is set; we uplift again the chalice;/ The priest is in purple; the bell booms to the sacrifice.' There could be no clearer statement of the parallel between the saving act of Jesus Christ and the action of the soldier in going to war.

Kettle is not a theologian and there are inconsistencies in his use of Old and New Testament references. Nevertheless, one can only conclude, from an examination of 'The Last Crusade' in particular that he sees the war as a holy war and the Christian man's duty to be a duty to fight, and that therefore the sacrifice of the soldier may be compared to the sacrifice of Christ. What his theology overlooks is the sense of the cross as an inclusive saving act for all human beings and not an act for some human beings and not others, the children of Cain or the slayers at the foot of the cross. His emphasis too is on the choice to suffer in the process of active resistance

---

[22] Kettle, 80–83.
[23] *New Jerusalem Bible*, John 20.14-16.
[24] *New Jerusalem Bible*, John 2.1-11.

rather than the passive resistance of Jesus Christ described in the New Testament.

Patrick MacGill, another Irish writer who fought in the British army came from a very different background from Kettle. He was born into a poor farming family in Glenmornan in west Donegal, and at a young age travelled to Scotland where he worked initially as a potato picker in Buteshire (as the particular district of the west of Scotland was then known), then on a series of jobs including the construction of the hydroelectric works at Kinlochleven, near Fort William, and as a plate layer for the Caledonian Railway Company, experiences recounted in his autobiographical novel, *Children of the Dead End*.[25] MacGill enlisted in the London Irish Rifles in 1914. He wrote several semi-autobiographical accounts of his wartime experience, both during and after the war, and poems, collected together in *Soldier Songs*.[26] In *Children of the Dead End,* MacGill's autobiographical central character Dermod Flynn express disillusion with official clerically dominated Catholicism and a lack of faith in a providential God. Nevertheless, he never abandoned Catholicism and his writing shows some level of continuing religious belief.

Both Robert Greacen and David Taylor suggest that MacGill's disillusion with the war emerges only in his postwar writings.[27] Nevertheless there are strong elements of such disillusion in *The Great Push,* the most powerful of his wartime accounts, which recounts the Battle of Loos. By the time of this battle, MacGill has become a stretcher-bearer, which as Brian D. Osborne suggests, in his introduction to the 2000 edition of the book, gave him, 'time to observe, to think and to write.'[28] *The Great Push* is prefaced by a very clear statement:

> The justice of the cause which endeavours to achieve its object by the murdering and maiming of Mankind is apt to be doubted by a man who has come through a bayonet charge. The dead lying on the fields seem to ask,

[25] Patrick MacGill, *Children of the Dead End* (London: Caliban Books, 1995).
[26] Patrick MacGill, *Soldier Songs* (New York: Dutton, 1917).
[27] Robert Greacen, 'Taking the Derry Boat', *A Journal of Irish Studies* 16, no. 1 (1981): 90–94.and David Taylor, *Memory, Narrative and The Great War: Rifleman Patrick MacGill and the Construction of Wartime Experience* (Liverpool: Liverpool University Press, 2013).
[28] Patrick MacGill, *The Great Push* (Edinburgh: Birlinn Limited, 1984), x.

"Why has this been done to us? Why have you done it, brothers? What purpose has it served?"[29]

The reference to 'brothers' although not in a specifically Christian context nevertheless may be seen as reflecting the religious belief which MacGill carries into the trenches.

On the eve of the battle, he encounters a mortally wounded German soldier in the trenches the London Irish have newly occupied. There is a very moving account of the incident, 'There was a look of mute appeal in his eyes, and for some reason I felt ashamed of myself for having intruded on the privacy of a dying man.' He gives the German soldier a drink. He speaks no English but nevertheless they communicate:

> When rummaging in my pocket I happened to bring out my rosary beads and he noticed them. He spoke and I guessed that he was inquiring if I was a Catholic.
>
> I nodded assent.
>
> He fumbled with his left hand in his tunic pocket and brought out a little mud-stained booklet and handed it to me. I noticed that the volume was a prayer-book. By his signs I concluded that he wanted me to keep it.[30]

The passage is remarkable for several reasons. It suggests an absence of hostility to the enemy, quite often reflected in the accounts of ordinary soldiers, and manifests nothing of the hostility of some of Kettle's writing. The shared Catholicism of the two men who have no other way of communicating other than by signs and symbols, suggests the Catholic emphasis on the universal church, which crosses national boundaries. The prayer book given by the dying soldier is seen as something to be kept. The writer may at this point have little faith in a God who will answer prayers, particularly in this context, but nevertheless feels the need of prayer, and carries rosary beads. To some, the carrying of the beads may appear little more than a superstitious practice, but it reflects something of the central character's recognition of his need to pray.

The crucifixion is a key motif in this novel, made physically present by the cross in Loos churchyard. The cross in the churchyard is used as a landmark, by which the advancing soldiers can find their way in their progress to the

---

[29] MacGill, Forward.
[30] MacGill, 44.

frontline trenches. Initially, this may suggest a symbolic representation of the soldier as a heroic and redemptive figure comparable with Christ:

> The sergeant seemed to be kneeling in prayer...In front the cloud cleared away, and the black crucifix standing over the graves of Loos became revealed.

> 'Advance, boys!' said the sergeant, 'Steady on to the foot of the Cross and rip the swine out of their trenches.' [31]

This comment, of course, raises contradictions in the minds of the Christian reader, who is likely to remember the much-quoted words, 'Father, forgive them; they do not know what they are doing.'[32] As the novel progresses it counters the ideas of those desperately trying to find a meaning for slaughter through the notion of purposeful sacrifice. It focuses instead on the notion of the crucified Christ as a suffering human being, a God prepared to take on the sufferings of His people.

After the battle, on his way to the dressing station, through the town of Loos, the narrator observes:

> In the midst of the ruin and desolation of the night of morbid fancies, in the centre of a square lined with unpeopled houses, I came across the Image of Supreme Pain, the Agony of the Cross. What suffering has Loos known? What torture, what sorrow, what agony? The crucifix was well in keeping with this scene of desolation. [33]

This suggests an emphasis on Christ as fellow-sufferer rather than redeemer. The link between the suffering and human Christ and the suffering soldier is made explicit in a quite remarkable passage, occurring shortly afterwards.

> I knew the dark grey bulk, it was He; for days and nights He had hung there, a huddled heap; the Futility of War.

> I was with Him in a moment endeavouring to help Him. In the dawn He was not repulsive, He was almost beautiful, but His beauty was that of the mirage which allures to a more sure destruction. The dew-drops were bright on His beard, His hair and His raiment; but His head sank low upon the wires and I could not see His face.[34]

---

[31] MacGill, 37.
[32] *New Jerusalem Bible*, Luke 23.34.
[33] MacGill, *The Great Push*, 133.
[34] MacGill, 137.

Contemplating a dead soldier on the wire, he elevates the soldier into a representative figure, by the use of capitalised pronouns. One interpretation of the archetype is that he represents the 'Futility of War'. However, the Christian reader, accustomed to seeing the capitalised pronoun to represent Christ, may see this as its meaning. It may be possible to merge these ideas. As has been seen in the sergeant urging his men to fight to the foot of the cross, Christianity is sometimes used as a reason to fight, and may be merged with the mirage of war. Nevertheless, the passage suggests the figure of Christ, not as saviour, but as fellow-sufferer, the final phrase suggesting he is sometimes hard to find in the midst of suffering.

MacGill's account of his experience as a stretcher-bearer at the Battle of Loos is above all else an account of great suffering. Through that suffering the central character feels links with the soldier on the other side who also suffers, an implicit recognition of the Christian teaching of the unity of the human race. His central character exhibits a need for prayer, though perhaps not sure in what way his prayer will be answered. Above all the predominance of the crucifix in the scenes of the novel demonstrates what for MacGill is the significance of the crucified Christ. He is a suffering human being whose suffering has significance for humanity.

David Jones is, of the writers under discussion, the most consciously aware of spiritual dimensions and theological implications. He served at the front from December 1915 until March 1918, and like many survivors remained strongly influenced by the experience for the rest of his life. Noted as an artist rather than a writer, he became a Catholic in 1921, and published his prose poem *In Parenthesis*, in 1937.[35] It is a curious and arguably unique work of art- the length of a novel and divided into seven parts, with important endnotes to help his readers understand the trench experience of twenty years earlier and illuminate the multiple references. The allusions are indeed plentiful. They encompass *Henry V,* and *Morte d'Arthur,* as well as the great Welsh epic, *Y Gododdin,* Welsh and English folklore, Norse Myth, *The Song of Roland*, Chaucer, Lewis Carroll*,* and, importantly for present purposes allusions drawn from the Bible and the Catholic liturgy. As Richard Griffiths points out, 'Catholicism is one among many cultural references here – but a particularly resonant one.'[36]

One of the strengths of *In Parenthesis* is the offering of multiple and shifting responses to a situation which was far from simple. The text is centred on

---

[35] David Jones, *In Parenthesis* (London: Faber and Faber, 1963).
[36] Richard Griffiths, *The Pen and the Cross* (London: Continuum, 2010), 199.

Private John Ball, an imaginary ordinary soldier named after the priest who led the Peasants Revolt in 1381,[37] and traces the movements and non-movements of Jones's regiment on the Western Front between December 1915 and July 1916, culminating in Ball's injury at Mametz Wood. It is narrated in the third person with a shifting viewpoint, mainly that of the group of soldiers being described and Ball himself.

The idea of the sacredness of all human life extends to different social classes. Much of the powerful and moving literature of this conflict is, inevitably in view of the levels of education at the time, written from the point of view of the officer class. However, the choice of Ball as a central character enables a focus on the experience and feelings of the ordinary soldier, including feelings related to religious belief. The Cockneys and chapel-going Welshmen who people the text call on biblical references and Christian teaching as a modern-day soldier might call on references to football or popular culture. Their attitude is unsophisticated, and, in some ways, their religious belief is simply part of the order into which they are born, without a great deal of power of choice or dissent. Thus, in the account of Sunday services in Part 5, a group of Anglican soldiers describe non-Anglicans as 'the fancy religions', suggesting, not any sectarianism, but just an observation on something different.[38]

As ordinary soldiers, recruited from the harsh conditions of the factory floor, or work as farm labourers or similar occupations, they have scant respect for their superiors or 'bosses'. There is a somewhat disparaging reference to 'sermons on the Bull Ring to further foster the offensive spirit' in Part 6,[39] and the author's note explains the reference to 'the large training ground at Rouen [...] A paradise for Staff Instructors; detested by all front-fighters...the object of its curriculum 'to foster the offensive spirit'[40]

There is more than a suggestion that attitudes of hatred for the enemy and his demonization, are not shared by the ordinary soldier. When the action of the enemy causes Ball to slip and fall to the ground, he describes how his companion 'remembers to halloo the official blasphemies.'[41] An endnote tells us that this was a reference to bayonet-fighting drill, 'Men were

---

[37] See Paul Fussell, *The Great War and Modern Memory* (Oxford: Oxford University Press, 1977), 147. Fussell suggests that he is chosen as 'the representative Briton.'
[38] Jones, *In Parenthesis*, 107.
[39] Jones, 143.
[40] Jones, 219.12.
[41] Jones, 167.

cautioned to look fiercely upon the enemy when engaging him and to shout some violent word- and not to spare his genitals. This attempt to stimulate an artificial hate by parade-ground Staff-Instruction was not popular among men fresh from actual contact with the enemy'[42]

The reference to 'actual contact with the enemy' reminds one of the familiar tale of the Christmas Truce of 1914, when groups of soldiers instinctively recognised the common humanity they shared with other groups of soldiers occupying various parts of the disputed frontline. While there may not have been a great deal of philosophy or theological thinking behind the attitude, it nevertheless suggests an instinctive sense that the German soldiers are, quite simply, just another group of human beings, part of the humanity shared with Christ. Indeed, there is an extended passage in Part 4, recounting Ball's two-hour night watch while his company are on the frontline in December, which does evoke the Christmas truce.[43] Noting a movement, but unsure what to do, Ball reflects, 'Leave him be on a winter's morning – let him bide.' He contemplates further:

> they were at breakfast and were cold as he, they too made their dole.
> And one played on an accordion:
> *Es ist ein' Ros' entsprungen*
> *Au seiner Wurzel zart*
> Since Boniface once walked in Odin's wood.[44]

The reference to the German Christmas carol establishes the Christian context and the reference to the story of an English saint much revered in Germany increases that sense of sympathy with the enemy. Then two men in the trench behind Ball start playing a popular song on their mouthorgans, further connecting them to the men on the opposite lines, and recalling the events of Christmas 1914. Ball's thoughts follow in a stream of consciousness which, while referring to the German soldiers in what Jones notes was a term used of them, 'bastard square-heads',[45] nevertheless acknowledges what the two sides have in common and culminates with a reference, which the author notes as being to Milton's, 'Hymn on the Morning of Christ's

---

[42] Jones, 222.18.

[43] In a recent article, Shane Emplaincourt points out that the Christmas Truce grew out of 'low-key fraternizing that happened a month prior to Christmas' in which the desire to sing together was one feature, Shane A. Emplaincourt, 'Joyeux Noël and Remembering the Christmas Truce of 1914', *War, Literature and the Arts* 27 (2015): 11.

[44] Jones, *In Parenthesis*, 67.

[45] Jones, 205.18.

Nativity', 'wot type's this of universall [sic] Peace/Through Sea and Land.'[46] Interestingly the lines which follow in Milton's poem are 'No war or battle's sound/Was heard the world around.' Ball's thoughts recognise the contradiction on Christmas morning of the two opposing sides, each singing in their own way, and ironically the enemy being the one who chooses to sing an acknowledgement of the universal Saviour. There is a very real sense in this incident of what unites human beings rather than what divides them, what ultimately the cross of Christ is about. Interestingly in the note here Jones speculates that the grey was always linked in the soldiers' minds with the grey wolf of Nordic literature and wonders 'what myth-conception our own ochre coats and saucer hats suggested to our antagonists'. [47]

The Christian belief in the incarnate Christ who became a fully human person, and dwells within us means that for the Christian all human life must be sacred.[48] This of course presents a challenge to the Christian engaged in warfare. The inescapable paradox of caring for another human being (in this case their children) by wishing for victory over an enemy is encapsulated in Part 6 by imagining the feelings of the Bavarian women. Ball considers their anxiety for their loved ones and imagines their prayers, understandable in the light of this: 'O Clemens, O pia and/ turn all out of alignment the English guns amen.'[49] This not only demonstrates understanding and sympathy, but by the paradox innate in the sympathy for those praying for the guns of one's own army to be turned away, emphasised by quoting the actual words of a hymn, suggests that such prayers are not only futile but based on a misunderstanding of the Christian Gospel.[50] This provides a good example of what Stephen McInerney considers the poem's focus on 'the moral, aesthetic and ultimately theological crisis confronting humankind.'[51]

In Part 7, there is a somewhat striking description of the German prisoners at Mametz Wood, not so much a description from the perspective of shared experience, as the above examples, more as an observation from the outside. They 'come in file, their lifted arm like Jansenist Redeemers, who would

---

[46] Jones, 68 and 205.19.
[47] Jones, 204-5.16.
[48] *New Jerusalem Bible*, John 1.12-14.
[49] The opening words are the from the final line of the Catholic hymn, 'Salve Regina'.
[50] Jones, *In Parenthesis*, 149.
[51] Stephen McInerney, 'David Jones's Blessed Rage for Order: The "Will Toward Shape."', *Logos: A Journal of Catholic Thought and Culture* 14, no. 2 (2011): 62.

save at least themselves.'[52] Jones's note informs the reader that crucifixes attributed to Jansenists have the arms of Christ 'stretched narrowly above the head indicative of their error concerning the exclusiveness of the redemptive act.',[53] highlighting a heretical view that encompasses predestination and therefore restricts Redemption and denies its universality. This sets up an interesting theological speculation for the alert reader. It recognises that soldiers from the Crusades onwards have been seen as in some way repeating the saving act of Christ in dying for others, but points to a paradox that Christ's sacrifice was universal, for all nations, and surely suggests that it cannot be appropriated by one side or another. Of course, it could be argued that the text is suggesting this was an error made by the German soldiers, and that the allied soldiers' sacrifice in the war to end wars was for the common good, but nothing else in the text of *In Parenthesis* suggests this.

The familiarity with death, an inevitable consequence of life on the battlefield, ensures at some level a link with the death of Christ. The entire text is overshadowed by suffering, both physical and psychological, whether the soldiers are enduring the fear and pain of the battlefield, or the hardships of life behind the lines. It evokes for anyone familiar with scripture or liturgy the suffering and death of Christ. This becomes particularly evident in Part 7 which deals with the opening day of the Battle of the Somme. John Ball's regiment is engaged at Mametz Wood, and Ball himself is severely wounded, possibly fatally. It opens with a Latin quotation from Psalm 136.6, [54] the theme of which is the search for God, and is immediately followed by a quotation from Lamentations (2.12), 'They say to their mothers,/"Where is bread and wine?"/as they faint like the wounded/in the streets of the city,/ as their lives ebb away in their mothers' arms.[55] This forms part of the liturgy for the Second Nocturne of Good Friday, a liturgy which marks the contemplation of the suffering of Christ and relates it to human suffering. The reference to the wounded, 'vulnerati' makes its relevance to the soldiers' suffering explicit. The liturgical reference continues with explicit reference to the words of two Psalms, 119 and 123, which are sung at the nocturne of Good Friday, 'coals that lay waste', from Psalm 119, and 'Our soul hath passed through a torrent' from Psalm 23.[56] Both Psalms express the idea that the anguished

---

[52] Jones, *In Parenthesis*, 169.
[53] Jones, 222.20.
[54] I refer here the Vulgate, which is the version referenced by Jones
[55] Jones, *In Parenthesis*, 153.
[56] Jones, 153.

prayers of those who have suffered have been heard but the two quotations refer only to suffering, with clear relevance to the suffering of the soldiers.

Indeed, this is a theme, which, while it becomes particularly significant in Part 7, has been present throughout. Part 3 opens with a liturgical reference which links the liturgy with the rituals of army procedures when John Ball's company undertake their first position on the Front Line, with a direct quotation from the liturgical instruction, 'Proceed...without lights... prostrate before it...he begins without title, silently, immediately...in a low voice, omitting all that is usually said. No blessing is asked, neither is the kiss of peace given...he sings alone.'[57] The tone is above all the tone of mourning,and the disparate references to the Complete Office of Holy Week echo the way in which on Good Friday the Church expresses sorrow for the death of Christ.

The biblical opening to Part 7, is, significantly, immediately followed by a reference to finding a soldier 'all gone to pieces.' It is followed by a description of how his friends, having upbraided him, 'You really can't behave like this in the face of the enemy', help him to calm down and come to terms with the situation. In the process of his calming, there is a very significant return to religious themes. It begins with a clear reference to the Epistle to the Hebrews, 'But he made them a little lower than the angels'[58] It is followed by:

> and their inventions are according to right reason even if you don't approve the end to which they proceed; so that there was rectitude even in this, which the mind perceived at the moment of weakest flesh and all the world shrunken to a point of fear that has affinity I suppose, to that state of deprivation predicate of souls forfeit of their final end, who nevertheless know a good thing when they see it.[59]

The opening words indicate clearly a sense that God (addressed as 'you') would not approve the use of weapons in war. What follows suggests that nevertheless it is understandable, if only because of human weakness and failure to trust in God. Although a certain understanding of the motives that lead to war is indicated, it is judged by the final somewhat cynical adoption

---

[57] Jones, 27.

[58] 'Thou hast made him a little lower than the angels: thou hast crowned him with glory and hour, and hast set him over the works of they hands:' *The Bible*, Douay-Rheims 1899, n.d., 2.7, www.biblegateway.com. This is the version used by Jones which is clearly referenced here.

[59] Jones, *In Parenthesis*, 153–54.

of a colloquial phrase, 'who nevertheless know a good thing when they see it.' There is also significance in the phrase, 'and all the world shrunken to a point of fear'. This may be related to ideas explored in Chapter 10 of the Gospel of St Matthew. This is the account of how Jesus instructs his apostles to go out and teach and warns them that they will be persecuted for what they teach. His instruction culminates with the instruction 'do not be afraid of them' and for several verses he continues to warn them against fear, a lack of trust in God which will cause them to sin.[60] I have quoted and discussed this passage at length because it is the basis for my view, that whatever Jones's views might have been when he joined the Royal Welch Fusiliers in 1915, by the time he came to write *In Parenthesis* he considered it wrong, and wrong for religious reasons, causing the suffering the soldiers are currently undergoing and manifesting a failure of trust in God. As they wait to adopt their positions for the long-awaited Somme Offensive, both those who experience doubt and those who do not, progress 'in a like condemnation/to the place of a skull.' For the Christian reader this of course means Golgotha, better known as Calvary, and signals the suffering which is to follow.

The following two to three pages capture the sense of fearful anticipation which is the prelude to the battle. While the biblical and liturgical references in the remainder of Part 7 are not as intense as in the first few pages, they nevertheless remain and above all link the suffering of the soldiers with the suffering of Christ. The soldiers wait for the battle to begin, having been warned that there are 'Two minutes to go' and Ball or one of his immediate companions reflects, 'Minutes to excuse me to make excuse./Responde mihi?' Jones references the Latin phrase as being from the 'Dominican Little Office of the Blessed Virgin Mary. Office of the Dead', and originally from the Book of Job, conveying a loss of faith in God, a sense of despair. [61] Shortly after this comes the expression of an improbable hope that the offensive might be cancelled. A significant comparison is made to Gethsemane, to that moment when the human Christ who embraces human frailty, prays that he won't have to endure his passion and crucifixion, 'Perhaps they'll cancel it [...] you can't believe the Cup wont [sic] pass from/or they wont [sic] make a better show/in the garden.'[62] The comparison of waiting for the battle to begin with the very moving Gospel accounts of the Garden of Gethsemane speaks for itself and demonstrates

---

[60] *New Jerusalem Bible*, Matthew 10.26-31.
[61] Jones, *In Parenthesis*, 157 and 220.5.
[62] Jones, 158.

what many would regard as the only relevance of the story of Christ to the battlefields of the Western Front.

By the 1930s, when Jones came to write *In Parenthesis*, he clearly saw a tension between the universality of Christ's incarnation, life and death and the act of one group of human beings fighting another. It was a division which divided Christians across Europe. In relation to this it is helpful to look at the portrayal of priests in *In Parenthesis*. Three priests are specifically mentioned, but only one by name. The Catholics are marched four kilometres to the next village because Father Larkin is up at the Aid Post 'with his Washbourne Rituale and the saving Oils'(a reference to the 1st edition of Burns Oates and Washbourne Missal published in 1912). Later Father Larkin and the unnamed Anglican are represented as carrying out the pastoral duties of the priest, caring for their troops, caring for the wounded and the dying. Father Larkin is described as giving the last sacraments to the dead: 'why is Father Larkin talking to the dead'[63] Earlier, at an Anglican service the unnamed chaplain preaches 'from Matthew text, of how He cares for us above the sparrows'. The inescapable irony here is reinforced by the fact that the service is held, 'behind the 8 in. siege, whose regular discharges made quite inaudible the careful artistry of the prayers he read.'[64]

Thus far the Church (in the broadest sense of the term, including both Catholics and Anglicans) is seen as representing love of neighbour manifested in the care of the soldiers. However, with some cynicism the text does not fail to represent the less attractive aspect of the Church's role (at least to this modern reader). In Part 6, as they prepare for the first day of the Somme offensive the ordinary soldiers discuss with some cynicism the idea that 'The Chaplain General will explain how it's a Christian act after all. Give 'em burial in St Paul's, there will be letters to The Times saying it should have been the Abbey...'[65] The passage conveys a tone of the drearily predictable reaction of the establishment which almost conceals the savage indictment of seeing the destruction of the Great War as a Christian act.

The Catholic Church fares no better. There is a sarcastic comment that Bertrand Russell (who was a noted campaigner against the war) should be garrotted with the Union Flag and that the powers that be should 'detail Fr Vaughan, O.C. Sergeant Instructors- to pr-reach [sic] a course of sermons

[63] Jones, 173.
[64] Jones, 107.
[65] Jones, 142–43.

on the Bull Ring to further foster the offensive spirit'. [66] Jones's note tells us that Vaughan was an eminent RC preacher 'reputed to have urged greater zeal in the destruction of enemy personnel.[67] In the light of the comments earlier about the detestation of the Bull Ring (the parade ground at Rouen) and of the attitude of Staff Instructors the condemnation of Vaughan seems clear.

The treatment of the clergy including chaplains is not a major theme of *In Parenthesis* but its consideration supports the view of the centrality of the suffering human being to the text rather than the idea that the war is a heroic and salvific action. The more militarist attitudes of some of their number, particularly those in high positions is acknowledged but does not win approval.

Of the three writers discussed, Kettle alone unambiguously endorses the view that the soldiers sacrifice their lives for the benefit of others, although he acknowledges the suffering endured in the process. His view is perhaps best summed up by his comment in *Ways of War*,

'The waste- the science of waste and bloodshed! How my heart loathes it and yet it is God's only way to justice'.[68] On first reading, it seems that MacGill's soldiers partake much more fully in heroic action than the soldiers Jones depicts. David Taylor, writing of 'the complex and dynamic ways' in which soldiers and others came to terms with the experience, argues that his earlier works, including *The Great Push* see the war in more positive ways. However, I would argue that in *The Great Push* pessimism ultimately dominates. [69] In my view, the heroism is challenged as mere killing by the presence of the cross, and the cross as representative of passive suffering with which the ordinary soldiers are identified ultimately comes to predominate in the text. The only truly heroic action in *The Great Push* is the succouring of the wounded, carried out in the name of the figure on the cross. Although Jones's soldiers too are often heroic, the text is dominated by a sense of suffering. Jones's text links the suffering soldiers with the suffering Christ more profoundly and extensively than MacGill's, but nevertheless makes a crucial distinction. It appears to me, ultimately to deny, not significance but purpose to their deaths. Yet no-one reading

---

[66] Jones, 143.
[67] Jones, 219.12.
[68] Kettle, *The Ways of War*, 6.
[69] Taylor, *Memory, Narrative and The Great War: Rifleman Patrick MacGill and the Construction of Wartime Experience.*

Jones's text in the light of his use of the cross can see it as wholly negative. It is its assertion of the sacredness of the human which renders it ultimately positive.

Bibliography

Appleby, R.Scott. 'How Christians Went to War'. *U.S.Catholic*, May 1999, 40–41.

Benedict XV, Pope. 'Apostolic Exhortation To the Peoples Now at War and to Their Rulers', 1915. http://w2.vatican.va/content/benedict-xv/en/apost_exhortations/documents/hf_ben-xv_exh_19150728_fummo-chiamati.html.

Emplaincourt, Shane A. 'Joyeux Noël and Remembering the Christmas Truce of 1914'. *War, Literature and the Arts* 27 (2015): 1–25.

Fussell, Paul. *The Great War and Modern Memory*. Oxford: Oxford University Press, 1977.

Graecen, robert. 'Taking the Derry Boat'. *A Journal of Irish Studies* 16, no. 1 (1981): 90–94.

Griffiths, Richard. *The Pen and the Cross*. London: Continuum, 2010.

Gwynn, Stephen, and Thomas Kettle. *Battle Songs of the Irish Brigades*. Dublin: Maunsel, 1915.

Jeffery, Keith. *Ireland and the Great War*. Cambridge: Cambridge University Press, 2000.

Jones, David. *In Parenthesis*. London: Faber and Faber, 1963.

Kettle, Thomas. *Poems and Parodies*. London: Duckworth, 1916.

—. *The Ways of War*. New York: Charles Scribner's Sons, 1917.

—. 'Under the Heel of the Hun'. In *The Ways of War*, 125–38. New York: Charles Scribner's Sons, 1917.

—. 'Why Ireland Fought'. In *The Ways of War*, 58–104. New York: Charles Scribner's Sons, 1917.

MacGill, Patrick. *Children of the Dead End*. London: Caliban Books, 1995.

—. *Soldier Songs*. New York: Dutton, 1917.

—. *The Great Push*. Edinburgh: Birlinn Limited, 1984.

McGarry, Fearghal. *The Rising*. Oxford: Oxford University Press, 2010.

McInerney, Stephen. 'David Jones's Blessed Rage for Order: The "Will Toward Shape."' *Logos: A Journal of Catholic Thought and Culture* 14, no. 2 (2011): 59–81.

New Jerusalem Bible, n.d. www.catholic.org.

Shannon, William H. 'Christian Conscience and Modern Warfare'. *America* 166, no. 5 (15 February 1992): 108–12.

Taylor, David. *Memory, Narrative and The Great War: Rifleman Patrick MacGill and the Construction of Wartime Experience*. Liverpool: Liverpool University Press, 2013.

The Bible. Douay-Rheims 1899., n.d. www.biblegateway.com.

Wells, H.G. *The War That Will End War*. London: F.&C.Palmer, 1914.

Winter, Jay. *The Great War and the British People*. Cambridge: Cambridge University Press, 1986.

THOMAS MANN:
THE STORY AND THE FEAST

MICHAEL KIRWAN

Or let us wait and see whether God will not one day honour himself in us by some great intervention and deliverance. The feast would then be there, ready to receive the story and ready for us to sing songs of rejoicing.[1]

Introduction

Great literature is able to disclose 'distinctive features of a Catholic philosophy of education and life'; so, at least, runs the thesis of the essays in this volume. Does the claim hold good for literary modernism, and its neglected religious dimension? Is there, as Mark Bosco suggests, a 'cultural confluence between three unlikely terms: Catholicism, literature, and modernism'? In its imperative to 'make it new', modernism has typically turned its back on religion as a spent force. Bosco maintains, to the contrary, that the aesthetic and religious commitments of major Catholic writers constitute 'a parallel narrative of engagement' during the rise of high modernist theory and artistic practice, from the late nineteenth century onwards.[2]

Introducing Thomas Mann into this debate requires special pleading, on two counts. Firstly, there is no sense that Mann can be plausibly introduced as a Christian, let alone a Catholic writer. 'I cannot say that I believe in God, and even if I did believe, it would be a long time before I said so'.[3]

---

[1] Thomas Mann, *Joseph and His Brothers* (New York: A.A. Knopf. 2005), 386.

[2] Mark Bosco SJ, "Shades of Greene in Catholic Literary Modernism." *Integritas* 6.3 (Fall 2015): 1-17. His article is on the novels of Graham Greene, but Bosco points to the flourishing of French literature in the late nineteenth century (Huysmans, Bloy, and Péguy), and into the twentieth (Claudel, Bernanos, and Mauriac).

[3] Erich Heller, *Thomas Mann: the Ironic German* (Cambridge: Cambridge University Press, 1981 [1958]), 148. Heller cites this statement from Mann, commenting that

Despite the profusion of Christian allusions in at least three of his fictional works especially, and in his letters and essays, the consensus is that Mann is a non-Christian or even anti-Christian writer.[4] Scaff cites two studies which seem to arrive at opposite verdicts: Wilhelm Kantzenbach asserts the 'theological thought structures' of Mann's work, while Werner Frizen maintains that *Doktor Faustus* represents a climactic and definitive repudiation of the Christian tradition.[5] Scaff's counter-arguments against the view of Mann as a blatant sceptic or even blasphemer will be examined in the next section. For the present, it must be acknowledged that Mann's most prominent philosophical and cultural guides are, surely, among the very architects of the Romantic and modernist displacement of Christianity: Schopenhauer, Nietzsche, Freud.

But if Mann's Christian 'credentials' are lacking, so too, it seems, are his modernist ones. Mann is aware of the cultural, political and artistic crises to which 'modernism' is a response; but his strategy is different from the experimentation of the acclaimed masters of modernism, such as Proust, Joyce, and Kafka. For these writers, the only coherent riposte to the incoherence of our time is radical innovation. Thomas Mann, by contrast, sets himself to work with traditional, even conservative literary forms- but with an ironical distance that charges them with new power. (Heller, *Thomas Mann: the Ironic German,* 22)

So if Mann is not writing out of a Christian commitment, and if he does not pursue modernist strategies of experimentation, how does his fiction exemplify Bosco's 'narrative of engagement'? More generally, where in

---

Mann 'religiously' embraces doubt in preference to false belief. See also "Thomas Mann's American Religion," accessed June 25, 2020, http://www.heinrichdetering.de/tagesfragen/thomas-manns-american-religion/, where Heinrich Detering gives an account of Mann's involvement with the First Unitarian Church of Los Angeles. Mann's personal and intellectual connection was strong: 'rarely, if ever, had he taken so lively and militant an interest in the activities of any religious group.'

[4] Susan von Rohr Scaff, "The Religious Base of Thomas Mann's Word View: Mythic Theology and the Problem of the Demonic," *Christianity and Literature,* 43.1 (Autumn 1993): 75-94. *Joseph and His Brothers, Doktor Faustus,* and *The Holy Sinner* are saturated with theological themes.

[5] Friedrich Wilhelm Kantzenbach, "Theologische Denkstrukturen bei Thomas Mann," *Neue Zeitschrift für Systematische Theologie und Religionsphilosophie* 9 (1967): 201-17; Werner Frizen, "Thomas Mann und das Christentum". In *Thomas-Mann- Handbuch,* ed. Helmut Koopman (Stuttgart: Alfred Kröner, 1995), 307-326.

Mann's work can we discern 'distinctive features of a Catholic philosophy of education and life'?

The evidence for a religious sensibility within Mann's writing will be drawn from two of his most important works, *The Magic Mountain* (1928) and the *Joseph* tetralogy (1926-42). The first of these is an intense novel of ideas which unfolds in a Swiss sanatorium for tubercular patients, their chronic sickness being a metaphor for Europe on the eve of the First World War. Its hero, Hans Castorp, is a young, fastidious burgher from Hamburg, whose short visit to the Bergdorf sanatorium becomes an extended stay of seven years when he is unexpectedly diagnosed and in need of treatment. His experiences- principally, the conversations with fellow patients, an intense but platonic love affair, and an extraordinary 'near-death' vision in the mountain snow- transform his narrative into a heroic quest, as he seeks to balance the competing enticements of the forces of life and death. *Joseph and His Brothers* is a more complex and elaborate work, utterly atypical in modern literature for its biblical subject matter. Mann renders the patriarchal narratives of Jacob and his son Joseph- the 'novella' of Genesis chapters 37-4- into an astonishing epic tetralogy of fifteen hundred pages. Joseph is portrayed herein as 'the type of the artist, in the tradition of the Old Testament patriarchs and prophets endeavouring both to understand his world and to change it by means of his interpretation of it'.[6]

Each of these works is an example of the peculiarly German literary form, the *Bildungsroman*, or story of the formation or initiation of a young, naïve hero. Mann's care for the two men- Hans Castorp, the innocent engineer, and Joseph, the patriarchal dreamer- shows a seriousness of ethical but also religious purpose: the 'parallel narrative of engagement' which Bosco identifies, as both an alternative to modernism and a variant of it.

Two themes are relevant here: Mann's 'ironical' style, and what Georg Lukács characterizes as Mann's 'search for *bürgerliche* (bourgeois) man'. Each of these, as we shall see, has a theological inflection, which will be explored with the help of Erich Heller and Johann Baptist Metz, respectively. Heller identifies the 'theology of irony' of the Joseph tetralogy as the distillation of Mann's ironic style; Metz offers an extensive theological critique of *bürgerliche* Christianity in the light of the Holocaust.

---

[6] Stephen Prickett, "Biblical and Literary Criticism: a History of Interaction." In *The Bible and Literature: a Reader*, eds. David Jasper and Stephen Prickett, (Oxford: Blackwell, 1999), 12-43: 39.

Firstly, the contrasting organising ideas of each of these *Bildungsromanen* will be introduced, to be explored further in a later section, 'from alchemy to typology'. The key to Hans Castorp's initiation, Mann proposes, is the legendary archetype of the eternal Quester, and of alchemical transformation or 'heightening'. The case of Joseph is more complex, but one of the guiding principles for interpreting Joseph's initiation is familiar from Christian biblical theology- even if Mann does not use this terminology- as figural or typological interpretation. The recovery of typological criticism by the French Jesuit theologians, Henri de Lubac and Jean Daniélou, at the same time as Mann is writing *Joseph and His Brothers* (and with a similar anti-Nazi intention), provides a further link between Mann's fiction and a Catholic theological imagination.

The two novels are considered here as a dialogue of question and response. *The Magic Mountain* asserts, but does not resolve, major tensions regarding aesthetic and religious meaning; *Joseph and His Brothers* offers some kind of reconciliation of these questions. The intellectual brilliance of *The Magic Mountain* is tragically undercut by the concluding chapter: Hans Castorp is last seen stumbling across a battlefield, his fate unspecified. By contrast, of course, the Joseph story ends in comedic blessing.

The genre of *Bildungsroman* requires careful attention to what happens to these two young men. Hans Castorp's unintended sojourn at the House Berghof sanitorium is a profound engagement with sickness and death. Hans comes to 'strike a pact' with the unknown world and its dark forces. These must not be rationalised away; but nor must one be overwhelmed or fascinated by them. Mann draws an analogy with the Quester legends of the search for the Grail, symbol of knowledge, wisdom, consecration. Castorp's unexpected encounters and experiences, are described by Mann as an alchemical enhancement or 'heightening' (*Steigerung*). This unexciting individual becomes 'interesting', transubstantiated into someone 'capable of adventures in sensual, moral, intellectual spheres.'[7]

Joseph and His Brothers is remarkably faithful to the biblical narrative. Its hero is recognizable from the Genesis narrrative as the naïve dreamer of destiny who overcomes his misfortunes to become the wise saviour- the 'provider'- for his people. There are hints of the trickster's ingenuity, but it is his steadfast faith in God's providential care for him which enables his forgiving and reconciling triumph. The hero's progress, according to Georg

---

[7] Thomas Mann, 'The Making of *The Magic Mountain*'. In *The Magic Mountain* (London: Vintage Classics, 1999), 725-26.

Lukács, imitates that of Goethe, 'from self-absorbed love via autobiographical confession to educative responsibility'.[8] On a more 'modernist' reading, Joseph's story records the birth of the ego out of the mythical collective, a journey toward artistic self-discovery and self-celebration.

The *Joseph* tetralogy is an extravagant deployment of Gnostic philosophy, history of religion, and Freudian theory- as well as a distinctive theological inflection which has been called a 'theology of irony', but is also discernible as the ancient and venerable practice of 'figural' or 'typological' interpretation. According to traditional figural reading, Joseph is a 'type' of Jesus. His story- the victimization by his brothers, his being cast down firstly into a pit and then into prison, his restoration, his forgiveness of and reconciliation with his brothers- traces the arc of Jesus' rejection, death and resurrection, and the grounding of a new conviviality.

But *Joseph and His Brothers* sets up an even starker typological contrast.[9] Written in exile, the *Joseph* novels tell the story of a 'dreamer' and 'leader/provider', alternative to the one laying waste to Germany and Europe. They narrate Joseph's education (*Bildung*) as a painful learning to overcome his sense of his own irresistible destiny. In his story we find true relationship between myth and reason, as Mann seeks to 'rescue myth from the hands of the Fascists'.

We will return to consider the implications of these respective frameworks- the alchemical 'heightening' in *The Magic Mountain*, and the typological signification which unites the Joseph novels. We will do so having first considered two specific *leitmotifen* of Mann's work: the 'theology of irony', and his 'quest for bourgeois man'.

The 'theology' of irony

To return to the question of modernism, and its ambiguity toward religion. Insofar as the movement marks a rupture of epistemological concerns from

---

[8] Georg Lukács, "The Tragedy of Modern Art". In *Georg Lukács, Essays on Thomas Mann* (London: Merlin Press, 1964). 47-97: 56.

[9] Mann's original title for the work, "Jacob and his sons", invites comparison with "Germany and its sons," that is, with the Aryan youth that Mann repeatedly tried, during the early Joseph years, to woo away from Hitler, the 'pseudo-patriarch.' William McDonald. 1999. *Thomas Mann's Joseph and His Brothers: Writing, Performance and the Politics of Loyalty* (Rochester, New York: Camden House, 1999), 3.

metaphysical categories, consequently a destabilization of social, and cultural conventions, then it is understandable that an oppositional or subversive stance toward religion is modernity's default position. Even when the search for a new coherence feels like a desperate gathering of the 'fragments shored up against [our] ruin' (Eliot), the assumption holds sway that this coherence can only be shaped independently of exhausted religious traditions- an assumption that Thomas Mann seems to share. His first novel, *Buddenbrooks*, opens with a family scene in which the young Toni has difficulty reciting her catechism answers, much to the amusement of her grandfather. Toni remarks that she is able to recite the formula correctly if she hurls herself into it, not paying attention to its meaning, like tobogganing down a hill. In *The Magic Mountain*, on his first evening at the sanatorium, Hans Castorp rubs his hands together before dinner 'in agreeable anticipation- a habit of his when he sat down to table, perhaps because his ancestors had said grace before meat.'

However, just as Mann deviates from modernist strategy by having a more complex relation to the traditions it rejects, so it is with regard to religious tradition. Scaff rests her case for a more nuanced view on two considerations: firstly, that in his later work Mann conceived of a religious identification of myth and literature which is remarkably consonant with that of the literary critic (and clergyman) Northrop Frye;[10] secondly, that Mann drew positively from the theologian Paul Tillich in his depiction of demonic vitality in *Doktor Faustus*. Paul Tillich helps us to understand the redemptive function of such a figure, as the demonic is integrated into the scheme of salvation.[11] While Mann is still some way from Christian orthodoxy, the parallel speculations of Northrop Frye and Paul Tillich within Christian theology suggest a closer alignment than normally recognised.

Erich Heller asserts that Mann shares the concerns of 'official' modernist writers- Proust, Joyce, Musil, and Kafka- but moves along a different trajectory. While these writers sought to forge a new and complex literary coherence, Mann undertook a more conservative strategy, as he 'set out to build a traditionally solid house on a metaphysically condemned site. ... clinging to a convention in the clear knowledge of its incongruity, and of desperately resisting despair'. (Heller, *The Ironic German*, 25) What saves

---

[10] Northrop Frye, *Anatomy of Criticism: Four Essays* (Toronto: University of Toronto Press, 2006 [1957]).

[11] Susan von Rohr Scaff, "The Religious Base of Thomas Mann's Word View", 77. She cites Paul Tillich's *The Interpretation of History* (1936), as well as Tillich's correspondence with Mann.

Mann's work from 'stale traditionalism' is the transformative power of matter and substance, ironically juxtaposed. Mann simulates the security of a tradition, even as the substance of the work undermines it.

'Irony' has a vast range of register in Mann's fiction and essays: equating with nihilism and cynicism, with contemplative bliss (Schopenhauer), or with a sceptical attitude toward scientism. (Heller: *The Ironic German*, 236-9) Of most interest for the present study, however, is Heller's chapter VI, where he describes the 'theology of irony' which comes to glorious fruition in *Joseph and His Brothers*. Here is 'the apotheosis of all previous ironies', where Mann

> resolves in serene irony the besetting dilemmas between faithful acceptance and disloyally creative critique, between the house and the journey, between the eternal recurrence and the adventure of the pilgrimage. (Heller, *The Ironic German*, 235)

The 'theological irony' here described means keeping in sight the 'still greater story' which Joseph anticipates, and within which Joseph's adventures are a kind of interlude.[12] The suffering of Mann's bourgeois heroes, such as Thomas Buddenbrook and Hans Castorp, is that of uprooted individuals, lamenting the loss of a tradition; but they are granted glimpses of a 'timeless presence'. In Jacob and Joseph, by contrast, we encounter men who wholly live in the mythic tense of the perfect present. The tensions between art and life, and so on, are resolved by means of a 'double blessing', which may be better described as humour. It is precisely the hermeneutical space to distinguish between what is and what is meant, to interpret and not simply receive meanings as given: the acknowledgment of 'points of view'.[13] Irony is the source of frivolity, arbitrariness and despair, but also of humility, humour and faith.[14]

---

[12] Thus comes into view the narrative of Tamar, who with persistence and cunning forces her way into the line of descent, and therefore into salvation history. She, like Mann, is aware of 'the story above the story'.

[13] See discussion below of Erich Auerbach, who describes the scriptural mode of representation in terms of 'multiplicity of meanings and the need for interpretation, universal-historical claims, development of the concept of the historically becoming, and preoccupation with the problematic.' Erich Auerbach, *Mimesis: The Representation of Reality in Western Literature* (Princeton: Princeton University Press, 2003),

[14] Heller, *Thomas Mann: the Ironoic German*, 251. For a robust critique of Mann's irony, see Gillian Rose, *The Broken Middle: Out of Our Ancient Society* (Oxford: Blackwell, 1992), 115-152.

Joseph, the 'first-born of irony', lives his life 'somewhere between humour and faith'. His alien status turns out to be a blessing, not a curse, as he is 'a *deraciné* with roots in the divine intelligence'. (Heller, *The Ironic German*, 251) He artfully plays the script written for him while skilfully improvising with 'divine allusiveness', in the many gaps left by 'that notoriously difficult playwright'. As Joseph rises to power in Egypt, he is subtly divested of mythological trappings. The more the world regards him as a god, the more human he becomes to himself, and the more humorously he acts, conscious that he is on stage with a responsibility for the success of the performance.

Humour is also Kierkegaard's name for 'the state of a soul existing at the approaches to faith'. This is, indeed, what we find at the end of the banquet which the disguised Joseph prepares for his brothers, when Benjamin is on the point of recognising his lost brother. Instead of attempting to describe the younger brother's feelings, Mann gives up on narration, and simply tells us of his facial expression: 'Just let someone try to describe what was happening now in Benjamin's heart- in a human heart so very close to belief!'' (Mann, *Joseph and His Brothers*, 1359)

Bürgerlich existence

We have noted the significance of *The Magic Mountain* as a *Bildungsroman*, a narrative of transformative growth of its young hero. The growth in question is Hans' transcending his bourgeois existence, and establishing a 'pact' with the forces of suffering and death. The conditions of this pact require a reckoning with *Bürgerlichkeit*: the ideology which prevents the union of life and art, and whose progressive reasonableness masks a potential for catastrophe. The argument bears comparison with the critique of bourgeois Christianity from the Catholic theologian, Johann Baptist Metz.

In a chapter entitled 'Snow', Mann presents us with what I would describe as a 'modernist parable'. Hans is lost and exhausted in the mountains, where he undergoes two hallucinations. The first is an extraordinary benign vision of a luxuriant park peopled by beautiful young human creatures, Mediterranean 'children of sun and sea'. This is immediately followed by a nightmare vision of two old, witch-like women, shouting obscenities at him in his own Hamburg dialect, as they dismember and devour a child. Hans reflects later that the two visions will always belong together- reason and recklessness; 'man's state, his courteous and enlightened social state; behind which, in the temple, the horrible blood sacrifice was contemplated'.

Transmuted, as it were, by alchemical 'heightening', Hans Castorp has been rendered capable of sacrifice: of dying and killing, alongside so many thousands of others. The paradisal dream of love, and the universal feast of death, are two sides of the same Nietzschean coin; consider Friedrich Nietzsche's contemptuous dismissal of 'this pseudo-humaneness called Christianity' which 'wants it established that no-one should sacrificed'.[15]

I have entitled the 'Snow' episode a 'modernist parable', because it exemplifies the modernist instinct for acknowledging, and coming to terms with, the dark forces which make up human existence. It also exemplifies the modernist case against Christianity, allegedly incapable of such comprehension of both aspects of existence. Thus Rainer Maria Rilke:

> I reproach all modern religions for having provided their believers with consolations and glossings-over of death, instead of giving them the means of coming to an understanding of it. With it and with its full, unmasked cruelty: this cruelty is so immense that it is precisely with *it* that the circle closes: it leads back into a mildness which is greater, purer, and more perfectly clear (all consolation is muddy!) than we have ever, even on the sweetest spring day, imagined mildness to be.[16]

Mann dramatizes this duel temptation in an equally shocking confrontation towards the end of the novel, when the disputations between two fellow tubercular patients at the sanatorium, Herr Naphta and Herr Settembrini, get out of hand. Leo Naphta is 'a peculiar sort of Jesuit' who has been invalided out of ministry, a fanatically misanthropic convert from Judaism; Settembrini is a shabbily chic rationalist and freemason. Both are 'talkers, the one luxurious and spiteful, the other for ever blowing on his penny pipe of reason.' Their heated altercations are a kind of morality play, in which they compete for the 'soul' of the naïve and impressionable Castorp. In the end, he rejects the arguments of both men- one intoxicated with the mysterious dark, one in enlightened denial of it. They are a mish-mash, a *guazzabuglio* of God and the devil, a 'confused noise of battle':

> You [Settembrini] are a wind-bag and a hand-organ man, to be sure. But you mean well, you mean much better, and more to my mind, than that

---

[15] Friedrich Nietzsche, para. 246, *The Will to Power* (New York: Vintage Books, 1968), 142.
[16] Rilke to Countess Margot Sizzo-Noris-Crouy (January 6th, 1923): Rainer Maria Rilke, *Selected Poetry* (London: Picador, 1987), 332.

knife-edged little Jesuit and Terrorist, apologist of the Inquisition and the knout, with his round eye-glasses- though he is nearly always right when you and he come to grips over my paltry soul, like God and the Devil in medieval legends. (Mann, *The Magic Mountain*, 478).

Castorp thinks he has done well to shake off both Herr Settebrini and Herr Naptha; but 'how much more powerfully the darkly insinuating Naptha speaks to humanity's ordinary soul'.[17] Settembrini, the man of progress, is in denial about the demonic nothingness to which his *Bürgerlichkeit* utimately tends; his clerical adversary insistently reminds him of it. Finally, Naphta challenges the other to a duel. The pacifist Settembrini thinks the whole business is ridiculous, but he goes along with the preparations. When they face each other with pistols, Settembrini fires his shot into the air and braces himself, ready for his opponent's turn. Naphta angrily demands that Settembrini fire again, properly. When Settembrini refuses, Naphta shrieks 'Coward!'- and shoots himself in the head.

Naptha's suicide is the 'terroristic deed of that desperate antagonist' (Mann, *The Magic Mountain*, 709). His spiritual intensification, his rejection of liberalism and espousal of Terror, strike us as Marxist in provenance, rather than Christian; and it does appear that Mann modelled this perverse figure on the Marxist literary critic George Lukács. But it is a 'demonic intensification of life [which] involves a re-ignition of the possibility of God'. (Fernie, "Something Rich and Strange", 7). As Hans Castorp acknowledges with disgust, 'that knife-edged little Jesuit and Terrorist ... is nearly always right'.

Hans Castorp disappears from our view on a battlefield, in the flash of an exploding shell: 'a man who, despite many warnings, had neglected to read the papers.' (Mann, *The Magic Mountain*, 709) Mann bids him a solemn farewell-'Farewell, honest Hans Castorp, farewell, Life's delicate child!':

Moments there were, when out of death, and the rebellion of the flesh, there came to thee, as thou tookest stock of thyself, a dream of love. Out of this universal feast of death, out of this extremity of fever, kindling the rain-washed evening sky to a fiery glow, may it be that Love one day shall mount? (Mann, *The Magic Mountain*, 716)

---

[17] Ewan Fernie, "Introduction: Something Rich and Strange (with a Note on Mann's Shakespeare, by Tobias Döring)". In *Thomas Mann and Shakespeare: Something Rich and Strange*, edited by Tobias Döring and Ewan Fernie, 1-22. (New York: Bloomsbury, 2015): 6.

Thomas Mann's 'search for bourgeois man' can be usefully compared with that of another thinker of the German catastrophe, Johann Baptist Metz. As Lübeck shaped Mann's imagination, so Metz's childhood- he was born in 1928- was spent in Auerbach, Bavaria, which he speaks of as a symbol of pre-Enlightenment Catholicism. It was a place which seemed caught in the Middle Ages, and while this culture had many fine aspects, Metz found himself having to make a 'journey from Auerbach', into the world of secular modernity.[18] Metz's development of a 'practical fundamental theology' centred on the need to respond to the question of Christianity's collapse in the face of the Nazi catastrophe. His diagnosis pointed to two related areas of crisis.

Firstly, in Enlightenment modernity a new, distorted version of the human subject has emerged. Because it defines its freedom independently of communal and traditional ties, this subject is- paradoxically- extremely vulnerable to manipulation and co-option. Modernity actually undermines the subject to which it gave birth, and threatens its very survival. The default instinct of the modern subject is an anaesthetic flinching from suffering and negativity- Charles Taylor's 'buffered self' of modernity.

Secondly, the same crisis has implications for the Christian community, in view of the privatization of Christianity in the Enlightenment era. Christianity's 'settlement' with modernity is described by Metz as a 'Pyrrhic victory' over the Enlightenment, the 'secret enthronement of the *bourgeois* subject in theology', which ultimately rendered the *bürgerliche* Church incapable of resisting fascism. (Metz, *Faith in History and Society*, 42-45)

Metz diagnoses the crisis of Christianity as a failure, both individual and collective, of its messengers. The individual Christian is called to embrace her vulnerability as freedom, not *from* suffering, but as a freedom 'to suffer the sufferings of others'. Similarly, the *bürgerliche* Church's incapacity to live an endangered identity is a forgetfulness of the interruptive and messianic 'dangerous memory' of Jesus Christ.

This diagnosis comes from the standpoint of Christian faith; but its scathing judgement upon the Church, and upon individual believers in the face of

---

[18] This 'journey' is illustrated by traumatic wartime experiences during his youth, which Metz called 'interruptions'. Metz was concerned by the failure of the revelation of the *Shoah* (Holocaust) to transform German theology and German society in the immediate post-war period. See Johann Baptist Metz, *Faith In History and Society: Toward a Practical Fundamental Theology* (New York: Crossroad, 2013 [1972]).

totalitarianism, coincides largely with the modernist case against traditional Christianity. Mann's own rejection of institutional religion would seem to stem from a similar view of the Church as a spent force; though as this chapter is seeking to argue, this is not at all the last word with regard to religion and its 'messianic' potential for human flourishing.

To conclude: in *The Magic Mountain*, the intoxicated love of death, and its secret nihilistic pact with *bürgerlich* existence, is exposed, but not resolved. Hans Castorp, we are told, has made a pact with the forces of life and death, in which he rejects both the denial of death (Settembrini) and the morbid fascination with it (Naphta). The vision in the snow anticipates *Joseph* as a moment of mythological clairvoyance, which releases Hans from his obsession with death, revealing to him the state and status of *Homo Dei*.

And yet; this is hardly a resolution of the issue. Hans grudgingly concedes that the 'Jesuit terrorist' is always right. The Marxist critic Georg Lukács-the alleged model for the fanatical Naphta- points out that Hans' transmutation is dearly bought, at the expense of immersion into instinctivism. The sanatorium is merely a 'holiday' from real life. In the end, Hans is 'a good honest soldier' who 'joined with the rest of the baccantes who had yielded up their will to the fascist hypothesis', to the 'wild dance' which almost became the death dance of civilization.[19]

From Alchemy to Typology

Castorp achieves a level of wisdom in being able to reject both Settembrini and Naphta. Naphta's malice is evident; Settembrini's danger is greater, perhaps, for being hidden, and I have suggested the political theology of Johann Baptist Metz as a complementary- or alternative- reading of Germany's *bürgerlich* vulnerability in the face of barbarism. The ideas of both men lead to disaster; but in what sense, then, is the odious Jesuit Terrorist 'nearly always right'? We need to turn attention to the Joseph volumes, as a kind of response to the unresolved drama of *The Magic Mountain*. Here, too, there is a Christian theological parallel- or alternative-to Mann's strategy.

Johannes von Goethe remarked of the Joseph narrative: 'How lovable this story is, and how natural. But it seems too short, and one feels called upon

---

[19] Georg Lukács, 'In Search of Bourgeois Man'. In *Georg Lukács, Essays on Thomas Mann* (London: Merlin Press, 1964), 13-46: 40.

to develop it in detail.[20] Mann's tetralogy could not be a more apt response; it is no coincidence that Mann's Joseph is an amalgam of Christ and Goethe, with his story following the Goethean path 'from self-absorbed love via autobiographical confession to educative responsibility.'

Mann's humanistic re-narration of the Joseph stories attempts to reunite time and history. The story moves, therefore, between two axes. Chronologically, Mann moves back and forth, because the past, present and future of myth are contemporaneous. But the psychological and gnostic patterning also requires that Mann move vertically, registering the 'heights and depths' as the sources of dark blessing.[21] It is in *Joseph and His Brothers* that Mann comes close to a realization of Schlegel's future *Universalpoesie*, that is, an oscillation of the 'uniquely interesting' and the 'mythologically bound and rooted'. For Hans Castorp, this is the 'alchemical heightening' of his life, above all as a result of his double vision in the mountains. Hans' bourgeois identity is transfigured by a momentary insight into the larger pattern which governs existence.

But the insight is fleeting, and in any case is swallowed up in the carnage of warfare.

This ephemeral and ambiguous glimpse into the truth of *homo Dei* in *The Magic Mountain* becomes, in the Joseph novels, a much more elaborate structuring principle, bringing the whole work toward a comedic conclusion. Its high point comes in a chapter entitled 'The Cretan Loggia', when Joseph is coming into his power in Egypt- his 'second resurrection from the pit'. As he interprets the dream of Amenhotep IV, the Pharaoh recognises the significance of the seer who stands before him, at this moment: 'in our own time we are the vessels of Eternity', meaning a mutual bestowal of gifts: 'the Eternal upon the Here and Now, the Unique and Particular, and the Here and Now upon the Eternal'.

Mann sees a dramatic co-responsibility between God and his patriarchal enablers. Abraham's covenant consists, precisely, in 'the freedom to fail

---

[20] Johannes von Goethe, *Dichtung und Wahrheit*, Part I Book IV; cited by Heller, *The Ironic German*, 30.

[21] This is emphasised by the two 'Preludes': firstly, the 'Descent into Hell', which introduces volume one, and contains at its centre the 'Romance of the Soul'; secondly, as its counterpart, the 'Prelude in the Higher Circles' which introduces the fourth volume, *Joseph the Provider*. This second prelude is a parodic rendition of the 'Prologue in Heaven' of Goethe's *Faust*- which in turn echoes the beginning of the Book of Job.

God's hope'. This is a break from humanity's mythically-determined repetitiveness. A naïve following of pattern is no longer acceptable. Every 'revolution of the sphere' must be scrutinized, to ensure that it really does accord with God's command, which may be requiring something different from what has gone before.

Jacob has inherited this 'divine anxiety': a constant guardianship over the established order of things on the one hand, and over the Creator's freedom on the other. This anxiety is dramatized in one of the most striking episodes of the tetralogy, in a chapter entitled 'The Test' (Mann, *Joseph and His Brothers*, 78-82) Here is a 'repetition' of the *Akedah*, or 'sacrifice of Abraham' in the life of the father of Joseph's father. Jacob has a terrifying dream, in which God requires of him the life of Joseph, his favoured son. Jacob knows the meaning of the dream, he knows that he both is and is not Abraham; but he fails the test, because he cannot brace himself to commit the deed, as Abraham had done.

Here the 'divine anxiety' makes itself felt: Jacob's dual custodianship of established pattern, but also of new departures. The poignant aspect is his divided love, for God and for Rachel (transferred onto Joseph), which leaves him fearful for his son at the hands of a jealous God who might require him after all.

Distressed, Jacob discusses with Joseph the meaning of his refusal. Jacob is convinced that God, like Molech, is fully entitled to the sacrifice asked of him; yet his knowledge of the Abraham story assures him that God does not 'really' desire this human immolation. But to believe this would be to place his trust, not in God, but in the legend. Besides, he is not Abraham, and he has no guarantee that his own case might not turn out differently. Perhaps this time God really *does* require the sacrifice to be carried out? Jacob regrets bitterly that his violent affection for Joseph was stronger than the violence of God's command to kill.

Joseph seeks to reassure his father, suggesting God's 'humanist' intention of finally doing away with the sacrificial immolation of infants. Jacob concludes that each of them is half-right: 'for man must not be too familiar with the progress of the drama; his part is made up of both familiarity and the suspense of waiting'.[22]

---

[22] Heller, *The Ironic German*, 246. The episode replicates, of course, Kierkegaard's arguments in *Fear and Trembling*, where the *Akedah* is explored from a multitude

Mann's weaving of the patriarchal narratives of Jacob and Joseph into a 'still greater story' is an impressive deployment of gnostic, idealist philosophical, psychoanalytic resources, in an alternative to Germany's *'Führer*-saviour' myth. But the enterprise has a parallel in twentieth-century theology, unacknowledged by Mann: the recovery of typological biblical interpretation by the French Jesuits Henri de Lubac and Jean Daniélou. De Lubac's 'spiritual resistance' in occupied France consisted in his work on an underground journal, with several of his co-workers being captured and executed. His post-war *Medieval Exegesis* is the scholarly fruit of his insistence that the Old Testament- the record of God's unique dealings with the Jewish people- remains theologically significant for Christians.[23]

Alongside this, mention must be made of Erich Auerbach's astonishing study of representation in western literature, up to and including modernism; the book includes chapters on Proust and Woolf. (Auerbach, *Mimesis*, 2003) *Mimesis* was largely written in Istanbul, after Auerbach had been expelled from the University of Marburg in 1935, and published after the war. The book famously opens with an essay, 'Odysseus' Scar', in which a comparison of a passage from Homer and one from the Book of Genesis (Abraham's sacrifice of Isaac) shows the distinctive representational potential of the biblical mode of narration:

> The two styles, in their opposition, represent basic types: on the one hand, fully externalized description, uniform illumination, uninterrupted connection, free expression, all events in the foreground, displaying unmistakable meanings, few elements of historical development and of psychological perspective; on the other hand, certain parts brought into high relief, others left obscure, abruptness, suggestive influence of the unexpressed, "background" quality, multiplicity of meanings and the need for interpretation, universal-historical claims, development of the concept of the historically becoming, and preoccupation with the problematic. (Auerbach, *Mimesis*: 23)

Here we have three writers upholding the continued significance of the Hebrew scriptures for western thought: Thomas Mann's *Joseph and His Brothers*; Erich Auerbach's *Mimesis*; and Henri de Lubac's work on scriptural allegory. Each of these authors, in very different contexts, was on

---

of perspectives. Like Kierkegaard, Jacob wants to take seriously the possibility that the ethical has been suspended.
[23] In his 1947 essay, de Lubac asserts, against Daniélou, that 'allegory' is a more appropriate, because more dynamic, category than typology'. Henri de Lubac, "Typologie et Allégorie," *Recherches de Sciences Religieuses* 34 (1947): 150-22.

the run from the Nazi terror; each of these enterprises was a riposte to the National Socialist determination to eradicate Judaism from sacred and secular history. Three attempts, therefore to 'rescue myth from the hands of the fascists.'

Conclusion

This essay has pursued an improbable quest, in seeking in the writings of Thomas Mann 'distinctive features of a Catholic philosophy of education and life'. There are hints of such a Catholic imaginary, I suggest, in Mann's convergence with Johann Baptist Metz on the diagnosis of *Bürgerlichkeit*; I also suggest that the Gnostic structure of the *Joseph* novels can be read in terms of the classical mode of typological biblical interpretation.

Nevertheless, Mann disavowed any real tie with church and dogma, including the Lutheranism of his youth. The 'godhead' in Joseph is a projection of the human psyche; Mann's religiousness, like that of Joseph, requires obedience to the divine human spirit that is God's will. What matters above all is for a man 'to recognize himself in the past, catch its echo in himself, and find in everything he is and does the familiar form and feel of humanity'.[24] Mann's tutelary angels are Schopenhauer, Nietzsche, and Goethe; even the biblical turn of *Joseph and His Brothers* is more a Freudian and gnostic journey than a Christian one.

On the other hand, Mann's relation to Christianity cannot be described as straightforwardly sceptical or antipathetic. In the two works considered in this essay, *The Magic Mountain* and *Joseph and His Brothers*, one can discern a shift 'from Nietzsche to Goethe'. Joseph, in his obedience to divine providence, is an amalgam of Christ and Goethe, and is Mann's attempt to resolve, in comedic form, the unhappy antinomies of the Bergdorf sanitorium.

Insofar as Mann pressed the need for a 'new humanism' which would incorporate the best impulses of Christian heritage, it is not surprising that the example of Goethe should come to the fore. His 'incarnation' in the well-known and much-loved figure of Joseph indicates Mann's concern, as a matter of urgency, to mobilise the spiritual and moral resources of western civilisation. Despite his rejection of Church and dogma, Mann saw the Judaeo-Christian heritage as synonymous with democracy, and to that

---

[24] Thomas Mann, *Essays of Three Decades* (New York: Alfred A. Knopf, 1947): 421.

extent was its defender. Thomas Jeffars alludes to Mann's conversation with a friend in 1941:

> We were talking about God and religion today, and I said that with the best will in the world I can't tell whether or not I believe. Nevertheless, I sometimes suspect myself of believing; for without a faith I don't suppose one could hate 'l'infâme' [Nazism] as much as I do.[25]

In other words, Mann's passionate horror and antipathy towards the ugly disfigurement of religion by National Socialism must, itself, signify a 'religious' outlook. A barbaric faith in a monstrous god can only be resisted by a civilized faith in the name of the true God. Mann uses the battle image of turning a captured gun around and directing it against the enemy. The stratagem is reminiscent of William Blake's denunciation of the Deists:

> Man must & will have Some Religion; if he has not the Religion of Jesus, he will have the Religion of Satan, & will erect the Synagogue of Satan, calling the Prince of this World, God; and destroying all who do not worship Satan under the Name of God![26]

Mann's strategy of building 'a traditionally solid house on a metaphysically condemned site' runs counter to the modernist mantra of 'make it new'. At a minimal level, the not giving up on history and tradition may be regarded as a 'Catholic' instinct. Jacob's double custodianship of home and pilgrimage, of fidelity and renewal, is mirrored in the contemporary Catholic Church's self-understanding as 'the pilgrim people of God', dialectically held in fidelity to past origins and present regeneration (*ressourcement* and *aggiornamiento*).

I have suggested two other points of connection with Catholic sensibility. Firstly, Mann recognises that Germany's existential struggle, and his own, are entwined in the phenomenon of *Bürgerlichkeit,* the reasoned and complacent progressivism which, frighteningly, is a breeding-ground for the

---

[25] Thomas L. Jeffars, "God, Man, the Devil—and Thomas Mann." Accessed June 25, 2020. https://www.commentarymagazine.com/articles/thomas-jeffers/god-man-the-devil-and-thomas-mann/

[26] William Blake, 'Jerusalem: to the Deists', *The Complete Poetry and Prose of William Blake* (Berkeley: University of California Press, 2008), 201. Thomas Mann's idiom is indeed reminiscent of Blake's, whose insistence on the 'Human Form Divine' was always a repudiation of any conception of deity separate from and opposed to humanity; Blake likewise regarded any ecclesiastical claims to mediate the divine as an outrageous imposition.

cruel irrationality which it denies. The Catholic theologian Johann Baptist Metz has diagnosed the Nazi catastrophe in terms of the Church's fateful settlement with *Bürgerlichkeit,* and its amnesia towards its 'messianic' calling to resist political idolatry.

I have also suggested that Mann's mythologising strategy is convergent with the recovery of 'figural' or 'typological' interpretation by de Lubac and Daniélou. As with Thomas Mann and Erich Auerbach, so with these *ressourcement* theologians: recovery of the Hebrew scriptures as a living tradition is a conscious gesture of resistance of Nazi virulence.

'I was he'. 'I am he'[27]

The issues of identity and repetition which Mann renders by means of an elaborate Gnostic scheme are the essence of figural interpretation. Jacob, as we have seen, is the double custodian, of established pattern, and of the divine freedom to depart from precedent; of home, and of pilgrimage. The anguish of his 'test'- replicated in Kierkegaard- consists in that Jacob both *is* and *is not* Abraham. Joseph's self-revelation to his brothers is the climactic example of this formula. Even as he utters it, the mythical still 'vibrates' within him, as he acknowledges the pattern which transcends his identity in the here and now. It foreshadows Paul's tremulous cry: 'It is no longer I that live, but Christ who lives in me'. (Galatians 2.20)

The typological method (or allegorical, to use de Lubac's preferred term) envisages a fidelity to the past and an openness to the future; in each case, being part of a 'still greater story'. This is beautifully rendered in an episode where, once again, Joseph is trying to console and encourage his father. Jacob the double custodian- of established pattern and of divine freedom- has scruples about a proposed feast in which primitive and idolatrous tribal memories are preserved. Once again, his son reassures him, with an answer which, Jacob recognises, speaks for 'both the custom and the future … awaiting that is also part of the journey'. Joseph counsels a generosity toward the future, and toward its narrative and liturgical possibilities:

> Might these [tribal stories] which over time may perhaps be replaced by some other, which you might then tell during the eating of the roast- the sparing of Isaak, for instance, which would be very fitting. Or let us simply

---

[27] Heller and McDonald note the significance of Mann's essay on Kleist's *Amphitryon*, written at the same time as he was working on the Joseph project. Mann was especially interested in Jupiter's enigmatic reply to Alcmene, as to whether she had slept with him or with her husband: 'I was he'.

wait until such time as God may glorify himself in some great act of deliverance and mercy, the story of which we will then make the basis of our feast, singing songs of jubilation. (Mann, *Joseph and His Brothers*, 386)

References

Auerbach, Erich. "Figura". In *Scenes from the Drama of European Literature*, 11-78. (Minneapolis: University of Minnesota Press, 1959).

Auerbach, Erich. 2003. *Mimesis: The Representation of Reality in Western Literature.* Fiftieth Anniversary Edition. Princeton: Princeton University Press.

Bell. Michael. "The Aesthetics of Modernism", In *The Cambridge Companion to Modernism*, edited by Michael Levenson, 9-32. (Cambridge: CUP, 1999).

Blake, William. 2008. *The Complete Poetry and Prose of William Blake*, edited by David V. Erdman. Berkeley: University of California Press.

Bosco SJ, Mark. "Shades of Greene in Catholic Literary Modernism." *Integritas* 6.3 (Fall 2015): 1-17.

Detering, Heinrich. "Thomas Mann's American Religion. *Ansprache* in der First Unitarian Church of Los Angeles." Accessed June 25, 2020. http://www.heinrichdetering.de/tagesfragen/thomas-manns-american-religion/.

Döring, Tobias, and Fernie, Ewan (eds.). 2015. *Thomas Mann and Shakespeare: Something Rich and Strange.* New York: Bloomsbury.

Fernie, Ewan. "Introduction: Something Rich and Strange (with a Note on Mann's Shakespeare, by Tobias Döring)". In *Thomas Mann and Shakespeare: Something Rich and Strange*, edited by Tobias Döring and Ewan Fernie, 1-22. (New York: Bloomsbury, 2015).

Fernie, Ewan. "'Yes-yes, no': Mann, Shakespeare and the Struggle for Affirmation". In *Thomas Mann and Shakespeare: Something Rich and Strange*, edited by Tobias Döring and Ewan Fernie, 171-190. (New York: Bloomsbury, 2015).

Frizen, Werner. "Thomas Mann und das Christentum". In *Thomas-Mann-Handbuch*, edited by Helmut Koopman, 307-326. (Stuttgart: Alfred Kröner, 1995).

Frye, Northrop. 2006 [1957]. *Anatomy of Criticism: Four Essays.* Toronto: University of Toronto Press.

Hamburger, Käte. 1987. *Thomas Mann's Biblisches Werk.* Frankfurt am Main: Fischer.

Heller, Erich. 1981 [1958]. *Thomas Mann: the Ironic German.* Cambridge: Cambridge University Press.

Jeffars, Thomas L. "God, Man, the Devil—and Thomas Mann." Accessed June 25, 2020. https://www.commentarymagazine.com/articles/thomas-jeffers/god-man-the-devil-and-thomas-mann/

Kantzenbach, Friedrich Wilhelm. "Theologische Denkstrukturen bei Thomas Mann." *Neue Zeitschrift für Systematische Theologie und Religionsphilosophie* 9 (1967): 201-17.

Kierkegaard, Søren. 1983. *Fear and Trembling; Repetition* [edited and translated Howard V. Hong and Edna H. Hong]. Princeton, NJ: Princeton University Press.

Lewis, Pericles. 2010. *Religious Experience and the Modernist Novel.* Cambridge: Cambridge University Press.

de Lubac, Henri. "Typologie et Allégorie." *Recherches de Sciences Religieuses* 34 (1947): 150-22.

de Lubac, Henri. 1998-2009. *Medieval Exegesis: the Four Senses of Scripture* [3 vols.]. Eerdmans: Grand Rapids, MI.

Lukács, Georg. "In Search of Bourgeois Man". In *Georg Lukács, Essays on Thomas Mann*, 13-46. (London: Merlin Press, 1964).

Lukács, Georg. "The Tragedy of Modern Art". In *Georg Lukács, Essays on Thomas Mann*, 47-97. (London: Merlin Press, 1964).

Mann, Thomas. 1947. *Essays of Three Decades*. New York: Alfred A. Knopf.

Mann, Thomas. 1996. *Essays*. Vol. 5, *Deutschland und die Deutschen 1938–1945*. Frankfurt am Main: Fischer Taschenbuch Verlag.

Mann, Thomas. 2008. *Thomas Mann's Addresses Delivered at the Library of Congress, 1942–1949*. Rockville, MD: Wildside Press.

Mann, Thomas. 1999. *The Magic Mountain*. London: Vintage Classics.

Mann, Thomas. 2005. *Joseph and His Brothers* [tr. John E. Woods]. Everyman's Library. New York: A.A. Knopf.

McDonald, William. 1999. *Thomas Mann's Joseph and His Brothers: Writing, Performance and the Politics of Loyalty*. Rochester, New York: Camden House.

Metz, Johann Baptist. 2013 [1972]. *Faith In History and Society: Toward a Practical Fundamental Theology* [new edition]. New York: Crossroad.

Nietzsche, Friedrich. 1968, *The Will to Power*. New York: Vintage Books.

Prater, Donald. 1995. *Thomas Mann: a Life*. Oxford: Oxford University Press.

Prickett, Stephen. "Biblical and Literary Criticism: a History of Interaction." In *The Bible and Literature: a Reader*, edited by David Jasper and Stephen Prickett., 12-43 (Oxford: Blackwell, 1999).

Rilke, Rainer Maria. 1987. *The Selected Poetry of Rainer Maria Rilke*; edited and translated by Stephen Mitchell. London: Picador.

Rose, Gillian. 1992. *The Broken Middle: Out of Our Ancient Society*. Oxford: Blackwell.

Scaff, Susan von Rohr. "The Religious Base of Thomas Mann's Word View: Mythic Theology and the Problem of the Demonic." *Christianity and Literature*, 43.1 (Autumn 1993): 75-94.

Scaff, Susan von Rohr. 1998. *History, Myth, and Music: Thomas Mann's Timely Fiction*. Columbia, S.C.: Camden House.

Tonning, Erik. 2014. *Modernism and Christianity*. New York: Palgrave Macmillan.

Webb, Eugene. "Review of *History, Myth, and Music: Thomas Mann's Timely Fiction*. By Susan von Rohr Scaff." Accessed June 25 2020. http://faculty.washington.edu/ewebb/R570/Mannrev.html

SPIRITUALITY AND HISTORICAL TRANSCENDENCE IN MANUEL BENÍTEZ CARRASCO'S *CASTILLO DE DIOS*

EMILIO JOSÉ ÁLVAREZ CASTAÑO

Introduction

This chapter is devoted to the play *Castillo de Dios* (1945) by Manuel Benítez Carrasco. Since it is an *auto sacramental* written in the first half of the 20th century in Spain, my analysis of the work will develop personal, literary and historical points. First, there is a brief introduction to the life and work of the author, useful data to be considered later. Second, the reader will be introduced to the revival of the *autos sacramentales* in Spain. Third, there will be critical comments on *Castillo de Dios*, which will analyse the play following the order in which the scenes and Acts are presented. Fourth, a final section will pay attention to the historical context as an important aspect of the development of *autos sacramentales*.

The Life and Work of Manuel Benítez Carrasco: A Brief Outline

Manuel Benítez Carrasco (1922-1999) was a Spanish poet and rhapsodist. He was raised in Granada, within a very religious family and was born in a rectory, where his parents lived and his uncle sheltered them there. Benítez Carrasco started his studies in a seminary owned by the Society of Jesus, but he gave up in 1940. At that moment he started to publish his first poems and he also wrote two plays and a novel. While doing military service he won several literary prizes thanks to his poems, one of them entitled "Salmo del agua preciosa", in honour of Saint John of the Cross. In 1947, he went to Madrid, where he worked as a rhapsodist and a year later he published *La muerte pequeña*, his first collection of poems. In 1953 he did a tour across different countries in Latin America. After this, he published the two parts of his work *El oro y el barro*, containing religious poems in the first part and poems of varied topics in the second. From 1955, he lived in Latin America, where he gave more than one thousand readings of his poems throughout that continent. From 1980 he started to spend more time in Granada, his hometown. In later years, he received many homages and awards appreciating his literary career as a poet and rhapsodist.[1]

Castillo de Dios was written when the author was still young and although it is not the most important literary genre for Manuel Benítez Carrasco, it is not an uninteresting work, considering the type of play which it is, an *auto sacramental* and the historical moment in which it was written. Sáinz de Robles said about Benítez Carrasco´s poetical work: "es, a nuestro gusto, uno de los poetas españoles contemporáneos más interesantes. Dentro de la lírica del neopopulismo, posee una voz propia, humildad cálida, colorido espléndido de gamas y matices" (1967, 2607) (he is, in our view, one of the most interesting contemporary Spanish poets. Within the lyrical poetry of neopopulism, he has a voice of his own, warm modesty, splendid colour of ranges and hints). One of the goals of this chapter is to evaluate to what extent *Castillo de Dios* is a semi-autobiographical creation by the author. Before commenting on the play, a section dealing with *autos sacramentales* in Spain's historical and literary contexts will follow in order to reach a better understanding of the work.

The *Auto Sacramental* in 20th Century Spanish Drama

In the first half of the 20th Century there was a revival of the *autos sacramentales* in Spanish drama. In 1926, Azorín published the article "Dos autos sacramentales" where he points to what was happening at that moment in Spanish drama:

> Asistimos al presente en Europa a un renacimiento de la fórmula calderoniana. Renace el teatro de ideas, de modalidades intelectivas, no de tesis sociales o políticas. Son cosas distintas. El teatro o es pasión o es idea, en el moderno renacimiento, a la pasión ha sucedido la idea abstracta, racional. Los autos calderonianos son el dechado del más abstracto e intelectual teatro. Luis Pirandello no hace nada más intelectual y abstracto. [...] Por ahí va toda la literatura dramática novísima (1926, 3-4). (Now we are witnessing a rebirth of the Calderonian formula in Europe. The theatre of ideas, of intellectual modalities, is reborn; not that of social or political thesis. They are two

---

[1] For more information about Manuel Benítez Carrasco´s life and work: Rafael Delgado Calvo, *Manuel Benítez Carrasco. Un destino en la poesía* (Granada: Ayuntamiento de Granada, 2007).

different things. Theatre is either passion or idea, in the modern renaissance, passion has been succeeded by the abstract rational idea. Calderonian autos are the paragon of the most abstract and intellectual theatre. Luigi Pirandello does nothing more intellectual and abstract. [...] The new dramatic literature follows that way).

Calderón de la Barca (1600-1681), a well-considered author, was highly influential on this genre and is regarded as the best example of this new type of drama where the focus is on ideas/philosophical abstraction and symbolism and the connections between these two elements.

After the prohibition of *autos sacramentales* in Spain in the 18th century due to their seeming irrelevance in the cultural context of Neoclassical rationalism, *El gran teatro del mundo* (1655) by Calderón de la Barca was performed again in Granada in 1927 (González 2009, 318), and in Madrid in 1930 (Rodrigo 1974, 165-166). Federico García Lorca also showed an interest in this type of play and *La vida es sueño* (1635) was performed in 1932, during the tour of the "La Barraca" theatre company (Sáenz 1998, 65-80).

Therefore, the *auto sacramental* has an important place in 20th century Spanish drama and in the work of some 20th Century Spanish dramatists there are clear signs of its influence. Sometimes there are references, sometimes allegorical meanings are prevalent and at other times, the original sense of *autos sacramentales,* particularly its form and background is followed, due to opportunism or conviction (Paco 2000, 112). Examples of each one of these three groups will now be provided.

It is fitting to consider those plays in which it is possible to find allusions to the *autos sacramentales*. Although the work has no relation with the *autos sacramentales, Un sueño de la razón* (1929) by Cipriano Rivas Cherif contains references to Calderón de la Barca in Acts II and III. Something similar happens to *Ni más ni menos* by Ignacio Sánchez Mejías, since Act III takes place on Resurrection Day. The second scene of *Amor de dos vidas* (1932) by Manuel Altolaguirre may also be considered to be like a draft of an *auto sacramental*.

The second group gathers together those plays which reflect the allegorical dimension of the *autos sacramentales,* but the intention is not always religious. *Teatro de almas* (1917) y *El primitivo auto sentimental* (1918) are two plays written by Federico García Lorca when he was a young author in which he is closer to the avant-garde than to classical drama. The same idea of renovation is present in *Judit* (1925) by Azorín, where the biblical character is placed in a modern context of miners and their working conditions. *El otro* (1926) by Unamuno is a symbolic work dealing with *doppelgängers* and the story of Cain and Abel. *Angelita* (1930) by Azorín is subtitled "auto sacramental" because it deals with the philosophical issue of the elimination of time. *El hombre deshabitado* (1931) by Rafael Alberti can be seen as an *auto sacramental,* but is far from its traditional sense in both form and content. *El director* (1936) by Pedro Salinas deals with the challenge of how human beings can reach happiness by themselves. For its part, *Pedro López García* (1936) by Max Aub contains a political message. The seven deadly sins are present in *El caballo griego* by Manuel Altolaguirre. And, finally, *El viaje del joven Tobías* (1938) by Gonzalo Torrente Ballester is a rewriting of this biblical character.

Lastly, it is possible to distinguish those plays which are closer to the original and traditional concept of *auto sacramental.* For example, *Corpus Christi. Poema sinfónico* (1925) by Gabriel Miró is connected to the traditional eucharistic plays. *Quién te ha visto y quién te ve y sombra de lo que eras* (1933), written by Miguel Hernández, is an *auto sacramental* following the pattern of Calderón de la Barca and the religious influence that the author had on the dramatist's youth. *El casamiento engañoso* (1939) by Gonzalo Torrente Ballester takes the same pattern to reflect on the relationships between humankind and technology. In *Farsa docente* (1942) by Azorín, the allocating of different roles when the characters start a new life on earth again reminds us of Calderón de la Barca´s *El gran teatro del mundo.*

All these are examples taken from plays in the first half of 20th century Spanish dramatic writings. As for the second half, it is possible to find works which, following the three points already mentioned, are also influenced by different avant-garde movements or by the political and social situation of the country. However, *Castillo de Dios* (1945) by Manuel Benítez Carrasco is a play written in the middle of the century and, within the classification already mentioned, belongs to the third group, one which follows the Christian Catholic tradition clearly.

Castillo de Dios: A Commentary

The influence of Calderón de la Barca is clearly present in *Castillo de Dios* (1945) by Manuel Benítez Carrasco. Both authors were educated with the Jesuits and, in this play, Benítez Carrasco follows the idea of "teach and delight". It is present in the definition of auto sacramental given by Calderón de la Barca:

Sermones
Puestos en verso, en idea
Representable, cuestiones
De la Santa Teología,
Que no alcanzan mis razones
A explicar ni comprender,
Y el regocijo dispone
En aplauso deste día (1984, 145).
(Sermons
Written in verse, in idea
Representable, issues
Of Holy Theology,
That my reasons are not enough
To explain or understand,
And the joy arranges
In applause of this day).

These lines belong to the prologue of *La segunda esposa* and are relevant to Benítez Carrasco, whose religious ideas emanated from Catholic theology.

The play *Castillo de Dios* by Manuel Benítez Carrasco is an original example of *auto sacramental*. As a matter of fact, the word appears in the subtitle – auto sacramental en verso (*auto sacramental* in verse). The originality of the play consists in three points. First, because the author was a poet, the play is written in verse, something which contemporary authors did not attempt. The most common stanzas used by the author are a combination of romance, *décima* (ten-line stanza), *quintilla* (five-line stanza) and quatrain. Quatrain and romance are the most usual and following again the example of Calderón de la Barca, are used in a flexible way. Second, unlike Calderón de la Barca´s *autos sacramentales* which only have one Act, *Castillo de Dios* has two scenes and three Acts. This is so because the scope of the plot is wider, something which is connected to my last point. The narrative shows different passages from the Old and New Testament remembering Salvation History: the Creation of the Universe, the Creation of Humanity, Temptation & Fall, the Exile, Jesus Christ, the Eucharist and the Last Judgment. In my commentary on *Castillo de Dios* which follows, I will show how the author introduces original reflections and elements in the development of the storyline. The analysis will follow the order of the five parts of the play.

Calderón de la Barca wrote two plays – *La vida es sueño* – a drama and an *auto sacramental*. There are allusions to both of them at the beginning of *Castillo de Dios*. The first part of this play by Benítez Carrasco is a scene entitled "En el jardín del Castillo" ("In the Castle´s Garden") where the first character on stage is Luzbel (Lucifer) who is alone, sad and exiled. In the drama by Calderón de la Barca, Segismundo says:

> Yo sueño que estoy aquí
> Destas prisiones cargado
> Y soñé que en otro estado
> Más lisonjero me vi.
> ¿Qué es la vida? Un frenesí (1961, 65).
> (I dream that I am in here
> with these chains and prisons burdened
> yet I dreamt that I in other,
> more fulsome state saw myself.
> What is life? A Frenzy).

These are famous lines in Spanish literature which can come to the reader's mind when Luzbel says in the opening of the play by Benítez Carrasco:

> Es esta cárcel oscura
> Donde sepultado fui,
> Todo es ira y frenesí
> Y rabia y fuego y locura.
> Y en mi eterna desventura,
> No sé qué pena es mayor:
> Si este fuego, este rigor,
> Esta llama, este gemido,
> O el recordar que yo he sido
> Príncipe de mi esplendor (Benítez 2001, 31).
> (Dark is this prison,
> Where I was buried,
> All is anger and frenzy
> And rage and fire and madness.
> And in my eternal misadventure,
> I don't know what pain is greater:
> If this fire, this rigour,
> This flame, this moan,
> Or to remember that I have been
> Prince of my brightness).

But Luzbel's complaints do not stop here. In the same speech, he will remember:

> Yo, el ángel que se adornaba
> Con nieve, gasas y plumas,
> De cuyas bellezas sumas
> Dios, con ser Dios, se admiraba.
> Yo, el que respeto causaba

A la corte del Creador,
Pues dudaban de los dos,
Al vernos tan igualados
Si era Dios el adorado
O el que adoraba era Dios (2001, 32).
(I, the angel who adorned himself
With snow, gauze, and feathers,
Of whose high beauties
God, being God, was admired.
I, the one who caused respect
To the court of the Creator,
As they doubted,
Seeing us so evenly matched
If it was God who was worshipped
Or the one who worshipped was God).

Luzbel´s fall occurs because pride (Soberbia) has resulted in him attempting to be on a par with God. Here, Benítez Carrasco follows the biblical story of the fallen angel and the author considers the basis of Luzbel´s sin, an idea also present in 1 Tim 3:6. In a symbolic way, Benítez Carrasco presents Soberbia dressed in peacock´s feathers (Chevalier and Gheerbrant 2007, 807), a visible contrast with the feathers of an angel.

As for the *auto sacramental La vida es sueño*, the spheres contain the characters which represent the four elements of matter which have clearly been influenced Benítez Carrasco´s scenography. A sphere is evident at the start of *Castillo de Dios*. Arquitecto (Architect) wants to show his glory by creating a fortress, with the help of Poder (Power), Ciencia (Science) y Hermosura (Beauty), an episode witnessed in *La vida es sueño*. In this *auto sacramental*, the character of Poder (Power) will tell Man: "Hombre que hice a imagen mía, / yo te saqué de la tierra; / en real alcázar te puse" (Calderón 1972, 194). (Man I made in my image, / I took you out of the ground; / in real fortress I put you). This fortress is the reason for the title of the play by Benítez Carrasco, something which the character of the Arquitecto expresses in the following way:

Quisiera hacer un alcázar,
En el que el Poder, la Ciencia
Y mi Hermosura infinitos
Compitan, poniendo a prueba
En virtud, milagro y gala,
Tú, de tus galas la fuerza,
Tú, la fuerza de tu brazo,
Tú, la de tu inteligencia (2001, 37).

(I would like to build a fortress,
In which Power, Science
And my Beauty infinite
Compete, testing
In virtue, miracle and elegance,
You, the strength of your elegance,
You, the strength of your arm,
You, your intelligence).

This fortress or castle will be the future dwelling of Man but, before this, Luzbel feels humiliated, so he calls his own company: Furor (Fury), Venganza (Revenge), Ira (Anger) and Fuego (Fire). A new battle is getting ready and the fortress becomes the place used to face the enemies. In this context, it is worth mentioning that Fire is also present when the four elements are called to create the world, something which can be seen in different *autos sacramentales* by Calderón de la Barca, like *La vida es sueño* or *El divino cazador*. In the case of *Castillo de Dios*, the double biblical sense of fire is used as one of the most precious discoveries, but also one of the most dangerous elements of matter - it is life *and* death, catharsis *and* punishment (Gerard 1995, 1181).

At this point, Poder, Ciencia and Hermosura control the four elements of matter to create the world, a situation which finds its counterpart again in *La vida es sueño*. In this *auto sacramental*, Poder, Sabiduría (Wisdom) and Amor (Love) will take on the same function and the elements make this comment:

AGUA: ...De suerte,
Que un mismo poder...
AIRE: que un mismo
saber...
TIERRA: ...que un mismo querer...
FUEGO: en tres personas distinto...
AGUA: y en sola una voluntad... (1972, 128).
(WATER: ...so that,
One power,
AIR: one knowledge...
EARTH: ...one love...
FIRE: in three different people...
WATER: and in one will...)

The elements proclaim the theological doctrine of the Trinity and Poder, Sabiduría and Amor are representations of it. In Benitez Carrasco´s play the elements are Poder, Ciencia and Hermosura. In both works, the conversations among the elements, either when they are arguing or in harmony, imitate the patterns of traditional lyric poetry: short poems with refrains and repetitions, like *cantigas de amigo* or carols (Beltrán 2002, 47 and 56).

The title of the second scene is "Creación del hombre" ("Creation of Man"). When Luzbel learns that the Arquitecto will go further in his purpose with the creation of Man, Luzbel asks his minions to react in some way. Soberbia tells him:

> Porque soy como serpiente
> Que entre la zarza y la espina,
> Espera astuta y ladina
> El momento y la ocasión
> De hincar mejor mi aguijón
> En su sandalia divina (2001, 62).
> (Because I'm like a snake
> That by the bramble and the thorn,
> Cunning and wily wait
> The moment and the occasion
> To better sink my sting
> In his divine sandal).

The reference to the snake points to the *Genesis* narrative, but it is also a piece of advice about the behaviour Luzbel has to follow if he wants revenge.

When Arquitecto has created Man and has given him the power over the world, he warns him about the "fragilidades del barro" (63) (mud fragilities). This reminder about being humble is connected to the original aim of *autos sacramentales* since these plays include such moral teaching (Alonso 2005, 22). At this moment, Luzbel feels his humiliation is even greater. But it is not his only feeling. Since he was near God and he is now a fallen angel and Man has been created from dust and his destiny is to reach heaven (Benítez, 2001, 64), they have followed opposite ways. So, in a new personal contribution of the author, Luzbel also feels envy and that is why he asks his company's help to insert chaos in the fortress.

One section of the play is the first Act is called "Del Castillo a la Dama" ("From the Castle to the Lady"). It is the moment when Temptation is prepared. Soberbia gives advice to Luzbel and he flatters Man, because it is the best way of convincing him of being better than he is. But Luzbel cannot wait for his revenge and wants to act quickly, so Soberbia asks him to be patient. This situation is repeated when Luzbel learns that Eve has been created. Soberbia asks Luzbel to be calm again and convinces him that it is better to flatter Eve and in this way, Man will also fall. The personal contribution of the author here is that Luzbel and his followers dress up as troubadours to begin their plan of flattering human beings.

The second Act is entitled "Ronda de trovadores y Castillo en ruinas" ("Group of troubadours and Castle in ruins") and corresponds to the moments of the Temptation, Fall and Exile. In the previous Act, Eve had been identified with the name of Curiosidad (Curiosity) and this is the name that she will keep here. Luzbel flatters Curiosidad who, in spite of being advised by Conciencia (Consciousness), is deceived with promises and songs. Since she is curious and moreover, has been convinced of being more than God, she eats the apple, which is offered by Soberbia. It is remarkable that although it took some time, Luzbel finally got his goal; what is also witnessed is the promptness with which Curiosidad convinces Man to eat the forbidden fruit. The Architect discovers what has happened and Man and Eve (thus called) learn of their destiny. The seven deadly sins take them to the castle, now without light and Luzbel laughs because he imagines that he has won.

Obviously, the ending cannot be so. There is a final act called "Reconquista del Castillo" ("Reconquest of the Castle"). In spite of Man being in a dungeon within the castle, he feels that he will be freed. It is as if there was a special connection between the Arquitecto and him. After the speech by the Annunciation Angel, Man feels braver and talks about the arrival of the Conquistador (Conqueror). Luzbel´s minions are confused because they did not know that the Conquistador would arrive in a humble way. Order is restored and the play ends with images of Jesus Christ, the Eucharist and the Last Judgment. For this reason, the Conquistador tells Man at the end of the play:

> Tú eres Castillo de Dios;
> Y porque eterno lo seas,
> En este pan hallarás
> Tu cimiento y tu cimera;
> Para el camino, alimento,
> Para la cruz, fortaleza,
> Como estímulo, el amor,
> Y por premio, Vida Eterna (2001, 153).
> (You are Castle of God;
> And for you to be eternal,
> You will find in this bread
> Your foundation and your crest;
> Food for the journey,

Fortitude for the cross,
Love as encouragement,
And for prize, Eternal Life.)

It is noteworthy that the *autos sacramentales* have a historical link to the Feast of *Corpus Christi* (Varey 1993, 357). In this way, the whole Salvation History is presented and recalled.

The Historical Context

Castillo de Dios is not the first play by Benítez Carrasco. In 1943 he wrote two other plays. *Luz de amanecer* was awarded the Teatro de Escuadra prize, a work in which there are six symbolic and real characters: Spain, the People, the Communism, a Falangist, a Soldier and a Poet. The plot is set in post-war Spain and ends with a praise to Spanish people because, thanks to their service and sacrifice, a new day´s light is coming to the country. The play is subtitled like a patriotic *auto,* so it can be argued that Benítez Carrasco was already testing some of the forms and concepts of the *autos sacramentales*. The second one was *Retablo de Colón,* where the author presented the figure of Christopher Columbus and the historical fact of the Discovery of America to a schoolchildren audience. Basically, the idea is to present and highlight one of the most important historical deeds in Spanish history. In this way, the patriotic sense is easily perceived again.

As for *Castillo de Dios*, in addition to Benítez Carrasco´s religious beliefs, the work was written only six years after the end of the Spanish Civil War, the same year in which World War II ended. In Spain, Francisco Franco was ruling the country. Much drama in the first years of Francoism was concerned about the formation of a new national Spanish identity through national exaltation (Fernández 2000, 30) and the *auto sacramental* was the ideal vehicle for that. In 1938 one of the *autos sacramentales* was chosen to be performed and was entitled *El hospital de los locos* by José de Valdivieso (1565-1638) directed by Luis Escobar. At that moment, the meaning of the battle between good and evil was extended to the political situation of the country. The performance of the play also included the participation of priests (Kasten 2011, 260-261), an example of how National Catholicism was starting to be seen. Moreover, a number of these performances of *autos sacramentales* which took place in the country attempted to warn people about their mortal condition and divine dependence. This situation fortified the revival of the *autos sacramentales* although, as it has been already stated, not all of them had the same goal because the *auto sacramental* also had links to the avant-garde, due to its use of allegory and abstract concepts.

However, the case of *Castillo de Dios* needs a clarification. In spite of *Luz de amanecer* y *Retablo de Colón*, a reading of *Castillo de Dios* shows that the goal of the play is eminently religious. However, this patriotism and religiousness certainly do not imply the support of Benítez Carrasco for Franco and National Catholicism.

Conclusion

Manuel Benítez Carrasco was an interesting 20th century Spanish poet. But he also wrote three plays and although his reputation as a playwright is less known, it is important to highlight this fact. As a poet, his plays are written in verse and can be better appreciated by understanding the personal and historical context in which they were created. Benítez Carrasco was born within a Catholic family, something which influenced deeply his later life and personality. When he decided to become an author, spiritual and religious dimensions were always present in his literary production. *Luz de amanecer* and *Retablo de Colón*, his first two plays, were written during the first years of Francoism and in both the influence of patriotic ideas can be witnessed, without showing any political support for the new Spanish government.

Thus, *Castillo de Dios* can be set in the development of the *autos sacramentales* during the first half of the 20th century in Spain. Although it is a type of play which is connected to the avant-garde due to its philosophical abstractions, it was also used with different aims during those years. However, *Castillo de Dios* is a peculiar case of *auto sacramental* since it is written in verse and has more than one scene or Act covering aspects of Salvation History. It therefore keeps to the original religious intention of *autos sacramentales* since the Middle Ages.

When Benítez Carrasco started his studies with the Jesuits, he had to go to the city of Loulé in Portugal, because the Jesuits were in the exile during the Spanish Second Republic since the Spanish Constitution of 1931 prohibited schools which belonged to religious orders. After this, he experienced the Spanish Civil War and its consequences. The lack of propaganda and any political message in *Castillo de Dios* involves a reading of the text which attends primarily to its religious and spiritual significance. In this sense, the play can be read as a reminder of humankind's limitations when the desires of power become present.

Bibliography

Alonso Rey, María Dolores. 2005. "Sincretismo y simbolismo en los autos sacramentales de Calderón: traje y atributos emblemáticos". *Estudios Humanísticos. Filología.* No. 27. 9-24.

Azorín. 1926. "Dos autos sacramentales". *Abc*, March 15th, 1926. 3-4.

Beltrán, Vicente. "Las formas con estribillo en la lírica oral del Medioevo". *Anuario Musical.* No. 57. 39-57.

Benítez Carrasco, Manuel. 2001. *Castillo de Dios.* In *Obra poética, vol. IV*, 29-153. Córdoba: Cajasur.

Calderón de la Barca, Pedro. 1984. *Una fiesta sacramental barroca. Loa para el auto entremés de los instrumentos. Auto sacramental "La segunda esposa" y "Triunfar muriendo". Mojiganga de "Las visiones de la muerte"*. Ed. José María Díez Borque. Barcelona: Taurus.

—. 1972. *La vida es sueño.* In *Autos Sacramentales.* Ed. Ángel Valbuena Prat. Madrid: Espasa Calpe.

—. 1961. *La vida es sueño.* Ed. Albert E. Sloman. Manchester: Manchester U.P.

Chevalier, Jean and Gheerbrant, Alain. 2007. *Diccionario de símbolos.* Trans, Manuel Silva and Arturo Rodríguez. Barcelona: Herder.

Delgado Calvo, Rafael. 2007. *Manuel Benítez Carrasco. Un destino en la poesía.* Granada: Ayuntamiento de Granada.

Fernández Torres, Alberto. 2000. "La piedra que cae en el agua: Breves reflexiones sobre la evolución del 'sistema teatral' español (1940-85)". *ADE Teatro: Revista de la Asociación de Directores de Escena de España.* No. 82. 28-39.

Gerard, André-Marie. 1995. *Dictionnaire de la Bible.* Madrid: Anaya & Mario Muchnik.

González Ramírez. David. 2009. "La escenificación de *El gran teatro del mundo* (Granada, 1927). Consideraciones sobre la 'vuelta a Calderón'". *Boletín Millares Caro.* No. 28. 305-324.

Kasten, Carey. 2011. "Tradición propagandística: el auto sacramental franquista". In *El Siglo de Oro en la España contemporánea*, edited by Hanno Ehrlicher and Stefan Schreckenberg, 255-272. Madrid: Iberoamericana.

Paco, Mariano de. 2000. "Ángel Valbuena y el auto sacramental en el teatro español del siglo XX". *Monteagudo.* No. 5. 97-112.

Rodrigo, Antonina. 1974. *Margarita Xirgú y su teatro.* Barcelona: Planeta.

Sáenz de la Calzada, Luis. 1998. *La Barraca. Teatro Universitario.* Madrid: Residencia de Estudiantes.

Sáinz de Robles, Federico Carlos. 1967. *Historia y antología de la poesía española (en lengua castellana)*. Madrid: Aguilar.

Varey, John. 1993. "Los autos sacramentales como celebración regia y popular". *Revista Canadiense de Estudios Hispánicos*. No. 17.2. 357-371.

FLANNERY O'CONNOR AS BAROQUE ARTIST: THEOLOGICAL AND LITERARY STRATEGIES

MARK BOSCO

Flannery O'Connor often described herself to friends and colleagues as a "thirteenth-century lady." Brad Gooch, in his biography of the writer, offers many instances of this in O'Connor's own correspondence, but the most striking is a second- hand reference in a letter written by the musicologist Edward Maisel to Yadoo director Mrs. Ames, encouraging her to invite O'Connor back for the winter term at the artists' retreat: "I have been on several evening walks with her, and find her immensely serious, with a sharp sense of humor; a very devout Catholic (thirteenth century, she describes herself)" [156].

Given her singularly Catholic literary vision, O'Connor's brand of religious orthodoxy is often discussed in light of the medieval philosopher-theologian Thomas Aquinas or by twentieth century interpreters of Aquinas, such as Jacques Maritain and Etienne Gilson. She took great pleasure in telling Robie Macauley in a 1955 letter that readers of *Wise Blood* think her a "hillbilly nihilist," when in fact the term "hillbilly Thomist" would be more accurate.[1] O'Connor, moreover, admits to Betty Hester that she "cut [her] aesthetic teeth" on Maritain's *Art and Scholasticism* and suggests that Hester read Gilson's *Art and Reality*.[2] Both of these seminal works of neo-scholasticism appropriate the Angelic Doctor's understanding of the nature and function of artistic creation. O'Connor imbibed the mysticism and synthesis of this medieval Catholicism, a philosophical and theological approach that saw reason and faith not as adversaries but as collaborators in the production of knowledge and the arts.

Yet as critic John Desmond suggests, O'Connor's identification as a hillbilly Thomist masks a more complex intellectual and artistic engagement with

---

[1] Flannery O'Connor, *The Habit of Being: Letters of Flannery O'Connor*. ed. Sally Fitzgerald (New York: Farrar, Straus & Giroux, 1979) 81.
[2] *Ibid.*, 216, 279.

modern and progressive writers of the 20th century, Catholic, Protestant, and Jewish.[3] She read Newman, von Hügel, and Maritain, but also Freud, Jung, and Buber. She recommended to Hester her own regimen of reading, including the crisis theologians of the Protestant tradition:

> They are the greatest of the Protestant theologians writing today and it is to our misfortune that they are much more alert and creative than their Catholic counterparts. We have very few thinkers to equal Barth and Tillich, perhaps none. This is not an age of great Catholic theology. We are living on our capital and it is past time for a new synthesis. What St. Thomas did for the new learning of the 13th century we are in bad need of someone to do for the 20[th][4]

Ted Spivey's claim about O'Connor is arguably the most accurate: "What is deepest in her writing is a tension that exists between her medieval self and her modernist self" (10). Though not a theologian, O'Connor sought in her art to embody the crisis of meaning in the 20th century, while simultaneously confronting, and perhaps embracing, the contours of a medieval Catholic vision of life. The dramatic settings of her short stories are riveting precisely because they extend outward and upward toward transcendent mystery. Her success in capturing this mystery depended on her ability to shock readers into acknowledging that the human and the divine literally, and sometimes violently, collide.

The pressure between O'Connor's synthesis of a medieval Catholic vision and her intellectual awareness of modernist thinkers made her art "counter, original, spare, strange," to borrow a phrase from Hopkins' poem "Pied Beauty." There is indeed something "counter" about O'Connor's art, akin to the Catholic Baroque aesthetics of the seventeenth century *Counter* Reformation. As an artistic and a religious response to a

culture reeling from the effects of the Protestant Reformation, the Catholic Baroque offered a theological vision that was as accessible as it was excessive in its sensory overload. Artists such as Caravaggio, Bernini, and Rubens communicated religious insight in strange, expressive ways, rendered in theatrical or revelatory moments in painting and sculpture. These artists looked back toward a medieval synthesis that fostered positive doctrines of Catholic faith and culture and yet offered this in innovative

---

[3] John F. Desmond, "By Force of Will: Flannery O'Connor, the Broken Synthesis, and the Problem with Rayber." *Flannery O'Connor Review* 6 (2008): 135-146. 138.
[4] O'Connor, *The Habit of Being*, 305-6.

ways that responded to the spiritual-cultural exigencies of a Catholic society living in the wake of a hegemonic Western Christendom.

An apt comparison can be drawn, for example, between Michelangelo Merisi da Caravaggio (1571-1610), an exemplar of a religious revival in painting during the early decades of the Church's Counter Reformation, and Flannery O'Connor, an exemplar of a Catholic literary revival during the Church's confrontation with modernity in the twentieth century. Both artists labored in cultural moments at odds with competing discourses on the validity and expression of religious faith. Caravaggio's works reacted against the Protestant reformation's distrust of art and, at the same time, resisted any easy congress with the more propagandistic desires of his Catholic patrons. O'Connor's texts reacted not against a Protestant dispensation but against an 'enlightened,' secularist distrust of faith by intellectuals on the one hand, and the pietistic aesthetics of a triumphant American culture on the other. Their artistic strategies challenged any religiosity that sought merely comfort and consolation from religious practice. In their use of the grotesque and their often violent epiphanies, Caravaggio and O'Connor, though centuries apart, nonetheless offer us a larger frame of artistic reference to excavate the contours of a Catholic Baroque aesthetic.

The Catholic Baroque

The word "baroque," from the Portuguese word *barroco* (an imperfect pearl) came to be applied to an artistic and architectural style of the 17th century that emphasized dramatic, often strained effects typified by bold, complex forms and elaborate ornamentation. The Oxford English Dictionary cites the adjectival form, "irregularly shaped, whimsical, grotesque, odd." Catholic Baroque was a conscious turn from the intellectual qualities of the previous generation of Mannerist style painters (Tintoretto, El Greco) to a visceral appeal aimed at the senses. With the emergence of new religious orders there rose an evangelical call to capture in art an experience of faith. Though historically the Baroque became an international fashion divested of religious content and purpose, the Catholic, often termed Italian, Baroque combined a virtuosic naturalism with kinetic emotionalism that was used in Churches as both a response to the Protestant Reformation and a pedagogical tool of faith formation.

The early Baroque was as much a political strategy of the Counter Reformation Church as it was an artistic one. The prelates and theological advisors at the Council of Trent (1545-1563) understood that art did not exist in some pure form, that it too had ideological implications. If the constant theme of John Calvin was that the senses cannot be trusted to lead one to faith, then the Catholic response was to accentuate the opposite, extending deeper the sacramental ramifications of the image as a way to understand art's effects on faith. The ideological strategies of the Catholic Baroque attempted to teach, to delight, and to persuade the viewer that a religious horizon impinged upon human life. In its simplest terms, it professed aesthetically the Jesuit argument that all the senses should engage empathetically with the events of religious martyrdom and ecstasy. Évonne Levy argues in her work *Propaganda and the Jesuit Baroque* that the aim of this counter- reformation tactic was the use of art as a "directed communication" of the Church's message.[5] Levy claims that the propagandistic element of Baroque art was essentially for forming subjects to respond positively to the Church's message of salvation. Through a highly developed naturalism that engaged the viewer both physically and emotionally, the Catholic Baroque drew on the theological doctrine of *Imago Dei*—made in God's image—as the foundational insight into mimetic reform, that process of conversion to God through sharing the image of Christ as one's own. Levy notes that St. Paul's statement, that "we reflect as in a mirror the glory of the Lord, thus we are transfigured into his likeness" [2 Cor 3:17-18], envisions salvation as a matter of becoming Christ's image.[6] The reform of the soul through mimesis made dramatization extremely important, for one must constantly perform—through story, ritual, and art—the ongoing conversion of the soul. Both the realism and the theatricality of the Catholic Baroque demanded something of the subject. The aesthetic is annunciatory, inviting the viewer into a decisive moment in the life of Christ or of His saints as a shared image of one's own life with God.[7] Imagination and artistic production were critical tools in the life of faith formation.

The energy of the Counter Reformation inspired great artists of the time, many of whom were sincere, conforming Christians. The cultural historian Kenneth Clarke assessed this revival in the early modern Catholic Church:

> Guercino spent much of his mornings in prayer; Bernini frequently went on retreats and practiced the Spiritual Exercises of St. Ignatius; Rubens went to Mass every day before beginning work. This conformity was not based on fear of the Inquisition, but on the perfectly simple belief that the faith

---

[5] Evonne Levy, *Propaganda and the Jesuit Baroque*. (Berkeley: U of California Press, 2004) 115.

[6] *Ibid.,* 116.

[7] *Ibid.,* 117.

which had inspired the great saints of the preceding generation was
something by which a man should regulate his life.[8]

Though Caravaggio is not on Clarke's list of artists, his work presents a
powerful illustration of the early Catholic Baroque. Caravaggio's revolutionary
realism; his dramatically intense form of chiaroscuro; and, his idiosyncratic—
and sometimes transgressive—reworking of traditional iconic piety; all of
these suggest his medieval theological vision was very much in tension with
his modern, secular way of reflecting on the spiritual.

Theological Implications: Aesthetics of Access and Excess

Counter-Reformation theology presumes that the presence of God is quite
accessible: the experience of the holy, of mystery, is available to everyone,
even the unlearned. The Catholic Baroque advocated a populist conception
of theology, one that eschewed abstraction and theory. Faith is not an
epistemological concept but a dramatic experience that moves the human
person to respond—in joy, triumph, pity, or fear.

Caravaggio's *Madonna of the Pilgrims* [1604] is a perfect example. The
painting reveals not a distant and ethereal Madonna but what Peter Robb
calls a "sexy young housewife coming to the front door of what looked like
a very ordinary Roman home" (265). Mary is a warm, fleshy, welcoming
mother. The poverty-stricken pilgrims look as if they have just arrived,
gazing up at the child Jesus who is ready to squirm from Mary's grasp.

Heaven's doorway is accessible to all who knock, a mere step away from
the pilgrims' earthly path. Both Mary and the pilgrims have dirty feet—a
provocation, certainly, in a painting that hangs over an altar during liturgical
celebrations in a city that feared the poor's growing presence. The painting
places the poor directly before the eyes of the clerical and courtly elites. The
theologian Nathan Mitchell suggests that Caravaggio is

"rewriting an icon, bringing the human condition—unwashed—smack into
the middle of the space for celebrating liturgy" (170). What Helen Langdon
calls Caravaggio's "harsh vernacular" creates a shock of humility for the
moneyed class of Rome (5).

---

[8] Quoted in Thomas E. Woods, *How the Catholic Church Built Western Civilization*
(Washington D.C.:Regnery Publishing, 2005) 127-8.

At the same time that the Catholic Baroque is accessible, it is often excessive, as the experience of the holy becomes an overwhelming encounter of the senses. Images stun the viewer with their vibrant color and dramatic lighting, transmitting theatrical energy and movement. Disequilibrium is fostered as clichéd categories of religious signification are destabilized. Caravaggio's *Martyrdom of St. Matthew* [1599], for instance, illustrates a Mass being interrupted by a murder. At its center is Matthew, already wounded and bleeding, catching his attacker's eye an instant before his death: "In that triangle of killer and victim locked together by their hands and their gaze and in the infinitesimal pause of mutual recognition before the murder, was a powerful immobility," in which the murderer stands "seemingly drained from all his strength."[9] Likewise, Caravaggio's *Seven Works of Mercy* [1607], which hangs above a Church altar in Naples, reinterprets acts of piety in the street life of the city. Instead of showing idealized virtue, it depicts "mercy as the satisfaction of basic needs." The starving old prisoner "sucked milk from his daughter's breast, hitched up the rest of her bodice as best she could" and looked around as if to dare anyone to comment.[10] Caravaggio depicts the dark conditions under which humanity works out its salvation in turbulent Neapolitan life. All this in an altarpiece intended to frame and interpret what the faithful are participating in at the liturgical celebration.

This notion of access and excess through visual representation responded directly to the Lutheran and Calvinist reformers whose theological stress focused on the absolute

transcendence of God, the unfathomable distance between the Lord in His heaven and the human person mired in earthly sin. The iconoclasm of the Protestant reformers is well documented. Churches removed statues and paintings in the cathedrals under Protestant principalities. The aesthetics of the Catholic Baroque, on the other hand, stood in direct contrast: heaven and earth are literally falling into one another and the Roman Catholic Church—its physical and ecclesial structure—is the place, the moment, where this crash happens. The sweeping sense of verticalization in many ceilings of Baroque churches suggests human passage toward some divine realm, but there is a counter effect as well, as if the heavens are tumbling down into the world. Andrea Pozzo's ceiling in the Church of St. Ignatius in Rome [1691] illustrates this well. The massive painting portrays the

---

[9] Peter Robb, *M: The Man Who Became Caravaggio*. (New York: Henry Holt and Co., 2000) 137.

[10] *Ibid.*, 371.

worldwide mission of the Jesuit order, dramatically visualizing Luke 12:49, when Christ said, "I have come to cast fire on the earth, would that it were already kindled!" The diffusion of the name of Jesus through Jesuit intermediaries to the four known continents connotes that the Church represents a portal that brings heaven and earth together, peopled with angelic figures grasping clouds, lest they plummet to the ground. This tumbling effect is evident in Caravaggio's *Martyrdom of Matthew* and his *Seven Works of Mercy* as well. In these paintings, heavenly figures are precariously balanced, reflecting not only the proximity of the divine, but the probability that the divine will collapse upon—and perhaps injure—those in the world below! The gap between the human and the hallowed, the natural and the supernatural, the secular and the religious, is momentarily glimpsed as fluid and indeterminate in these artistic manifestations.

Interpreting Catholic Baroque 1600

Caravaggio's preeminent biographers—Peter Robb and Helen Langdon—argue that the painter, however reckless his life, was thoroughly conversant with current artistic practice and theory. Working in Rome before his sudden departure in 1606, for having killed a man in a brawl, he spent his early years assimilating the aesthetics of religious art but never gave way to the easy triumphalism that marked the efforts of later artists patronized by the institutional Church. Though critics are quick to argue that Caravaggio's personal religious experience is unimportant to his work or at odds with any orthodox religious faith, such criticism falters when one views his compositions.

That he does not fit into the easy categories of religious piety of the age does not deny the significance of his Catholic vision and its influence on his creativity. What can be said with certainty is that he uses his genius to awaken the imagination to an entirely new way of comprehending the experience of faith in art. Such provocation is due in part to his technique. Caravaggio perfected a heightened chiaroscuro, called tenebrism, which intersperses dark, murky spaces with areas of spectacular intensity. The violent contrasts of light bring high drama to his subjects. Illumination directs the viewer's attention both to the subject and to a source outside the painting, effecting a momentary revelation on the faces or on the bodies of his subject. In this cast of luminosity, the force of the figure's psychological interaction is directed toward a momentary glimpse of the divine. Here, the divine is represented as a literal and realistic enlightenment on the human plane, revealing a highly intimate, incarnational vision of reality.

Along with chiaroscuro, Caravaggio reinterpreted the use of the grotesque in painting. The motif had been prevalent since the fourteenth century artist Hieronymus Bosch, whose eschatological themes about heaven and hell, the seven deadly sins, and the Last Judgment express a shockingly indeterminate and alien landscape. Where Bosch presents the natural order subverted to produce a surreal world of alienation and depravity, Caravaggio uses the grotesque to accentuate the outward expression of his subject's inner anxieties. His biblically inspired paintings transgress static notions of religious meaning by making the familiar seem unfamiliar in the faces and actions of his characters. Indeed, the stories of salvation are drawn from a perspective that suddenly renders them strange in either a terrifying or sometimes comic manner. This distortion demands a fresh perspective toward the work of art and its underlying and essentially theological inspiration.

The faces of Caravaggio's figures often disclose such interiority fraught with sympathy, danger, or surprise. In his *Judith Beheading Holofernes* [1598], all three faces capture different emotional responses. One senses the horror and surprise of a violent death in the face of the Assyrian warrior; in Judith's courtly countenance resides fascination, even a reflective concern for what she is doing; and in the hardened visage of Judith's maid, there is an ugly and almost greedy satisfaction with vengeance. This is seen, too, in Caravaggio's *Call of St. Matthew* [1599]: the light from outside the edge of the painting falls upon the tax collector's startled, incredulous expression as Christ's hand reaches out to claim him. In the *Martyrdom of St. Matthew*, which hangs opposite the *Call of St. Matthew* in San Luigi dei Francesi in Rome, every face, every limb on the canvas is held in a momentary shock of recognition at the immensity of Matthew's murder. In both of the St. Matthew paintings, the demanding implications of religious faith are felt and realized in the prosaic rituals of ordinary life (Matthew collecting taxes, Matthew celebrating the Mass).

Caravaggio draws upon violent or melodramatic biblical tableaus that bow to realism at the same time that they give anagogical possibilities of meaning. The magnification of light and action through these episodes becomes an epiphany of grace, often in an expression that leaves the subjects in the painting—and the viewer— unprepared for the consequences of such divine intervention. His use of chiaroscuro and the grotesque subvert the natural order, yet the effects of this disharmony paradoxically imply a transcending principle of order underneath or behind the surface events.

Caravaggio deconstructs the culturally normative paradigms in which one engages the religious imagination for the sake of a harsh *metanoia*, a recognition of religious mystery breaking forth in the Roman manners of his day. The vitality of his art lies precisely in holding together the negative aspects of this grotesque disruption and the affirmation of mystery. The viewer is caught between these extremes.

Interpreting Catholic Baroque 1950

To claim that Flannery O'Connor's methods are comparable to those of Caravaggio is to suggest that both the religious properties of counter-reformation ideology, and the techniques by which those principles were rendered, have an affinity to the cultural ideologies of literary modernism that O'Connor creatively reworked from within her pre-modern (medieval) Catholic sensibility. As Caravaggio created a fresh, accessible aesthetic that developed from new modes of artistic theory and practice, so too does O'Connor fashion an accessible mode of literary realism that reflects her modernist, formalist credentials and places them at the service of an orthodox Christian faith often at odds with a complacent and compromising American culture.

By the time *Wise Blood* was published in 1952, O'Connor was already commenting on ways to write about the movement of grace in the lives of her characters. In a letter to Winifred McCarthy, she notes, "There is a moment in every great story in which the presence of grace can be felt as it waits to be accepted or rejected, even though the reader may not recognize this moment."[11] Her most famous pronouncement on this particular kind of grace is at the center of her work:

> I have found that violence is strangely capable of returning my characters to reality and preparing them to accept their moment of grace....This idea, that reality is something to which we must be returned at considerable cost, is one which is seldom understood by the casual reader, but is one which is implicit in the Christian view of the world.[12]

O'Connor's artistic strategy is, in part, a response to her assessment of the mores of a post-World War II America that had frequently displaced religious discourse into narratives of economic progress and psychological therapies. Her critique of modern America echoes her contemporary, the

---

[11] O'Connor, *The Habit of Being*,118.
[12] *Ibid.,* 112.

Protestant theologian H. Richard Niebuhr, who claimed that American religious communities had come to understand faith as a story where "a God without wrath brings man without sin into a kingdom without judgment through the ministrations of a Christ without a cross."[13]

The incongruity between religious faith and a secularized modern world produces many of the tensions within her texts. As a Catholic and a literary modernist, O'Connor self-consciously steeped herself in the task of fashioning a religious vision of art within the confines and concerns of the formalist theory of the New Criticism in mid-century America. Her regard for the fundamentals championed by Allen Tate, Caroline Gordon, and John Crowe Ransom, resonated with her Christian impulses. She created jewels of formalist structure, modern day Christian parables situated in the manners of Southern life that generate the internal paradoxes and ironic contrasts so important to New Critical analysis. Her short stories climax with the disordered thoughts, words, and actions of her characters, upended of their significance, only to reveal to the reader, if not the character, an ordered, even hierarchical structure of religious meaning. A character's internal conflicts suggest some finalizing insight partially revealed through grotesque, and often fierce, action. Like Caravaggio's brutal canvases, which draw the viewer in and force a revaluation of the biblical stories he paints, O'Connor's parabolic storylines violently deconstruct preconceived notions of righteousness and social order, drawing her characters into the real struggles and costs that come with attempts to live a coherent and authentic life.

The logic of O'Connor's purpose is asserted in her essay, "The Fiction Writer and His Country":

> The novelist with Christian concerns will find in modern life distortions which are repugnant to him, and his problem will be to make them appear as distortions to an audience which is used to seeing them as natural; and he may be forced to take ever more violent means to get his vision across to this hostile audience. When you can assume that your audience holds the same beliefs you do, you can relax a little and use more normal ways of talking to it; when you have to assume that it does not, then you have to make your vision apparent by shock—to the hard of hearing you shout, and for the blind you draw large and startling figures.[14]

---

[13] Richard H. Niebuhr, *The Kingdom of God in America*, (Wesleyan UP, 1937), 193.
[14] O'Connor, *Mystery and Manners: Occasional Prose*, ed. Sally Fitzgerald and Robert Fitzgerald (New York: Farrar, 1969) 30.

In order to shake the reader out of such false conceptions, O'Connor affects a realistic narrative style that routinely ends in horrendous, freak fatalities or, at the very least, a character's emotional instability. These grotesque distortions shine a light, in a manner much like a painter's use of chiaroscuro, on a moment that penetrates the self-delusions of her characters. The revelatory flash of insight unexpectedly becomes the interpretive centers of her stories.

Like Caravaggio's naturalism, O'Connor's level of specificity in her narratives gives her an opportunity to manipulate her characters until their surplus of potential meanings becomes apparent. Farrell O'Gorman describes the aesthetic as an "emphasis on the concrete and a faith that the immediate world itself holds a mystery and a meaning that does not have to be imposed by the artist but is already present, if only recognized."[15] It is the function of her grotesque characters to engage the reader in this present mystery. And Paul Giles argues that the grotesque affects a gap between what is surface realism and the mystery within the complex motivations of her characters: "The traditional function of the literary grotesque is to rip things open, to render moribund systems vulnerable to the very forces they are seeking to exclude... [this is] the advent of 'mystery' alongside 'manners,' the interruption of observable social reality by the latent force of divine truth."[16] O'Connor says as much in her essay, "The Regional Writer," affirming that "What appears on the surface is only of interest to the artist insofar as it can be gone through to an experience of mystery itself" so that her art is "always pushing its own limitations outward toward the limits of mystery...until it touches that realm that is the concern of prophets and poets."[17] Mystery, she claims, must be described, realized, and felt on the literal level of natural events, if it is to have any real power.

Hence, where Caravaggio's works are accessible to the viewer immediately as a religious moment that is nonetheless destabilized in his refusal to sanitize his subjects or their situations, O'Connor's tactic is to "maneuver her characters through dark and impenetrable mazes which seemingly lead to nowhere, but which unexpectedly reveal an exit into Christianity's back

---

[15] Farrell O'Gorman, *Peculiar Crossroads: Flannery O'Connor, Walker Percy, and Catholic Vision inPostwar Southern Fiction* (Baton Rouge: Louisiana State UP, 2004) 108.
[16] Paul Giles, *American Catholic Arts and Fictions: Culture, Ideology, Aesthetics* (New York: CambridgeUP, 1992) 361.
[17] O'Connor, *Mystery and Manners,* 44-45.

yard."[18] Her stories are not built upon biblical moments but rather conform to the biblical structures of a parable. We gain easy access to her realistic settings and psychological portrayals, only to have the dramatic action magnified to the point that she achieves what she calls "the essential displacement of the reader."[19] If her art is effective, then, readers experience a transformation of consciousness in which the story—on the surface horrific and nihilistic—becomes imbued with a new perspective, a deeper possibility of meaning. Her aim is to affect this aesthetic moment, much as Caravaggio did on canvas. He deconstructs iconic forms of religious faith, only to re- inscribe them in realistic, natural expressions of human life; O'Connor conceals the orthodox notions of Catholic faith within the Protestant mores of her southern characters, only to have them tested and evaluated, accepted or rejected, in light of the grotesque ruptures within the plot. Both Caravaggio and O'Connor explore the way the shock of divine grace complements suffering humanity.

Access, Excess, and Heaven's Crash upon the Christian South

The aesthetic strategies of the Catholic Baroque—an accessible experience of God through the lens of realism, an excessively dramatic action that leads to a surplus of meaning, and the violent crash of a transcendent moment falling or opening upon characters—provide a fascinating way to understand O'Connor's context within the larger artistic responses to Catholic faith. If, as Levy suggests, the Catholic Baroque of the Counter Reformation created an emotional response to religious martyrdom and ecstasy, then one can find this quest in all of O'Connor's fiction. She uses her own "harsh vernacular" to critique contemporary Christianity's self-satisfied manners. A brief look at four of her short stories—"A Good Man Is Hard to Find," "The River," "A Temple of the Holy Ghost," and "Revelation"—reveals this Baroque strategy.

The Breaking Point of Grace: Violence in "A Good Man Is Hard to Find"

O'Connor's most famous story has a fairly simple plot line: a deceitful and scheming grandmother presides over a dysfunctional family on their way to

---

[18] Gilbert H. Muller, *Nightmares and Visions: Flannery O'Connor and the Catholic Grotesque* (Athens: Uof Georgia Press, 1972) 18.
[19] O'Connor, *Mystery and Manners*, 45.

Florida for vacation and ends up causing the death of her entire family at the hands of an escaped convict called "the Misfit." We laugh at the reactions of her son Bailey and her grandchildren—June Star and Wesley— as the grandmother complains, scolds, and wears them down in order to get her way. But when the grandmother meets the Misfit, it is, quite literally, the beginning of the end for them. Having entered the story through O'Connor's familiar humor and detail, the reader experiences a sharp reversal of role expectation. After the Grandmother witnesses each member of her family being escorted into the woods and shot by the convicts, she summons up every bit of religious virtue she possesses in order to save herself. But despite her pleas that the Misfit "turn to Jesus," we discover how narrow and naïve the Grandmother's faith actually is when confronting this diabolical criminal. Her rhetoric of Christian conversion—"turn to Jesus"—fails to understand the religious crisis that haunts the Misfit, while at the same time revealing the banal, complacent religiosity of the grandmother's own call to be a Christian.

The Misfit replies to the Grandmother that Jesus "thrown everything off balance," and that there are only two choices for us:

> If He did what He said, then it's nothing for you to do but throw away everything and follow him, and if he didn't, then it's nothing for you to do but enjoy the few minutes you got left the best way you can—by killing somebody or burning down his house or doing some other meanness to him.[20]

There is a grotesque, if genuine, logic to the Misfit's words. In discerning the brutal truth of what he says, the grandmother's own religious scaffolding falls apart: she mumbles that the Misfit might be right. And here O'Connor captures a moment of literary chiaroscuro gracing the scene: the Misfit, suddenly aware of his own moral bankruptcy, cries out, "Listen Lady…if I had of been there I would of known and I wouldn't be like I am now." The grandmother, feeling real compassion for the Misfit for the first time, murmurs "Why, you're one of my babies. You're one of my own children!" and touches him on the shoulder. The Misfit's precarious sanity is shattered by this touch and he shoots her, for as O'Connor comments on her story in a letter to Andrew Lytle, "This moment of grace excites the devil to frenzy."[21] O'Connor stretches the notion of grace to the breaking point: grace smashes into all of the familiar categories—even moral categories—

---

[20] O'Connor, "A Good Man Is Hard to Find." in *Flannery O'Connor: Collected Works*, ed. SallyFitzgerald, (New York: Library of America, 1988) 152.
[21] O'Connor,*The Habit of Being*, 373.

that the grandmother holds. In her own disequilibrium she sees what she did not see before—a person in need. She is left dead but with "her face smiling up at the cloudless sky" affecting an intimacy with the heavens above with the earth below.

The Sacrament of Baptism in "The River"

O'Connor's "The River" builds more explicitly on a portal where the natural and the divine merge, this time in the baptismal waters of a river. As Caravaggio's paintings are framed by the Churches where they hang, the liturgical discourse of baptism structures the dramatic ending of this story. O'Connor suggests that the young Harry Ashfield's drowning is a spiritual encounter of baptism, and readers are startled by any staid associations he or she might have about its significance for Christian life. Harry doesn't seem to understand the workings of grace any more than the adults in the story, but he manages to penetrate the surface of the sacramental ritual in his deadly plunge toward the "Kingdom of Christ." In terms of a Baroque aesthetic, O'Connor dramatizes a strange combination of Catholic sacramentalism with fundamentalist practice. A sacrament is a visible "sign" [*sacramentum*] that both bears within itself and simultaneously points beyond itself to an invisible "reality" [*res*] that is, in the final analysis, the Creator. It implies a vision of the world as a composite of two interpenetrating planes of reality: seen and unseen, created and uncreated, natural and supernatural. Within the story, then, the river becomes the composite site, both place and moment when these two planes of reality merge. O'Connor pushes the sacramental system to its precarious edge, for now the unseen, the uncreated, and the supernatural reality of baptism [the *res*] is not discovered in the performance of formal ritual but in Harry's tragic death.

Once again, O'Connor's humorous portrayal of dialectically opposed worlds—the urban wasteland of Harry's family life and the rural, religious home of his babysitter Mrs. Connin—draws us into the child's predicament, for Harry is a mere afterthought in his parents' lives and looks forward to an adventurous day away from them. Mrs. Connin sets him on a new course of discovery, culminating in his baptism at the river by the preacher. Early on, Harry hears mention of the itinerant preacher's name, Bevel Summers, and the boy unthinkingly takes the name as his own. The naming ritual of baptism is evoked here, and biblical name changing, often accompanied by violence (Saul becomes Paul, and is at once blinded on the road to Damascus) sets the stage for the violent ending of the story.

O'Connor's characterization develops a realistic psychology in the newly named Bevel. Though divorced from any initial spiritual experience, the boy weaves together the information that he has collected over the course of his day. He learns that Jesus Christ is a carpenter and has made him (and is not a curse word like he has heard the name used at home). This same Jesus makes pigs come out of a man. A pig has snorted in his face and chased him into Mrs. Connin's arms. He then learns that a man named Mr. Paradise with a cancerous growth on his ear resembles a pig. At the river he hears that being baptized "is not a joke," that he now counts when "he didn't even count before." Finally, when he returns to his parents and reports that he has been baptized, they mock and belittle his experience. Bevel's desire to go back to the river the next morning seems inevitable as he awakens to the apartment's stale smell of cigarettes and alcohol. He decides that this time he will go back and not "fool with preachers any more but Baptize himself and keep on going until he found the Kingdom of Christ in the river."[22] In his second attempt, Bevel sees what looks like a giant pig bounding after him. On one level, Bevel is reliving the pursuit of the shoat from the day before, but on a more significant level, O'Connor suggests that in fleeing Mr. Paradise, Bevel instinctively is fleeing the devil. And in that effort to swim away from the false Mr. Paradise, the child finds himself pulled toward the paradise he is seeking.

Heaven does not come crashing down upon Bevel; rather, he must go in search of a more promising future beneath the water's surface. A Baroque aesthetic is evident, for the encounter with the river becomes the indeterminate place where the temporal and the eternal meet. As Bevel gets pulled under the current, the reader is left with the image of Mr. Paradise touched by the mystery before him, staring "with dull eyes as far down the river line as he could see."[23] The ramifications of such a liturgical act—that in baptismal waters one dies and is reborn into the death and resurrection of Christ—is provocatively rendered. The tragedy of the boy's drowning is countered by the reader's overwhelming conviction that his naïve faith has somehow led him to God, just as surely as Mr. Paradise emerges from the river of life "empty handed."

(Trans)Figuring the Body in "A Temple of the Holy Ghost"

If the grandmother in "A Good Man Is Hard to Find" looks up above to the blue sky in her moment of death, and if young Bevel in "The River" meets his supernatural fate in the undertow of a stream, then in "A Temple of the

---

[22] O'Connor, "The River" in *Flannery O'Connor: Collected Works,* 170.
[23] *Ibid.*, 171.

Holy Ghost" O'Connor anchors the human-divine encounter in bodies: sexual bodies, martyred bodies, sacramental bodies. O'Connor builds all the disparate threads of the story to a moment of revelation in which the Body of Christ—the consecrated Host of Eucharistic adoration— becomes the transcendent reality that, paradoxically, holds together the secular body of a hermaphrodite and the body of these young girls as dwelling places of God.

The unnamed twelve-year-old protagonist, naïve about sexuality and filled with "ugly" thoughts, must help her mother host her two fourteen-year-old cousins from Mount St. Scholastica Convent school for the weekend. The older girls—Susan and Joanne—call themselves "Temple One and Temple Two," mocking their teacher Sr.

Perpetua, who told them what to do in the face of ungentlemanly behavior: "Stop, Sir, I am a temple of the Holy Ghost."[24] From the beginning of the story there is this transgressive comedy on the theological anthropology of the human person—made in the image and likeness of God—and the sexual awakening of the teenage girls. The reader laughs at the sharp-witted child as she pokes fun at her older cousins and attempts to put together the many dissociated facts that she has accumulate this day. With her cousins still away at the fair, she is reminded of the grotesque bodies on the circus tent advertisements. Thinking that the freaks look like the pained bodies of the martyrs of the early church, the young girl ruminates on her future career. She moves from wanting to be a doctor to an engineer to a saint and settles on a romantically comical reverie of martyrdom as the only option for her proud and ornery disposition. The story dances around this notion of vocation, of the consequences of being called a temple of the Holy Ghost.

O'Connor affects something akin to the Baroque strategies of Caravaggio in the wonderful play between Protestant and Catholic discourses. Catholic girls Susan and Joanne are wooed by the Church of God boys, Wendell and Cory Wilkins. In the midst of their flirtation, the reader senses *counter*-imaginations at work: the young men sing their evangelical hymns, "I've Got a Friend in Jesus" and "The Old Rugged Cross," to which the young women literally chant the *Tantum Ergo* in response. The Protestant hymns of personal righteousness and witness to Jesus are juxtaposed to the Catholic

---

[24] O'Connor, "A Temple of the Holy Ghost" in *Flannery O'Connor: Collected Works*, 199.

contemplative hymn of Eucharistic adoration. And when the cousins arrive home from the fair and report to the young girl that the hermaphrodite told them not to laugh, because "God may strike you the same way,"[25] the twelve-year-old is left wondering how the freak could be a man and a woman both. Unable to fathom this, the young girl's dream merges the circus tent with that of a Protestant revival, as the freak becomes "a temple of the Holy Ghost," preaching a sermon about the holiness of the body and the ruin that comes from desecrating it.

We see this *counter*-imagination at its fullest in the final scene of Benediction at the convent school. The young girl's "ugly thoughts" halt and she realizes she is "in the presence of God," which provokes her to confess her sins mindlessly. But her mechanical thoughts turn to something unimaginable as she sees the priest raise the monstrance with the Host shining ivory-colored like the sun, and immediately she thinks of the Hermaphrodite saying at the fair, "I don't dispute hit. This is the way He wanted me to be."[26] The Eucharist becomes the mysterious place in which two dissimilar realities are held together. It is wonderfully transgressive at the same time absolutely orthodox: the strangeness of the Incarnation of Christ's dual nature as divine and human is found in the strangeness of the Hermaphrodite's intersexed abnormality. O'Connor juxtaposes the hermaphrodite's suffering of indignities to the incarnate Christ suffering on the cross, and made present in the sacramental bread as the broken body of Christ in the Eucharist. It is, I think, O'Connor's most daring analogy, revealing in an original and striking way something about the nature of God and of human life that the reader has not seen before. Indeed, the story suggests that God is to be found enfleshed in the freak, the stranger, and the alienated of society.

A final story, "Revelation," is a fitting illustration of O'Connor's Baroque aesthetic sensibility for it highlights more than any other her disdain for conventional Christian piety in her work. Where Caravaggio's aesthetic re-imagines acts of charity and Christian piety in representations that profoundly undermine the comfortable orthodox considerations of faith, O'Connor's aesthetic makes Christian piety an object of satire and travesty. As a triumph of the comic grotesque, O'Connor structures the story like a parable in which God's providence violently overturns the proud Ruby Turpin in her conceit.

---

[25] *Ibid.*, 206.
[26] *Ibid.*, 209.

Like the grandmother in "A Good Man Is Hard to Find," the self-indulgent
Ruby Turpin is made grotesque largely from her own doing. Ruby confuses
the righteousness of faith with the hypocrisy and pride she feels as a white,
Christian lady, whose sense of moral superiority is wrapped up in her race
and economic class. O'Connor builds up Ruby's spiritual deformity in the
first part of the story as the character sits in a doctor's office, assessing the
worth of various representatives of the South's class structure. The reader
witnesses her duplicity as she comments aloud about her "good
disposition," in contrast to her classist and racist inner monologue about
those around her. The Wellesley girl, Mary Grace, strikes Ruby in the eye
with a book and tries to strangle her. Mary Grace tells Ruby to, "Go back to
hell where you came from, you old wart hog,"[27] a violent revelation that
Ruby finds hard to understand but cannot deny the force of truth in it. The
key theological turn in the text is thus set as the paradox of a Christian
anthropology: how is Ruby Turpin "a hog and me both"? How is she saved
and from hell too? Or put in theological language, how is she redeemed in
her identity with Christ and yet a sinner identified with the wart hogs from
hell?

Ruby wrestles with her revelation in the second part of the story as she
marches out to her pig parlor "going single-handed, weaponless, into
battle."[28] O'Connor's use of the realistic, natural setting reinforces a
chiaroscuro-like moment in the story, as if a transformative light shines
upon this duplicitous Christian woman as she journeys out to meet her
apocalypse. From the brightness of the late afternoon setting to the
deepening blue hue of evening, Ruby rages at God for giving her such a
revelation, as she angrily hoses down her pigs:

> The color of everything, field and crimson sky, burned for a moment with a
> transparent intensity....Mrs. Turpin stood there, her gaze fixed on the
> highway, all her muscles rigid.... Then like a monumental statue coming to
> life, she bent her head slowly and gazed, as if through the very heart of
> mystery, down into the pig parlor at the hogs. They had settled all in one
> corner around the old sow who was grunting softly. A red glow suffused
> them. They appeared to pant with a secret life.[29]

There is a perfect blend of literary realism and religious vision as Ruby's
long view of the highway at the edge of the horizon is juxtaposed to the

---

[27] O'Connor, "Revelation" in *Flannery O'Connor: Collected Works*, 646.
[28] *Ibid.*, 651.
[29] *Ibid.*, 653.

close view of the pigs panting beneath her.

O'Connor literally paints with words the final revelation where the heavens and the earth open up before the reader:

> There was only a purple streak in the sky, cutting through a field of crimson and leading, like an extension of the highway, into the descending dusk.
>   A visionary light settled in her eyes. She saw the streak as a vast swinging bridge extending upward from the earth through a field of living fire.[30]

In this visionary light the "battalions of freaks and lunatics" are ahead of her and her husband Claude, on their way through the purgatorial living fire. Ruby stands immobile in this verticalized, reordered vision, where the last shall be first and the first shall be last is dramatically rendered as the spiritual corrective to Ruby's journey of faith. O'Connor suggests that this theological vision must not only be perceived but felt as a harsh conversion, a metanoia that recomposes one's vision in a critical moment of time.

Conclusion

O'Connor paints familiar scenes in realistic terms, but invites the viewer/reader into a transformed perception of such scenes. It mirrors a Baroque aesthetic because it suggests that reality has not changed; rather, the measure of that reality has been changed by the grotesque and violent dramas that reorient one's perspective. Whether in the chiaroscuro paintings of Caravaggio or in the parable-like stories of O'Connor, Catholic Baroque modes of expression force one to recognize and respond to it. The ideology of the Baroque requires conversion, an interior turning that is not merely a psychological act but a dramatic turning of the self out to the otherness of reality (which for Caravaggio and O'Connor ultimately means God). Conversion is thus a re-composition—in canvas or text—in which we move from the accessibly smug, comfortable versions of religious experience to a moment of excessive, sensory overload. In this moment, we return to a reformulation of the promise of salvation as something in our very proximity but made distant by our disordered sensibility. Both O'Connor and Caravaggio create an aesthetic strategy that deconstructs these preconceptions of what we think religion is and how we evaluate religious experience. Their work forces one to take off the blinders of a rationalized and distorted faith in order to see clearly the image of God in unlikely

---

[30] *Ibid.,* 654.

places, among an unworthy, unwanted, ungrateful, and ungodly people. In doing so, they reawaken the risks, the stakes of Christian witness, allowing a moment of participation in the drama of salvation while still in the flesh.

CHILDHOOD AND THE TERRAIN OF TRANSFORMATION: A TALE OF TWO O'CONNORS

MICHAEL P. MURPHY

"Anybody who has survived his childhood has enough information about life to last him the rest of his days."
—Flannery O'Connor[1]

Home

The mid-twentieth century was graced by two virtuosi of the short story who shared the same last name: "O'Connor."[2] These two O'Connors—Flannery (1925-1964) and Frank (1903-1966)—while they were related neither by blood nor the environments that marked their personal formation and artistic vision, they nonetheless shared a similar literary focus: the critically dynamic "character space" inhabited by children. The examples are almost too numerous to adduce in the work each writer. From Flannery O'Connor's

---

[1] Flannery O'Connor, "The Nature and Aim of Fiction" in *Mystery and Manners: Occasional Prose* (New York: Farrar, Strauss and Giroux, 1970), 84.

[2] One important biographical note on these two O'Connors. Frank O'Connor was born Michael O'Donovan and took his mother's maiden name as his *nom de plume*. Former British Prime Minister Harold Macmillan provides a keen insight into the writer's life and work in his "Rorward" to a collection of essays on Frank O'Connor:

Frank O'Connor had two names and lived a life of many facets. Yet everything he did, however unexpected or even contradictory it might seem, was informed by the same single-minded and passionate integrity. The young Irish rebel and the mature war-time friend of Britain, the eccentric librarian, the enthusiastic man of the theatre and the meticulous self-taught scholar, the sonorous translator of Irish poetry and the superlative short-story writer, the inspiring public lecturer and the dogged master of the seminar – all were unquestionably the same unique and original man." "Foreword," *Michael/Frank: Studies of Frank O'Connor with a Bibliography of his Writing,* ed. Sheehy, Maurice (Dublin: Gill and Macmillan, 1969), vii.

earlier tales (specifically "The Turkey," "The River," "A Circle in the Fire," and so many others), to her middle works (specifically "A Temple of the Holy Ghost" and "The Artificial Nigger"), and beyond, the experience of child protagonists—and the idea that childhood is a mysterious, transformative place rife with theological vitality—are of special concern to her. Likewise, Frank O'Connor's literary imagination makes astute and evolved observations about the interior lives of children, especially when children are in threshold states pregnant with conflict and transformational energy. From the Larry Delaney tales to the famous "First Confession" to the high theological realism of "The Face of Evil"—Frank O'Connor demonstrates that the experience of childhood is no minor affair, no one dimensional Dickensian expression of "seen but not heard" Victorian neglect. Childhood in these stories is instead a fecundating site filled with indelible experiences of suffering, moments of epiphany, and deep encounters with the spiritual life in a Catholic key.

This chapter will focus on a series of revelatory moments in the experience of child characters. Flannery's "A Temple of the Holy Ghost" (1953) will be set alongside Frank's "The Face of Evil" (1954) as main texts so that we might distill three theologically charged themes in three snapshots. These themes—sanctity, solidarity, and mysterious moments of insight begotten by the navigation of opposites (i.e., the *complexio oppositorum*)—are not only fundamental to a Catholic philosophy of life, but they are also located in a theological aesthetics that both precede and invigorate any notion of such a philosophy.

The care with which the two O'Connors navigate the transformative and redemptive aspects of these phenomena, specifically as they are encountered and performed in the seemingly circumscribed territory of childhood, emerges as unique and distinct. In so many cases, children are represented in literature in polarized terms—either purely good or purely evil—and rarely painted with an integrated inner life that honors the rich complexity of the childhood experience.[3] Of course, this makes sense given the developmental issues that attend all stages of life, particularly in childhood;

---

[3] In his book, *Evil Children in Religion, Literature, and Art* (New York: Palgrave, 2001), Eric Ziolkowski argues that authors reiterate metaphorical shorthand by portraying children as flat characters—and more often as evil than good. This convention stems from the "Adamic sin" inscribed on humanity (7). The two O'Connors face this stamp head on; and, while Edenic fall is a most vital topic and presence in their stories, they also provide a space for gracious realism or the liberating agency that comes from authentic encounter and understanding.

but it also may reveal either a troubling amnesia or a lack of imagination in adult artists. Generally speaking, conventional depictions of children in literature, up until the mid-twentieth century anyway, illustrate time and again how adults fail to realistically comprehend childhood and its many conflicting dynamics; and these gaps, left untended, are shuttled into adulthood where they continue to exert psychological and spiritual influence. No matter the drama or gravity we experience in adult life, no matter the "tracks" that adults follow, proudly "in the wrong direction," as the ten-year old Nelson observes in "The Artificial Nigger," we know that childhood makes vital, lasting impressions and that its boundaries are porous.[4] As Flannery wrote in 1956, "I am much younger now than I was at twelve or anyway, less burdened. The weight of centuries lies on children, I'm sure of it"—a sentence that Frank could have easily written just as well.[5]

In their fiction, both O'Connors demonstrate persuasively how childhood is not so much an era as it is a geographical place—a location with scents and sights, a shared terrain to be navigated by us all. Because childhood is more a region than an epoch, it becomes flattener of distances and a place for unexpected and expansive encounter. Childhood is a place to which we circle back as we grow older—motivated, perhaps, by a nostalgia that exists in a kind of never-ending present. In his late poem "A Herbal," written not long after a debilitating stroke, Seamus Heaney meditates on a dialogical intimacy of place, of his Irish home: "I had my existence. I was there./Me in place and the place in me."[6] This kind of nostalgia, to follow the Greek trope of *nostos*, is a longing that comes with a deep sense of displaced physicality, one that exerts a visceral, full-bodied force on human memory.[7]

---

[4] Flannery O'Connor, *The Complete Stories*, ed. Robert Giroux (New York: Farrar, Strauss and Giroux, 1971), 263. I quote the title and the hateful "N-word" for reasons of scholarly integrity. A note here as well on the specter of racism in Flannery O'Connor, a topic which has become again an embattled subject for so many. The topic is outside the scope of this chapter, but for those who would like to read a scholarly treatment, see Angela Alaimo O'Donnell, Radical Ambivalence: Race in Flannery O'Connor (New York: Fordham University Press, 2020).

[5] Flannery O'Connor, *The Habit of Being: Letters of Flannery O'Connor*, ed. Sally Fitzgerald (New York: Farrar, Strauss and Giroux, 1979), 136-37.

[6] Seamus Heaney, from "A Herbal" in *Human Chain* (New York: Farrar, Strauss, Giroux, 2010), 41.

[7] For a novel length distillation of this phenomenon, Alain-Fournier's *Le Grand Meaulnes* (1913), remains the late modern gold standard of this kind of *nostos*. Of course, there are other excellent late modern novels that take *nostos* up in creative, penetrating ways, notably James Joyce, *Ulysses* (1922), Gabriel Garcia Marquez, *100 Years of Solitude* (1967), and Kazuo Ishiguro, *The Remains of the Day* (1989).

The interpenetrating circles of "home" that characterize the various stages of our lives are therefore deeply theological and speak to a phenomenon that energizes the Catholic imagination, that of *exitus* and *reditus*—the pilgrim *procession from* and *return to* God, to our home, that fires the heart of trinitarian theology.[8] This being a premise in both O'Connors sets us quite naturally in a terrain-- in a geography of childhood as place set by the God who offers cartographical clues in speaking about the importance of this location in no uncertain terms:

> "Who, then, is the greatest in the kingdom of heaven?" He called a little child to him, and placed the child among them. And he said: "Truly I tell you, unless you change and become like little children, you will never enter the kingdom of heaven.[9]

Seeing the Form: A Theological Aesthetics of Childhood

> "Only the Christian religion, which in its essence is communicated by the eternal child of God, keeps alive in its believers the lifelong awareness of their being children, and therefore of having to ask and give thanks for things."
> —Hand Urs von Balthasar[10]

The many settings in our lives that play host to the formation of our personal and communal identities—all of the physical places that beget experiences of encounter and intimacy—speak to another phenomenon that fires the Catholic imagination: that theological mystery takes root in finite spaces. And what is more, this mystery unfolds dramatically and is midwifed

---

[8] As *exitus et reditus* (the Latin of *proodos/epistrophe*) is a fundamental theological dynamic it is threaded through the whole of the Christian tradition—from St. Paul to Pseudo Dionysius (i.e., Denys) to St. Hildegard of Bingen to St. Thomas Aquinas to Hans Urs von Balthasar who writes, meditating on Denys and the *Divine Names*, "so all is in accordance with the great flowing movement of being itself as procession and return, *proodos* and *epistrophe*, so that what is ultimately important is to trust oneself to the direction of this flow, recognizing in the procession the source, and in the return the goal." Balthasar, *The Glory of the Studies in Theological Style: Clerical Styles*. Vol. 2 of *The Glory of the Lord: A Theological Aesthetics*, ed. John Riches, trs. Andrew Louth, Francis McDonough, and Brian McNeil (San Francisco: Ignatius Press, 1984), 165.

[9] MT 18:1-5.

[10] Hans Urs von Balthasar, *Unless you Become Like This Child* (San Francisco: Ignatius Press, 1991), 49.

intelligibly through the sensible topographies and carved-out languages of a place or region. This is to say that the terrain of childhood takes place amidst other local terrains—villages and cities, alleys and meadows, schools, doctor's offices, trains, and so on. This kind of navigation—between the local and the universal, the regional and the cosmopolitan—has a fundamentally liturgical quality and speaks to a theological aesthetics at work in both O'Connors. Such an aesthetics is often short-handed by critics with theological sensibilities, at turns, as either "incarnational" or "sacramental" and is very much awash in the cultural contexts and intellectual discourses in which both O'Connors lived and wrote—contexts and discourses that illuminate a Catholic philosophy of life even as they show various impediments to it.

Flannery, more than Frank, is instructive here. While both O'Connors wrote fiction imbued with theological life and advents of spiritual transformation, Frank, writing from the context of mid-century County Cork in an Ireland where the church has taken an entrenched, authoritarian, and pharisaical posture, is more critical of the Church as institution than Flannery, who writes from the Protestant South in the United States. Flannery has a different set of fish to fry than Frank does. She is less concerned with the middle-manager power intrigues of clerics in the local diocese; instead she has her literary sights fixed on the spiritual displacement of a pervasive "Christ-hauntedness" that she discerns in her native Georgia and surrounding environs. Famously, Flannery lasers in on this point in her in her 1960 essay "Some Aspects of the Grotesque in Southern Fiction":

> But approaching the subject from the standpoint of the writer, I think it is safe to say that while the South is hardly Christ-centered, it is most certainly Christ-haunted. The Southerner, who isn't convinced of it, is very much afraid that he may have been formed in the image and likeness of God. Ghosts can be very fierce and instructive. They cast strange shadows, particularly in our literature.[11]

She expands on the issue in a 1962 letter to poet Alfred Corn, anticipating well the contemporary diminution of religion we see today into a kind of moral therapeutic deism as opposed to a relational, vivifying encounter with the living God:

> One of the effects of modern liberal Protestantism has been gradually to turn religion into poetry and therapy, to make truth vaguer and vaguer and more

---

[11] "Some Aspects of the Grotesque in Southern Fiction" in *Mystery and Manners: Occasional Prose,* 44-45.

and more relative, to banish intellectual distinctions, to depend on feeling instead of thought, and gradually to come to believe that God has no power, that he cannot communicate with us, cannot reveal himself to us, indeed has not done so and that religion is our own sweet invention.[12]

Flannery's strong critique of those "for whom the supernatural has become an embarrassment and for whom religion has become a department of sociology or culture or personality development" becomes an even more apt description of much thought traffic today.[13] Many seek to reduce Flannery's sacramental aesthetics to the cultural or political or psychological, as is found in some contemporary critical writing on the subject.[14] For Flannery, though, sacramentality is not a cultural or aesthetic novelty, but an epistemology—a way of knowing par excellence and a way of seeing the world. To this end, many critics with religious sensibilities have done well to locate and illuminate the mystery of the Incarnation of God that explains and undergirds O'Connor's sacramental imagination.[15] The best of these critics approach her work as she did—as an aesthetic of Christian realism. O'Connor wrote in a letter to Betty Hester in 1955 that there is only "one Reality"; and her fiction points to and participates in the transcendent mystery, not of "what" is true, but of the Who that is True, a markedly

---

[12] Flannery O'Connor, *The Habit of Being*, 479.

[13] Flannery O'Connor, "In the Protestant South," *Mystery and Manners: Occasional Prose,* 207.

[14] For instance, see Katherine Prown, *Revising Flannery O'Connor: Southern Literary Culture and the Problem of Female Authorship* (Charlottesville: U of Virginia, 2001) and Sarah Gordon, *Flannery O'Connor: The Obedient Imagination* (Athens: University of Georgia Press, 2003). Both of these texts are original studies that expand the scope of O'Connor criticism; but they are also at times too dismissive of O'Connor's theological vision and often confuse theology with psychology or conflate it with the byproducts of gender politics. I write at length on this topic in "Breaking Bodies: Flannery O'Connor and the Aesthetics of Consecration" in *Revelation &Convergence: Flannery O'Connor and Her Catholic Heritage* (M. Bosco and B. Little, eds., Washington DC: Catholic University Press, 2017). Paragraph excerpted here.

[15] There are several excellent texts to cite in this regard dating back to second wave of O'Connor criticism in the 1980's—Marion Montgomery, Richard Giannone, Frederick Asals, and others. More recent scholarship indicates both amplification of and increased theological precision with the topic, and O'Connor's Sacramental imagination is taken up in various ways by Susan Srigley (in Flannery O'Connor's Sacramental Art, 2004), Christina Bieber-Lake (in *The Incarnational Art of Flannery O'Connor*, 2005), and Farrell O'Gorman (in *A Peculiar Crossroads: Flannery O'Connor, Walker Percy, and Catholic Vision in Postwar Southern Fiction*, 2008).

different kind of "turning to the subject" than what normally preoccupies most late modern critical discourse.[16] O'Connor's fiction moves from the *concretum* of her Southern subject matter to the *concretum universal* of the Transcendent God, which is to say she is sacramental from the ground up. Frank shares this orientation as well especially in his profound suspicion for the abstract, for the excarnate. His approach to the short story, articulated expansively in *The Lonely Voice* (1963), discloses a stylistic principle and practice that becomes a theological aesthetics: unfiltered depictions of the Irish quotidian that disclose the immediacy of our lives in God. It is in this way that these two O'Connors reveal childhood for what it is: a concrete (even if it is interstitial and liminal) space packed with implicit mystery and transformational clout of a high theological register.

Sanctity

"The only real sadness, the only real failure, the only great tragedy in life, is not to become a saint."
—Léon Bloy [17]

Flannery's "A Temple of the Holy Ghost" and Frank's story "The Face of Evil" were written within a year of each other. There must have been something in the long secret pipeline that connects clan O'Connor because the stories concern themselves essentially with the same questions: What is sanctity? What is it not? What is sainthood? What is it not? How do our notions of sanctity shape our theologies and Christologies, our ethics and aesthetics? These questions are stitched into the fine seams of both tales— one narrative focusing on the interior life of a child protagonist (in "Temple of the Holy Ghost") and one tale narrated in the form of a detached autobiographical recollection of a speaker remembering a critical moment of his childhood (in "The Face of Evil"). In both stories, sanctity—and an evolving appreciation of its mysterious character—occupies both the arc and the focal point of each author's concern.

In Flannery's recently published *A Prayer Journal*, which, among other things, invites readers to consider and connect an author's juvenilia with care, Flannery provides details about who she is reading as she matriculates through the Iowa Writers Workshop to her MFA degree in 1947. Of all the writers she cites—from Kafka to James to Katherine Ann Porter, it is the French "pilgrim of the absolute," Léon Bloy, who occupies a significant

---

[16] Flannery O'Connor, *The Habit of Being*, 92.
[17] Léon Bloy, from *La Femme Pauvre* (1897).

space at this time in the development of her Catholic imagination, a development that was in full bloom by 1946. It was Bloy who instructed Jacques and Raissa Maritain (and Raissa's sister) in Catholic thought and spirituality. It was Bloy who critically intervened in the life of the Maritains; Bloy who was their Godfather. Jacques Maritain and his heart-solid Neo-Thomism is essential in any discussion about O'Connor's thought and work and his philosophical and aesthetic influence on Flannery is without parallel—and there is no Jacques Maritain without Léon Bloy. In *A Prayer Journal*, Bloy also teaches O'Connor about refining her narrative art—particularly in regards to characterization: "These modern 'Christs' pictured on war posters & in poems—'every man is Jesus; every woman Mary' [--] would have made Bloy retch. The rest of us have lost the power to vomit"—a kind of theological psychology that will serve as a subtext of so many of O'Connor stories.[18]

But sanctity was of uppermost concern to the adolescent Flannery in those graduate school days. Another stunning observation of Léon Bloy can serve as pillar and subtext here: "The only real sadness," he writes, "the only real failure, the *only* great tragedy in life, is not to become a saint," a call (and premise) upon which Georges Bernanos builds his 1936 novel, *The Diary of a Country Priest*, a novel Flannery also read in Iowa.[19] In *A Prayer Journal*, one sees the fingerprints of both Bloy and Bernanos as a twenty-one year old Flannery writes about sanctity:

> What I am asking for is really very ridiculous. Oh Lord, I am saying, at present I am a cheese, make me a mystic, immediately. But then God can do that — make mystics out of cheeses. But why should he do it for an ingrate slothful & dirty creature like me. ...The rosary is mere rote for me while I think of other and usually impious things. But I would like to be a mystic and immediately...If I am the one to wash the second step everyday, let me know it and I will wash it and let my heart overflow with love washing it. (My Soul is) a moth who would be king, a stupid slothful thing,

---

[18] Flannery O'Connor, *A Prayer Journal*, ed. W.A. Sessions (New York: Farrar, Strauss and Giroux, 2013), 34.
[19] The wise but often ranting curé de Torcy amplifies the sacramental power of childhood in Bernanos's novel: "The shabbiest tuppeny doll will rejoice a baby's heart for half the year, but your mature gentleman'll go yawning his head off at a five-hundred franc gadget. And why? Because he has lost the soul of childhood. Well, God has entrusted the Church to keep that soul alive, to safeguard our candour and freshness." Georges Bernanos, *The Diary of a Country Priest*, trans. Pamela Morris (New York: Carroll and Graf, 2002), 20.

a foolish thing, who wants God, who made the earth, to be its Lover immediately.[20]

Of the several moments in *A Prayer Journal* that can be classified as explicit, uttered prayers, this one is most noteworthy for its honesty and gravity. The desire for sanctity—in this case for the intimacy with God that comes with the gift of mysticism—is on full display. Yet there is also an authentic tension disclosed, one between desire and sloth, one between explosive spirituality and the tedium of rote prayers that so often become a crucible of spiritual life at any age.

We see also this tension developed and rendered with more dimension and texture eight years later in the fictional space of "A Temple of the Holy Ghost." In the story, a twelve-year old protagonist is confronted with a series of related threshold experiences that bear decisive theological significance. It is essential to note that, throughout the story, O'Connor refers her protagonist as "the child" while her fourteen-year old cousins are called "girls." Like the adolescent Flannery we behold in self-narration of *A Prayer Journal*, in "The Temple of the Holy Ghost," the child outlines her desire for sanctity; unlike Flannery in the journal, the child imagines the pathway with to martyrdom, one that drips with the kind of humor present in so much of her fiction, letters, and occasional prose:

> She would have to be a saint because that was the occupation that included everything you could know; and yet she knew she would never be a saint. She did not steal or murder but she was a born liar and slothful and she sassed her mother and was deliberately ugly to almost everybody. She was eaten up also with the sin of Pride, the worst one. She made fun of the Baptist preacher who came to the school at commencement to give the devotional. She would pull down her mouth and hold her forehead as if she were in agony and groan, "Fawther, we thank Thee," exactly the way he did and she had been told many times not to do it. She could never be a saint, but she thought she could be a martyr if they killed her quick.[21]

The child continues in this vein, vividly imagining several heroic ways her martyrdom might go down:

> She could stand to be shot but not to be burned in oil. She didn't know if she could stand to be torn to pieces by lions or not. She began to prepare her martyrdom, seeing herself in a pair of tights in a great arena, lit by the early Christians hanging in cages of fire, making a gold dusty light that fell on her

---

[20] Flannery O'Connor, *A Prayer Journal*, 38.
[21] Flannery O'Connor, *The Complete Stories*, 243.

and the lions….to their astonishment she would not burn down and finding she was so hard to kill, they finally cut off her head very quickly with a sword and she went immediately to heaven[22]

In the vast array of 20th century short fiction, mirth-provoking level of piety exuded by this child is hard to equal, but Frank is up to the task with his narrator in "The Face of Evil." In the (rarely anthologized) story, which first appeared in *The New Yorker* in 1954, the narrator leads with a characteristic pompousness that can attend people of any age, not least of whom early adolescent boys endowed with unique precociousness. The story begins:

I could never understand all the old talk about how hard it is to be a saint. I was a saint for quite a bit of my life and I never saw anything hard in it. And when I stopped being a saint, it wasn't because the life was too hard.[23]

The pompousness, of course, masks the deeper reality of the situation and sets the ground for the transformational moment in which the text culminates. The narrator's conception of sanctity is upside down. It is, to allude to a famous Flannery moment in "Revelation," as if he were looking at it through the "wrong end of a telescope."[24] For this young narrator, sanctity—and idea of being a saint—is but a kitsch-grade and romanticized dime-store quest, "like no other hobby," he reports, but a hobby all the same. Sainthood for him is formulaic and procedural—a state acquired by a prescribed set of actions: "For me," the boy observes, "the main attraction of being a saint was the way it always gave you something to do…put everything neatly back into place, scour it," and so on.[25] This brand of lift-yourself-up-by-your own-bootstraps Pelagianism is well expressed in the literary work of both authors and is also, of course, a notorious red herring interrupting the spiritual quest of many pilgrims in human history, literary or otherwise. Moreover, like so many Flannery tales, this late modern Pelegianism, serious as it is, is depicted with deft humor. In the vast majority of any O'Connor story, it is as Chesterton famously quipped: "'funny' is not the opposite of 'serious;' it is the opposite of 'not-funny.'"

[22] Flannery O'Connor, *The Complete Stories*, 243.
[23] Frank O'Connor, "The Face of Evil" (1954), accessed July 15, 2020. https://archives.newyorker.com/newyorker/1954-04-03/flipbook/024/, 24.
[24] Flannery O'Connor, *The Complete Stories*
[25] "The Face of Evil" (1954), accessed July 15, 2020. https://archives.newyorker.com/newyorker/1954-04-03/flipbook/024/, 24.

Still, in "The Face of Evil" the narrator's task-derived sanctity demands our scrutiny. It is a typical expression of what it might mean to be a "good Catholic" not only in mid-20th century Ireland, but well beyond. The narrator likes to be thought of as a saint, likes to be known in the lanes for how he copes with his "little book of transgressions," the contents of which he offloads scrupulously to the ear of his priest each week. He is certain that grace is a thing that is merited. That he delights in being envied by his colleagues for being a saint, that he, in the central reveal of the tale, has "no inclination to mix with other kids who might be saints as well," shines direct light on the poverty of his understanding, his solipsism, and his naiveté.[26]

But naïveté works at least two ways and is not confined to children. If we are to appreciate the spirituality and intellectual life of children—and the authentic ways in which they encounter their experiences of culpability and growth—we also would be well advised to be as clear as possible when we consider conceptual differences between naïveté and, say, purity. O'Connor touched on this phenomenon in a 1956 letter to Betty Hester and speculates that the dynamic is essentially theological in nature and that it exists *outside* the boundaries of age or stage:

> Always you renounce a lesser good for a greater; the opposite is what sin is. And along this line, I think the phrase naïve purity is a contradiction in terms. I don't think purity is mere innocence. I don't think babies and idiots possess it. I take it to be something that comes either with experience or with Grace so that it can never be naïve.[27]

The great work for child protagonists in both Frank and Flannery is not only to confront incipient pride and narcissism, but also to reject the bourgeois prescriptions of sanctity and the cheap antidotes to sin prescribed by such narrow and myopic theologies. This, as it happens, is also the great work for adults. There is a latent neo-puritanism, it can be argued, that attends and continues to shape the social milieu of "Christian" countries evangelized under corpse-cold, pharisaical versions of the faith, another element that links the two O'Connors—links 20th century Cork to 20th century Milledgeville— and it is a phenomenon about which both were profoundly critical. We fail to fully inhabit a Catholic philosophy of life when we reiterate this kind of puritanism, when we view sanctity as a prize to be won in competition as opposed to the gracious and relational development of an authentically holy innocence. Still, it is the typical course

---

[26] "The Face of Evil" (1954), accessed July 15[t,] 2020.
https://archives.newyorker.com/newyorker/1954-04-03/flipbook/024/, 24.
[27] *The Habit of Being*, 126.

at any stage of life, or as Frank observes: "Even if there were only two men left in the world and both of them saints they wouldn't be happy. One of them would be bound to try and improve the other. That is the nature of things."[28] In Flannery, if a character presumes to be about the work of improving her neighbor under such clinical conditions, she gets a textbook in human development thrown at her.[29]

Solidarity

"Knowing later, when smitten at last with the Christ, he had been always turning, unconsciously, to face him, flinching already from the embrace."
—John F. Deane[30]

The theological context of the "The Face of Evil" is one characterized precisely by unbridled pride and narcissism; and in the tale, naïveté, while essential to the moment of transformation, retreats in significance rather quickly—in the very moment that the human capacity for God is revealed, in the very moment that the narrator begins to have an inkling that the title of the tale may be referring to him, an untested *poseur* of a saint. When he beholds his neighbor, Charlie Dalton, a policeman's son but "easily the most vicious kid in the province," struggling in prayer (just after he condescends to Charlie, we are quick to note, in a sanctimonious peer-to peer exercise in spiritual direction)—when he encounters Charlie "kneeling up front, before the altar" in authentic compunction—the narrator suddenly realizes the limits to the sphere of his personal influence and the impotence of his misdiagnosed attributes of sanctity. He realizes his failure: "It was no good...I wanted to go with Charlie and share his fate. For the first time I

---

[28] Frank O'Connor, from "Song without Words" in *Collected Stories* (New York: Vintage, 1982), 33.

[29] Flannery O'Connor, from "Revelation": "If it's one thing I am," Mrs. Turpin said with feeling, "It's grateful. When I think who all I could have been besides myself and what all I got, a little of everything, and a good disposition besides, I just feel like shouting, 'Thank you, Jesus, for making everything the way it is!' It could have been different!" For one thing, somebody else could have got Claud. At the thought of this, she was flooded with gratitude and a terrible pang of joy ran through her.
"Oh thank you, Jesus, Jesus, thank you!" she cried aloud.
The book struck her directly, over her left eye. It struck almost at the same instant that she realized the girl was about to hurl it. (*The Complete Stories*, 499).

[30] John F. Deane, from "A Boy Child" in *Like the Dewfall* (Cornwall: Guillemot Press, 2019), 24.

realized that the life before me would have complexities of emotion which I couldn't even imagine."[31]

Frank O'Connor's narrator in "The Face of Evil" encounters a kid—Charlie Dalton—with real problems, problems that confound the rote prescriptions of sanctity offered by the catechetical manuals. This is one revelation; the other is that the narrator begins to see his own face inscribed in another— begins to see his need for grace—inscribed in Charlie and Charlie's authentic, if vacillating, desire. Such a revelation makes available the chance for true solidarity for, again, it flattens distances between God's creatures—whether young, old, or in between—and cracks the self-fashioned shells of our egotism. Such a revelation also discloses local impressions and expressions of the *Imago Dei*, the face of the merciful Maker inscribed upon us all, and draws us nearer to our lives in God "in whom we live move and have our being."[32] Such a revelation, perhaps most importantly, is also faithful to the hardscrabble truths engendered by literary art because it teaches the unflinching credibility of Christian realism. We learn that the following week after the church experience, Charlie Dalton "ran away from home again…and, after being arrested seventy-five miles from Cork in a little village on the coast, and was sent to an industrial school."[33] My guess is that Charlie ended up in Flannery's Georgia. "It's no real pleasure in life," he keeps saying and the plot of his pilgrimage thickens.[34]

Compared to the novel, the short story, it can be argued, is a more regional space and is therefore a canvas where sacramental dynamics—and central Christian themes like false pride, solidarity, and mercy—may be set free to work a small course more starkly and directly. Frank muses in this direction in the introduction to his *The Lonely Voice: A Study of the Short Story* (1963): "Always in the short story," he argues, "there is a sense of outlawed figures wandering about the fringes of society." "We see in the short story," he continues, a confederacy of the marginalized and excluded, "submerged population groups, whatever these may be at the given time—tramps, lonely idealists, dreamers, and spoiled priests." This rag-tag community is the very

---

[31] "The Face of Evil" (1954), accessed July 15[t,] 2020.
https://archives.newyorker.com/newyorker/1954-04-03/flipbook/024/, 28.
[32] Acts, 17:8
[33] "The Face of Evil" (1954), accessed July 15[t,] 2020.
https://archives.newyorker.com/newyorker/1954-04-03/flipbook/024/, 28.
[34] Perhaps melding too liberally here the two O'Connors and their work. Still, The Charlie Daltons of the world may well be the Irish prototype of Flannery's Misfit in "A Good Man is Hard to Find" (1953).

Body of Christ in a Catholic philosophy of life as Frank gleans and then declares in no uncertain terms: "Across the abyss that separates me from them I seem to hear the voice of Gogol's copying clerk, crying, "I am your brother." [35]

In the world of grace, we observe again how distances are flattened. This may be the central quality of a truly Christocentric teleology. In "The Face of Evil," a young person has a first-row experience of suffering and it broadens his view of sanctity and solidarity. That suffering educates in this way is not a particularly new or astute insight; but it is striking to recognize the ways that these writing O'Connors respect the movement of suffering in young people. As a quick aside, I am a fan of the films of Wes Anderson and find that his work meditates consistently and constructively on this theme. In Anderson's films, particularly in *Rushmore* (1998), but in so many other of his films besides, not only is the authenticity of suffering of young people taken seriously (and humorously, which again, as readers of both O'Connors know, is an entirely consonant depiction), but distinctions in age are laid to waste by the acknowledgement of shared trial. Creatures young and old stand side by side in the common event of having encountered something painful—having come face to face with the mystery of suffering— which, in the Christian milieu, discloses and engenders a primary attribute of the God of relationship who reaches out to us in kenotic self-donation. As Frank observes: "I suppose we all have our little hiding-hole if the truth was known, but as small as it is, the whole world is in it, and bit by bit grows on us again till the day You find us out." And Flannery follows, "Please help me to get down under things and find where you are."[36]

Navigating Opposites

Nothing was changed, all was revealed otherwise;
not that horror was not, not that the killings did not continue;
not that I thought there was to be no more despair,
but that as if transparent all disclosed
an otherness that was blessèd, that was bliss,
I saw Paradise in the dust of the street.
—Denise Levertov[37]

---

[35] Frank O'Connor, *The Lonely Voice: A Study of the Short Story* (New York: Melville House, 2011), 20; 40.

[36] Frank O'Connor, *The Collected Stories*; Flannery O'Connor, *A Prayer Journal*, 4.

[37] Denise Levertov, from "City Psalm" in Selected Poems, ed. Paul Lacey (New York: New Directions, 2003), 36.

Such a prayerful and redemptive theory of suffering—and the sanctity, mercy, and solidarity born of it—is rendered in a particularly adept way by Flannery in her 1955 story in "The Artificial Nigger." Mr. Head is washed in the insight upon the advent of a gracious catastrophe while lost in the streets of the Atlanta setting: "He understood that it (mercy) grew out of agony, which is not denied to any man and which is given in strange ways to children."[38] The entire piece pulsates with questions of sanctity and solidarity and is a story that has also has at its center the flattening of the distances of age. The story, it is also well known was Flannery's "favorite" and, as she wrote in a letter to Maryat Lee, was "probably the best thing I'll ever write."[39] Age is displaced when grace is afoot and signals an even deeper solidarity between characters—between a recalcitrant grandfather and a grandson who deserves better—and the loving God who makes them in in His image:

> Mr. Head looked like an ancient child and Nelson like a miniature old man. They stood gazing at the artificial Negro as if they were faced with some great mystery, some monument to another's victory that brought them together in their common defeat. They could both feel it dissolving their differences like an action of mercy.[40]

To discern a quadrupled inscription of divine action is no small feat; to render it expertly in prose is even one better. Distance in this moment is annihilated not only between grandfather and grandson, but also between their present moment in Atlanta and the darker twists and turns of a collective Southern history. It is one that connects, ultimately, to transcendental justice. In this way we witness ever deepening ways that the dynamic concept of the concrete universal enlightens understanding. Sanctity and sin are held together with solidarity and separation in one moment.

To hold two seemingly opposing ideas up together and proceed as if they are not is perhaps the most demanding feature in a Catholic philosophy of life. In their art, both O'Connors derive much fruit from this paradox as it has everything to do with the incarnational and sacramental realism the makes the whole thing go. Flannery, fixing again on its wisdom one last time in her (arguably best) short story, "Revelation" (1964), paints a stark (but ultimately loving, as always) picture of Ruby Turpin, a self-congratulatory hog-farming Christian assured of her own salvation. Late in the story—and after a life-changing encounter with an adolescent girl in a

[38] CS, 269
[39] Flannery O'Connor, *The Habit of Being*, 209.
[40] Flannery O'Connor, *The Complete Stories*, 269.

doctor's office—she learns better. Her husband was the patient, but it is the state of Ruby's spiritual health that is the issue here. Reflecting upon the violence that had been visited upon her by the girl, she shakes her fist at God: "What do you send me a message like that for? How am I a hog and me both? How am I saved and from hell too?"[41]

Flannery's "A Temple of the Holy Ghost" is likewise oriented around seminal both/and questions and the child protagonist is confronted with the complexity of a larger theological algebra. Upon hearing about the side show freak at the carnival, her mind is stretched. How can it be that there are hermaphrodites in this world? How can it be that here is something that is two things at the same time? Why would a God traffic in such messy streets? As Flannery well knew, the *complexio oppositorum* is both *in* and *of* the *Imago Dei* and expresses itself as a fundamental attribute of the divine. But neat Neoplatonic propositions often collide with the reality of the Gospel as God enters into humankind not as unity, but as conflict. God is both a disruptive and fecundating "advent of a gracious catastrophe" to say it how Flannery says it, appearing almost always in Flannery, as Denise Levertov, another witness to the *complexio* has it, as "destructive construction" where apparent opposites dissolve into the unity of theological mystery.[42] In "A Temple of the Holy Ghost," the child is initiated into this complicated Christology in an innovative nature and grace move that highlights Flannery's devotion to classical Thomism-- but also in a way that also in a way that honors its implicit energy and adaptability. The hermaphrodite stretches the theological vision of the child and orients it rightly—on the God who is two natures at once: fully human and fully divine. It is God alone who negotiates contraries in ways that "burn our virtues away," put "bottom rails on top," and make straight crooked things—especially things (and people) hubristically convinced of their own moral rectitude or spiritual merit.[43]

Flannery's devotion to St. Thomas Aquinas is famous—so much so that she claimed the title "Hillbilly Thomist" with humor and pride.[44] She read Thomas daily and quotes him regularly in her letters and occasional prose.

---

[41] Flannery O'Connor, *The Complete Stories*, 269.

[42] Denise Levertov, from "In California: Morning, Evening, Late January," in *A Door in the Hive* (New York: New Directions, 1989), 42.

[43] Cf. Flannery O'Connor from "Revelation." Ruby gets her "virtues burned clean" in the hierophanic vision that concludes the tale.

[44] Flannery O'Connor, *The Habit of Being*, 81. "Everybody who has read *Wise Blood* thinks I'm a hillbilly nihilist, whereas. . .I'm a hillbilly Thomist."

In the story, the child's Catholic school cousins, Joann and Susan, sing St. Thomas's hymn, "The Tantum Ergo," to the Protestant boys, Wendell and Cory, who think the Latin chant is "Jew singing." The hymn, as it encapsulates the action of eucharistic encounter, becomes a keystone of understanding for the child:

> Down in adoration falling,
> Lo!the sacred Host we hail,
> Lo! o'er ancient forms departing
> Newer rites of grace prevail;
> Faith for all defects supplying
> Where the feeble senses fail.

The child's second-hand encounter with hermaphrodite is received as a kind of Gospel news—reported by fallible witnesses and received by the child with a heart prepared for transformation:

> This is the way [God] wanted me to be, and I ain't disputing His way. I'm showing you because I got to make the best of it. I expect you to act like ladies and gentlemen. I never done it to myself nor had a thing to do with it but I'm making the best of it. I don't dispute hit.[45]

Like so many of the outcast and marginalized in O'Connor's fiction, the carnival freak becomes a sacramental element that draws a protagonist deeper into faith and mystery where "newer rites of grace prevail": "Raise yourself up. A temple of the Holy Ghost. You! You are God's temple, don't you know? God's spirit has a dwelling in you, don't you know?"[46]

In *A Prayer Journal*, Flannery the graduate student prays for aid in understanding the mystery of such things:

> Please help me to get down under things and find where you are. I do not mean to deny the traditional prayers I have said all my life; but I have been saying them and not feeling them. My attention is always very fugitive.[47]

The prayer seems to anticipate the issue as it is later presented in "Temple":

> Hep me not to be so mean, she began mechanically. Hep me not to give her so much sass. Hep me not to talk like I do. Her mind began to get quiet and then empty but when the priest raised the monstrance with the Host shining ivory-colored in the center of it, she was thinking of the tent at the fair that

[45] Flannery O'Connor, *The Complete Stories*, 245.
[46] Flannery O'Connor, *The Complete Stories*, 246.
[47] Flannery O'Connor, *A Prayer Journal*, 4.

had the freak in it. The freak was saying, "I don't dispute hit. This is the way He wanted me to be."[48]

To get down under things may require a certain habit of seeing. Certainly, it requires habits of mercy and compassion; and it is God who inscribes these virtues upon all of creation, sharing with us always in grace His image and likeness. So how fitting it is that our young protagonist gets written upon in the final movement of the tale: "The big nun swooped down on her mischievously and nearly smothered her in the black habit, mashing the side of her face into the crucifix hitched onto her belt and then holding her off and looking at her with her little periwinkle eyes."[49] Solidarity with others is written upon the soul in the same moment that the image of Christ is impressed upon the soft cheek of the child. A sacramental aesthetics *par excellence* precisely because it one that leaves a deep impression and one that will last.

"There are some things," says cousin Susan to the child in "A Temple of the Holy Ghost," that "a child your age doesn't know."[50] Certainly, there are things that children do not know, but then there are also as many things that adults do not know, have forgotten, or are too hardened to hear. Flannery, like Frank, demonstrates that the capacity for God transcends age and impresses upon so deeply—not in our time, but in God's. To see oneself inscribed in another is to see the face of God in all creation. It is to reconcile the space between nearness and distance, a grace certainly, but one meaningful at any age—or to return to where we began and the last word for Flannery: "Anybody who has survived his childhood has enough information about life to last him the rest of his days."

---

[48] Flannery O'Connor, *The Complete Stories*, 245.
[49] Flannery O'Connor, *The Complete Stories*, 209.
[50] Flannery O'Connor, *The Complete Stories*, 245.

THE CATHOLIC VISION
AND PRACTICE OF TONI MORRISON:
MOMENT AND RITUAL IN *BELOVED*

CAROLYN MEDINE

In 1998, I attended the first Biennial Conference of the Toni Morrison society, "Toni Morrison and the American South."[1] Morrison, at that moment, had not spoken openly about her Catholicism. During the meeting, I overheard a conversation between two participants in which one said that "Toni" was not Morrison's birth name, that her real name was Chloe Ardelia. I thought, "Well, she must be Catholic, and Anthony is her confirmation name." Later, we all learned that St. Anthony of Padua is her patron. St. Anthony is the patron saint of lost things. Many of us invoke him in a child's prayer, "Tony, Tony, come (or look) around/Something's lost and must be found."[2] Though at my house, we generally beg St. Anthony to find our keys, the losses he assuages may be of lost people and lost matters in our lives—that is, of something that unsettles our "peace and tranquility of mind."[3] It seems logical to me that he is Morrison's patron: her work has

---

[1] Toni Morrison Society, "Programs,"
https://www.tonimorrisonsociety.org/conference.html.

[2] See, for example, Loyola Press Catholic Resources. Accessed July 31, 2020. https://www.loyolapress.com/catholic-resources/prayer/childrens-prayers/prayers-for-gods-care-and-guidance/oops-st-anthony-i-lost-something-childs-prayer/. The more "grown-up" version of this prayer is: "Dear St. Anthony, please come around: something is lost and it cannot be found." One longer prayer is:

> St. Anthony, perfect imitator of Jesus, who received from God the special power of restoring lost things, grant that I may find **[name the item]** which has been lost. At least restore to me peace and tranquility of mind, the loss of which has afflicted me even more than my material loss. To this favor, I ask another of you: that I may always remain in possession of the true good that is God. Let me rather lose all things than lose God, my supreme good. Let me never suffer the loss of my greatest treasure, eternal life with God. Amen

[3] Ibid.

been the search for those who are lost, the "Sixty Million and more"[4] of the Middle Passage and also what is lost in our understanding of African American life, particularly the life of enslaved women.

In this chapter, I will focus on two Catholic practices that characterize Morrison's work: the breaking into ordinary life of a power that transforms that life in what I call "moments" and her ritual sense, which encompasses rites of passage. These practices run throughout her oeuvre, but, here, I will discuss them in *Beloved*, which Nick Ripatrazone has called Morrison's most Catholic book, in his discussion of the body, another important trope, in the novel.[5]

Morrison's Catholicism became public knowledge in a 2003 in a *New Yorker* article, "Toni Morrison and the Ghosts in the House," by Hilton Als: "When she was twelve years old, Morrison converted to Catholicism, taking Anthony as her baptismal name, after St. Anthony. Her friends shortened it to Toni."[6] Morrison, in 2015, openly discussed her distance from the Church after Vatican II and the loss of the Latin mass, her aesthetic appreciation of Catholicism, and her recent reattraction to the Church led by Pope Francis.[7]

---

[4] Toni Morrison, *Beloved* (New York: Signet Books/Penguin, 1987), 2. Dedication. Henceforth, this volume will be cited parenthetically.
[5] Nadra Nittle, "The Ghosts of Toni Morrison: A Catholic Writer Confronts the Legacy of Slavery," *America: The Jesuit Review,* November 3, 2017. https://www.americamagazine.org/arts-culture/2017/11/03/ghosts-toni-morrison-catholic-writer-confronts-legacy-slavery.
[6] Hilton Als, "Toni Morrison and the Ghosts in the House," *The New Yorker*, October 27, 2003. https://www.newyorker.com/magazine/2003/10/27/ghosts-in-the-house. See also Ripatrazone, in "On the Paradoxes of Toni Morrison's Catholicism," that Morrison had Catholic family members, including one cousin. *Literary Hub*, March 2, 2020. https://lithub.com/on-the-paradoxes-of-toni-morrisons-catholicism/#:~:text =Toni%20Morrison%20converted%20to%20Catholicism,Anthony%20of%20Padu a.&text=She%20loved%20her%20mother's%20singing,the%20particular%20pray er%20of%20song.
[7] Ripatrazone, "On the Paradoxes of Toni Morrison's Catholicism." He talks about language, history and tradition in Morrison's work, and her focus on the body. He argues her Catholicism is one of the Passion. Nittle reviews some of the comments on Morrison's Catholicism.
Morrison told Terry Gross that she could be "easily seduced to go back to church," and she liked the "controversy as well as the beauty of this particular Pope." "He's very interesting to me," she said. "'I Regret Everything': Toni Morrison Looks Back on Her Personal Life." Fresh Air,20 April 20, 2015. https://www.npr.org/2015/08/24/434132724/i-regret-everything-toni-morrison-looks-back-on-her-personal-life.

Ripatrazone, assessing this, describes her as a lapsed Catholic "in practice," but, he continues, "she was culturally—and therefore socially, morally—Catholic."[8] M. Shawn Copeland, in "A Catholic Reading of the Spirituality in Toni Morrison's *Song of Solomon*," unpacks the cultural, social, and moral implications of Morrison's Catholicism strongly:

> Catholicism is, of course, a religion, yet, to put it radically, Catholicism is a spirituality. In other words, first and foremost, Catholicism is a way of life, a way of living, a way of being in and moving with and through the world. Thus, as a way of life, a way of living, Catholic spirituality enfleshes and sacralizes memory and word, mystery (sacrament) and materiality (sacramentals), community and communion. Moreover, this way of life and living extends the presence of the Word made Flesh through community and communion in and through and beyond time.[9]

Morrison, therefore, exercises a Catholic imagination, but a Black one, one that infuses her Catholicism with her identity.[10] She asks, "What would Catholic Studies"—and, indeed, the study of American history and literature, as she demonstrates in *Playing in the Dark*—look like if we, as Matthew Cressler puts it, "considered race, racism, and white supremacy as constitutive

---

[8] Ripatrazone, "On the Paradoxes of Toni Morrison's Catholicism." One facet of American Catholicism that the Pew Center found is that even if Catholics are not practicing—indeed, if they have chosen another religion, they still call themselves Catholic because they are "indelibly Catholic by culture, ancestry, ethnicity or family tradition." The Atlantic explores this phenomenon in Lincoln Mullen, "Catholics Who Aren't Catholic," *The Atlantic* September 8, 2015. https://www.theatlantic.com/politics/archive/2015/09/catholics-who-arent-catholic/404113/?gclid=Cj0KCQjwvb75BRD1ARIsAP6LcqsTfPzy-HSETJBtOz9L8uHqtY1ZeXQ51qdAtWlId79xBkqAZl9t6QsaAuTkEALw_wcB.

[9] M. Shawn Copeland, "A Catholic Reading of the Spirituality in Toni Morrison's *Song of Solomon, Church Life Journal* (17 March 2020). https://churchlifejournal.nd.edu/articles/a-catholic-reading-of-the-spirituality-in-toni-morrisons-song-of-solomon/.

[10] There is so much to say about this question. As Copeland points out, "Catholicism in the United States presents itself, almost exclusively, as the faith of European immigrants, thus, separate from or exterior to African American experience." While some slaves who came into the United States were Catholic, like those from the Kingdom of Kongo, Catholicism, before the influx of Irish immigrants, was implicated in the slave system. Maura Jane Farrelly, in "American Slavery, American Freedom, American Catholicism," *Early American Studies* No. 10 (Winter 2012): 69-100, that "the Church not only tolerated, but actually supported the institution of slavery" and actively opposed abolition.

categories for the study of U. S. Catholicism?"[11] And, if we asked how Black Catholic spirituality has negotiated these. Fr. Cyprian Davis argues that African American spirituality is grounded in hospitality emerging from a sense of community, the experience of prayer, the gift of holiness, and the place of the Word, of Scripture.[12] All these are put to work, as Brian Massingale writes, in a particular way for Black Catholic intellectuals in manifesting an ongoing concern for the legacy of slavery for church and society; in maintaining an organic connection to the faith community; in speaking truth to and within the Church as a means towards justice; in exhibiting a generosity of spirit towards racial adversaries—even in the Church; in maintain universalism, a broadly inclusive perspective; and, in exhibiting a concern for the ordinary, the absent, and the invisible as one witnesses to hope.[13]

This concern intersects with Morrison's Catholic practice as a writer. I see particular characteristics in the work of modern Catholic writers from Flannery O'Connor to Walker Percy to J. R. R. Tolkien to Toni Morrison. Here, I want to focus on two: moments, when a power enters the ordinary reality to transform it, revealing a larger reality and ritual, the ordered movement through time and space that transforms and recreates.

The Catholic imagination, I think, trusts in the inherent goodness of creation and that the material world can be enchanted, can reveal the divine. I see this in moments in which God's power enters—indeed, breaks into—everyday life, human history: moments like the Grandmother's recognition of the Misfit as her son or Walker Percy's car accident in The *Moviegoer*, or the sudden changes of fortune, which Tolkien calls eucatastrophe. This breaking in characterizes the monotheisms, which are religions of revelation, of God's intervention into and shaping of history. In Morrison's work, sheer beauty or a moment of radical insight by a character signal the presence of something Other, of power beyond our making, breaking into human space-time. These *Kairos* moments signal change. I will examine two here: the nephew's experience as he sees Sethe standing over her dead

---

[11] Matthew J. Cressler, "Forum: Race, White Supremacy, and the Making of American Catholicism: Introduction," *American Catholic Studies* No. 127 (Fall 2016): 1-5.
[12] Cyprian Davis, "Some Reflections on African American Catholic Spirituality," *U. S. Catholic Historian* No.19 (Spring 2001): 7-14.
[13] Bryan N. Massingale, "Cyprian Davis and the Black Catholic Intellectual Tradition," *U. S. Catholic Historian* No. 28 (Winter 2010): 76-80.

child and the spores in the birth of Denver in *Beloved*. These moments suggest, as Copeland's comments do, that the Catholic imagination lives here and now, working out salvation in the world and maintaining hope even in the face of our fallenness.

Second, the Catholic imagination is a ritual one, as I will suggest in looking at the rescue by the Thirty Women at the end of *Beloved*. Ritual and liturgy, bind us into a community. As the *Catechism of the Catholic Church* teaches, the whole community celebrates the liturgy: "Liturgy is an 'action' of the *whole Christ* (*Christus totus*). Those who even now celebrate it without signs are already in the heavenly liturgy, where celebration is wholly communion and feast" (1136).[14] Liturgy includes symbols and signs (1146) that teach us as we move through an ordered, sacramental act. While Morrison's characters may not have access to such order, they enter ritual space, created by the writer. John Randolph LeBlanc and I have written that, in ritual altered space of diaspora becomes "altared" space of potential healing.[15] Morrison turns our gaze to the site of fracture, slavery. Since slaves were only units of energy, many of the "Sixty Million and more" diasporic lives are erased. Morrison refuses this erasure, refuses to lose them, following in the sense of her patron, St. Anthony, any traces of those lost to tell their stories and, if possible, to bring them home.[16] Just as sacraments involve matter, form, and action, the writer uses these elements from her own life, acting as what Tolkien calls a sub-creator who creates a fictional world that mirrors Reality,[17] not for escape, but for engagement that takes the reader back into the ordinary world with a baptized imagination. Morrison, performs this work, bringing the matter of her African American life into the form of her work so that the reader's imagination can grasp what his or her reason may miss or deny.[18]

---

[14] *The Catechism of the Catholic Church* City of the Vatican: Libreria Editrice Vaticana, 1997. Paragraph 1135.

[15] John Randolph LeBlanc and Carolyn M. Jones Medine, *Ancient and Modern Politics: Negotiating Transitive Spaces and Hybrid Identities* (New York: Palgrave Macmillan, 2102), 128.

[16] Ibid., 129.

[17] J. R. R. Tolkien, "On Fairy Stories," in *Tree and Leaf* (London: HarperCollins, 2001).

[18] See, C. S. Lewis, *The Pilgrim's Regress*. 3rd. Edition (Eerdmans, 1943), 13.

God Breaking In: Transformative Moments in *Beloved*

One characteristic of Morrison's fiction is the sudden breaking through of insight or power into the ordinary world. Her work suggests that time and space are greater than we regularly acknowledge: the dead occupy the space with the living and interact with us. Baby Suggs says to Sethe, America is a haunted landscape: "'Not a house in the country ain't packed to its rafters with some dead Negro's grief'" (5). In *Beloved*, the house is haunted by the dead—and not just the dead baby girl. For Denver, for example, Baby Suggs as ancestor and saint helps to guide her life, telling her that Black life is a "'rout'" and that the only choice is to know that and to live (244).

While these hauntings and the world of whites surround black life, Morrison suggests there is more. In particular moments, in *Kairos* moments, there is a strong breaking through ordinary life and history—a bending down of God into the world, as St. Francis of Assisi saw it, or an interpenetration of realms or, as Karla F. C. Holloway, a criss-crossing of dimensions,[19] that, potentially, brings transformation to the character, but also brings clarity, of seeing the complex reality of Black life, to the reader. These moments are not always peaceful ones. As Richard Hardack wrote of violence in Morrison's *Jazz*, she "reenvisions the use of violence to oppose violence."[20] In our first example, we see violence potentially undoing violence, as Schoolteacher's nephew witnesses the scene of Beloved's death. In a more peaceful, but nevertheless charged moment, we experience the beautiful but complicated and dangerous moment of the birth of Denver.

Schoolteacher's Nephew

Sethe's murder of her daughter is the event that sets the plot of *Beloved* in motion. It is recounted about mid-way through the novel, acting as the pivot that ties the novel's action together. As Schoolteacher and the slave catchers enter the yard and, finally, the shed at 124, seeking to recapture Sethe and the children, they characterize the black people they encounter as animal and as mad. For example, they see Stamp Paid as a "crazy old nigger," and they think that Baby Suggs, who is "standing stock-still—but fanning her hands as though pushing cobwebs out of her way," is crazy too (149). When they see what Sethe has done, Schoolteacher characterizes her as an animal,

[19] Karla F. C. Holloway, "Beloved, A Spiritual," *Callaloo* 13.3 (Summer 1990): 521.
[20] Richard Hardack, "'A Music Seeking Its Words: Double-Timing and Double Consciousness in Toni Morrison's Jazz," *Black Warrior Review*. No.19 (1993): 160. 151-71.

made useless because she is "mishandled," severely beaten, by one of his nephews (150) who, because of his act, is not allowed on the "hunt" (150).

In a small, curious moment, however, the nephew who has been allowed to come (150), has a moment of compassionate horror. This is the nephew who "nursed" Sethe "while his brother held her down" (150). Hence, he is the cause of her deepest sense of violation, that they took her milk (17). This is the violation of her role as mother, and it is linked to Halle, who watches. Sethe learns from Paul D that, as Sethe is whipped and, I think, raped by the boys, that Halle, her husband, witnessed her violation and it "'broke'" him: he lost his mind (68-69), vanishing into Sweet Home's terrible vortex of suffering.

The nephew, seeing that Sethe has killed her child, is shaking, experiencing a "kind of confusion" (150) that lets him see Sethe as human—indeed, as one like himself--not just as an animal to be raped, nursed on, hunted, and captured. He thinks,

> What she go and do that for? On account of a beating? Hell, he'd been beat a million times and he was white…But no beating ever made him… I mean no way he could have…
>
> What she go and do that for? (150)

The nephew asks the sheriff this question, but he does not get an answer. The sheriff only tells Schoolteacher and his mob to go.

How might we read this moment? Like the Grandmother's confusion in *A Good Man is Hard to Find*, the nephew's confusion undoes the category of Sethe as animal and, even, as slave. He never calls her "nigger" or any other racist term in his musing. Instead, he recognizes that she, like him, has been beaten and seeks to know why the beating leads to death. He does not understand what she has done, but he understands that it is connected to a kind of pain beyond mere physical pain. He has experienced this. He tells us that he had been beaten so badly that it made him smash the well bucket and take it out on Samson, probably a dog. I would suggest that, in this moment, he aligns Sethe's action with his own and sees Sethe as human: he knows they both have been beaten viciously and that something, which he cannot define, has moved her to a level of violence he did not reach: one that makes her kill another human being. He sees the slaves not as "crazy niggers" or "creatures," but as people. This recognition makes him shake with emotion and, more importantly, wonder.

We do not know if this breaking in of power changes the nephew. He disappears from the narrative. But this moment of what another Catholic writer, Joseph Conrad calls "human fellow feeling" that opens up a "moment of vision" that contains all the truth of life[21]--an awareness of the whole. There are many such moments of realization in Morrison's work, as when Violet and Alice, in *Jazz,* for example, can laugh at themselves and realize that "laughter is more serious. More complicated, more serious than tears;"[22] or, when the Blacksmith tells Florens that she has become a slave by choice, that her head is empty and her body is wild—that she is "wilderness"— and that she is a slave to him.[23] That recognition, first, makes her violent, but, later, facilitates her writing her story as she sorts out what he means. These epiphanies, are, in religious terms, personal revelation, intuitive, clarifying grasps on reality that can alter the direction of a life,[24] but they also show us the intersectional reality of that life in the social, political, and cultural.

The Bluefern

A second, beautiful and significant, moment in *Beloved* is the birth of Denver. This is a moment fraught with danger for the two women, Sethe and Amy Denver, who bring this baby into the world. Both are women on the run for their freedom. Amy Denver is an indentured servant who finds herself sexually exploited and kept in bondage by Mr. Buddy who owns her papers. She is doing what her mother desired to do--heading to Boston, looking for velvet (80), something soft and rich. Like Sethe, Amy, with her "fugitive eyes" (78) is crossing the river to freedom. Amy Denver, like Sethe has been beaten, by Mr. Buddy's "'right evil hand'" (79) and she has been or is threatened with sexual violence. She is the one who names the Sethe's bloody back a chokecherry tree (79) and who touches her with her "good hands" (79), working on Sethe's back and feet, warning her that

---

[21] Joseph Conrad, *The Nigger of the Narcissus: A Tale of the Forecastle* (New York: Doubleday, Page and Company, 1897, 1914), 18.

[22] Toni Morrison, *Jazz* (New York: Penguin Books, 1992), 113.

[23] Toni Morrison, *A Mercy* (New York: Alfred A. Knopf, 2008), 150.

[24] Maya Angelou defines epiphany as "the occurrence when the mind, the body, the heart and the soul focus together and see an old thing in a new way." Quoted in Ellise Ballard, "How Do You, We, I Define Epiphany, Exactly?" *Psychology Today* (25 January 2011), https://www.psychologytoday.com/us/blog/epiphany/201101/how-do-you-we-i-define-epiphany-exactly.

"'Anything dead coming back to life hurts'" (35), a truth Sethe will experience in relation to Beloved.

When the baby comes, the women work together to bring her into the world, "appropriately and well" (83). Their full attention is on bringing this child into the world and caring for it so that the child may survive. As in the quotation that is sometimes attributed to St. Augustine and sometimes to St. Ignatius Loyola says, they are working like everything depends on them. Their work becomes prayer. They practice the presence of God, to use Brother Lawrence's phrase, and in a moment of faith working in love,[25] they love the neighbor. Thomas Merton writes, "There is no contradiction between action and contemplation when Christian apostolic activity is raised to the level of pure charity. On that level, action and contemplation are fused into one entity by the love of God and of our brother in Christ."[26] The work of these women signals a moment of the presence of the divine and of hope--they "thirst"[27] for freedom in a broken, fallen world that enslaves them. Each of these two women recognizes the dignity of the other—a dignity not recognized by the society that exploits them. As they work, the narrative voice steps back to ponder them and this moment:

> Spores of bluefern growing in the hollows along the riverbank float toward the water in silver-blue lines hard to see unless you are in or near them…Often they are mistook for insects—but they are seeds in which the whole generation sleeps confident of a future. And for a moment it is easy to believe each one has one—will become all of what is contained in the spore: will live out its days as planned. This moment of certainty lasts no longer than that; longer, perhaps than the spore itself (84).

The spores that surround them signal the "breaking in" of the divine into history or the bending down of God into this moment. Not all the spores will come to flower. But Denver will. In this passage, therefore, Morrison connects the baby—and, perhaps Sethe and Amy, as well--to the spores, reminding us that the promise of generations is tenuous, particularly for an indentured servant and a slave woman on the run and for a newborn baby.

There is a vertical dimension in this moment. The women wonder what God has in mind (79, 84), when a pregnant woman is so viciously beaten that her back is torn open to look like a tree. What does God have in mind in bringing

---

[25] Brother Lawrence, *The Practice of the Presence of God*, p.6, 8.
[26] Ibid., 93.
[27] Thomas Merton, *Contemplative Prayer* (New York: Image Books/Doubleday, 1969, 1996), p. 94.

them together in this charged moment? Denver, as Sethe tells Paul D, is a child of this promise, a "'charmed child'" (41). Denver is an incarnation, representing a transitional moment. Denver, born in the water, is born as baptized, in a sense: she is born free. She is, as I say when I teach the novel, the "Reconstruction baby," born into—and as we see at the end of the novel—and taking on the possibilities of freedom as she heads to college at Oberlin. Her name, Denver, is a memory of Amy Denver. Amy is concerned that the baby knows who helped bring her into the world. She tells Sethe, "'You better tell her...Miss Amy Denver. Of Boston'" (85), and Denver bears her name.

Amy's name—Denver—suggests frontiers, spaces of freedom that, of course, as American moves West, will become spaces of terror. But, Sethe has claimed this promise of freedom in bestowing this name on baby Denver. Morrison rewrites the notion of frontier here, giving it not just a sense of movement across space, horizontally from east to west, but a vertical sense as well. Denver's birth is a Kairos moment. She practices, the "Catholic incarnational and sacramental imagination"[28] which reads the "signs" of an animated world. As Toni Morrison said in an interview, "You have to be very still to understand these...signs, in addition to which they inform you about your own behavior."[29] The readers, encountering one moment of terror and one moment of promise, may be changed. These moments are symbols in the ritual movement of the novel. Ritual, in the sense that, for example, Victor Turner writes about it, are acts that create transformation, but, overseen by (male) ritual specialists, they reinforce the social. Morrison's reconstruction of ritual challenges the social for the purposes of affirming Black women's lives.

Rituals: Pride, Rememory and the Death of Beloved

Toni Morrison, in an interview on *Beloved*, pauses and muses about her work:

> There's so much to remember... For purposes of exorcism and purposes of rites... celebratory rites of passage... Things must be made...some fixing

---

[28] Anthony J. Godzieba, "Secretary's Report: The 63rd Annual Convention, CTSA Proceedings 63 (2008): 192.
[29] Charles Ruas, "Toni Morrison," in Danielle Taylor-Guthrie, *Conversations with Toni Morrison* (Jackson, MS: University Press of Mississippi, 1994), 100.

ceremony... some memorial... some thing... some altar... somewhere... where things can be released...thought and felt.[30]

One feature in her work, a feature that is characteristically Catholic, is her construction and use of ritual as healing for her characters. Morrison "affirms her attraction to, and fascination with, Catholic ritual" even as she has become distanced from the church.[31] From the Candomblé/Catholic/Indigenous ritual that Consolata creates for the wounded women in *Paradise*[32] to the "kitchen table" ritual of ironing and talking and the entry of Felice as a substitute for the murdered Dorcas in *Jazz*[33]—a substitute[34] that stops the violence that the narrator expects—Morrison constructs artistic repetitions that take us into the darkness of the American past to face the abject in order to break the tragic cycle of violation and nemesis. She makes repetitions that create.

Morrison takes Sethe from a life of emotional paralysis and stasis to a potential new beginning. Pride, that most deadly of the mortal sins, figures prominently in the death of Beloved. As I have written about this in another piece, Sethe's pride is the issue for the community, which also becomes prideful. Sethe compounds this sin of pride and alienation when Baby Suggs dies. The community will not enter the house, so Sethe refuses to go to the

---

[30] Toni Morrison, "Profile of A Writer," RM Arts Productions/Homevision, Released 2000.

[31] Nick Ripatrazone, *Longing for An Absent God: Faith and Doubt in Great American Fiction* (Minneapolis, MN: Fortress Press, 2020), 119-120.

[32] Toni Morrison, *Paradise* (New York: Vintage Books, 1997, 2014), 262-266. Consolata makes a ritual meal, and the women draw their own vèvè, working through issues in their lives. Vèvè are a feature of Vodun, also a mixture of indigenous and African religious elements and Catholicism. We see a mixture of practices in what the women do. For the syncretic nature of Candomblé, see Rachel Harding, *A Refuge in Thunder: Candomblé and Alternative Spaces of Blackness* (Bloomington: Indiana University Press, 2003), 38. Harding notes that "creole Catholicism and indigenous Brazilian (Indian) traditions were important elements of Bahian religiosity in the period of Candomblé's formation" (38).

[33] Toni Morrison, *Jazz* (New York: Penguin Books, 1993), 205ff. The narrator expects a second murder: "What turned out different was who shot whom" (6). But this does not happen. Felice becomes like a daughter to Violet and Joe, and she appreciates both of them so that they can begin to heal.

[34] I use this term recognizing Christ as substitute in atonement theory but not a penal substitution. One might also think of Emmanuel Levinas' sense that substitution is the core of the ethical encounter. Emmanuel Levinas, *Otherwise Than Being, Or Beyond Essence* trans. Alphonso Lingis (Pittsburgh, PA: Duquesne University Press, 1998), Chapter IV.

funeral. At the graveside, the community does not sing for Baby and to support Sethe, so Sethe does not eat their food, and they do not eat hers.[35]

The community became suspicious of Baby Suggs, particularly of the bounty bestowed in the celebration of Denver's birth. Baby Suggs, whose understanding of life is that good is knowing when to stop (87), a Greek understanding of "Nothing too much." Excess leads one not to know the self and its limits. The community sees that Baby has been excessive and that her power to multiply the blackberries is taking God's power, and it "made them furious" (137). Therefore, they do not warn the household that the slavecatchers are coming, participating in the death of the child (157). This leaves Sethe, when Beloved appears and becomes her sole obsession, trapped in the past and in the haunted house, unable to atone for her killing of the baby, and learning that the role by which she defined herself, mother, is deadly:

> The moment of recognition and reunion with the dead child, the destroyed fragment of a past self, is rapturous and satisfying. Yet it must remain a stepping stone and not the ground of existence.[36]

As Trudier Harris so aptly puts it, "If Sethe is to live, Beloved must depart."[37]

Denver begins to break this sin of pride when she goes in humility to the community, confessing that her mother is not well, and seeking support and food. Food arrives at 124, with the names of the women on their plates and pans (149), opening the way for Denver to continue the conversation and the reintegration of 124 into the group as she returns the containers. The community women begin to see that "the personal pride, the arrogant claim staked out at 124 seemed…to have run its course" (249).

Led by Ella, who has been the captive of two white men, a father and a son who shared her sexually and whom she calls "'the lowest yet'" (256), the

---

[35] Carolyn M. Jones [Medine], "Sula and Beloved: Images of Cain in the Novels of Toni Morrison," *African American Review* No. 27 (Winter 1993), 617.
[36] Barbara Offutt Mathieson, "Memory and Mother Love in Morrison's *Beloved*," *American Imago* No. 47 (Spring 1990), 14.
[37] Trudier Harris, "Beloved: Woman, Thy Name is Demon," in *Beloved: A Casebook*, ed. William L. Andrews and Nellie Y. McKay (New York: Oxford University Press, 1999), 137. Harris also gives a magnificent reading of what Beloved sees, which is her mother trying to save her.

women decide that they must mount a rescue for Sethe. Ella's fury turns to a kind of righteous anger and love:

> Whatever Sethe had done, Ella didn't like the idea of past errors taking possession of the present. Sethe's crime was staggering and her pride outstripped even that; but she could not countenance the possibility of sin moving on in the house, unleashed and sassy. Daily life took as much as she had. (256)

In a life in which "every day was a test and a trial" (256), and "invasion" of the world by an evil spirit is not acceptable. It constitutes an excess that has to be eliminated.

The Thirty Women approach 124 on Friday afternoon at three, the hour of the death of Jesus. Here, we see the syncretic nature of African American faith and a silent signaling of the depth and texture of this moment. Unsure of what they will need or do, they bring "what they could and what they believed would work" (257). They bring their mojo bags and wear their amulets. Some bring Christian faith. "Most brought a little of both" (257).

Entering the yard, the women are ritually transported to the original moment of wounding, the founding moment of this ritual: they see Baby Sugg's party. They see themselves "younger [,] stronger" (258) and happy. They smell the food. They see Baby Suggs moving among them, and they see their mothers. There is no envy, only celebration and love.

At 124, some pray. Ella does not. Instead, she engages in what Morrison calls "rememory." Just as Baby Sugg's celebration is "'[r]ight in the place where it happened'" (36) and can be reexperienced, the horror of slavery, as Sethe warns Denver, never dies either. This layered existence means that nothing ever dies. History is not past, and time is not linear. As Sethe tells Denver about Sweet Home:

> "Where I was before I came here, that place is real. It's never going away…and what's more, if you go there—you who never was there—if you go there and stand in the place where it was. It will happen again; it will be there for you, waiting for you." (36)[38]

Ella, stepping into a rememory, overlays/intersects 124 with her own past. She remembers her own enslavement, how she lost her bottom teeth, the

---

[38] Ashraf H. A. Rushdy, "'Rememory': Primal Scenes and Constructions in Toni Morrison's Novels," *Contemporary Literature* No. 31 (Autumn, 1990): 300-323, calls these "primal scenes."

beatings, and how she had delivered and let die a baby of the "'lowest yet'" (258-59). Sethe is not the only slave woman to kill a child or to let a child die. All this memory gathers in Ella, and she hollers—in rage and in resistance, at memory so traumatic that no words can contain it. But, when the women join her, something happens.

> took a step back to the beginning. In the beginning there were no words. In the beginning was the sound, and they all knew what that sound sounded like. (259)

This sound, like the spirit of God moving over the face of the waters, signals a creation.[39] It is a "the key, the code, the sound that broke the back of words" (261). They enter the origin, an arche.

At the same time, Edward Bodwin, the owner of the house and an abolitionist, rides toward the house. Again, a white man will enter the yard. Bodwin was born in 124; it surfaces in his dreams (261), and he remembers that it is a place where the women of his family died (259). Morrison signals a solidarity with women's pain here, across race. This house is haunted by women's spirits.

As Bodwin approaches the house, Sethe is breaking up a chunk of ice with an icepick, reminding us of Baby Suggs' having ice sent to 124 when Denver was born. Sethe hears the women and opens the door. What follows is a baptism of sound, one that returns her to Baby Suggs as well, as the Clearing in which Baby preached seems to come to her. The sound the women make, one so powerful that it is "wide enough to sound deep water and knock the pods off chestnut trees" (261), breaks over Sethe, opening a liminal space, a clearing.

When Beloved steps onto the porch, she is beautiful and pregnant and has vines of hair all over head, in what seems like an image of Medusa. As Satish Kumar suggests, in this image of a demonic spirit, the women see "history: the uncanny glory of the figure of the black woman in slavery."[40]

---

[39] See Lars Eckstein, "A Love Supreme: Jazzthetic Strategies in Toni Morrison's *Beloved*," *African American Review* No. 40 (Summer 2006), 271-283. Eckstein connects this passage to Morrison's statements that she wants her novels to be like African American music. Eckstein sees this passage as an "ironic subversion of John 1.1," one that emphasizes African American sound over English words: the sound breaks the back of words (271).

[40] S. Satish Kumar, *An Ethics of Empathy and An Aesthetics of Alterity: The Other and Otherness in the Study of Literature.* PhDdiss, University of Georgia, 2020.

They also see themselves as whites, particularly men, see them[41]: a captive body that is naked, black, pregnant and, to use the image from *Jazz* and *A Mercy*, "wild"—that is sexual with a "dazzling" smile that may be interpreted, in the old sense of the word, as overpowering and stupefying. If black women are just body, they cannot be raped and so welcome white men's sexual violence.

Sethe, seeing the white man enter her yard experiences the death of Beloved once again: "…he is coming for her best thing" (262). Instead of turning to kill her child, she runs, icepick in her hand, towards the white man. This time, she attacks the white master and not the child. Denver runs towards her mother and throws her to the ground, and the Thirty Women pile on them. This action, as I have suggested, honors Baby Suggs even as it saves Sethe and confirms that Denver is now a grown woman. Community is reestablished with Sethe, potentially, a part of it.

For Beloved, however, there is no place. She sees only the slave ship: the loss of her mother, the "man without skin," with a whip in his hand, looking at her (262). She runs away. If Beloved is, as many critics have argued, the spirit of slavery. As Karla F. C. Holloway so beautifully puts it, if Beloved is the slave past, Morrison does not let her die, but poses her as a "liminal 'text,'" a "confrontation of a killing history and a disabling present" in lives haunted by black death.[42] Hence, Beloved's is not a story "to pass on," in the sense that ordinary life has to go on, but hers is not a story to "pass on," in the Black sense of something that must be told (274). For the women, seeing themselves in Beloved, this image of the black woman as body—as producer who creates marketable product--has to be exorcised, and the problematic vanishing of Beloved signals that the ordinary life, beyond slavery, that Ella discusses cannot go on with this image in the house. But, this means existing in a paradox. As Baby Suggs tells Denver, know it and go on. Therefore, Beloved, the "disremembered and unaccounted for" is just the "wind in the eaves or spring ice thawing too quickly" (175). No one "clamoring for a kiss" is there; it is "just weather." But all know, simultaneously, that she is there: they "can touch her if they like, but don't, because they know things will never be the same if they do" (175), as they are for the nephew who touches Sethe's pain. Almost all Morrison's novels

---

[41] See, for example, the discussion in Mary Paniccia Carden's "Models of Memory and Romance: The Dual Endings of Toni Morrison's Beloved," *Twentieth Century Literature* No. 45 (Winter 1999), 401-427, particularly her discussion of Hortense Spillers's insights, pp. 403ff.
[42] Holloway, 522, 523.

signal that the ritual cycle continues. Beloved vanishes, therefore, but does not.   But there is a chance to begin again: the end of *Beloved* signals beginnings—though fragile for Sethe.[43]

As Martha Cutter puts it, Morrison resists closure, "the totalizing impulse of narrative and of readers themselves."[44] She brings back the character of Beloved—or seems to—in *Jazz*, Cutter notes, ripping "open the sutures a reader may have imposed over the ending of Beloved."[45] And, though *Paradise* had not been printed when Cutter wrote her article, Morrison does not allow the reader to rest in *Jazz* either. In *Jazz*, Morrison puts the story in the hands of the readers "through its awareness of a reader's need for closure and its simultaneous insistence that closure itself is a delusion," an impulse that must be deconstructed.[46] Cutter suggests that to close a story is to say that it can be forgotten, and Morrison will not let us forget the story of slavery that shapes the New World. And, in a Catholic sense, we, as pilgrims on earth, move through multiple cycles of rite of passage—both formal and personal.

Some Final Thoughts

Toni Morrison writes out of her Catholic tradition, but, as an African American writer, with duties that other Catholic writers might not carry. She described herself, in a *Washington Post* interview, as a "disaffected Catholic," but one "'sensitive to ghosts and spirits.'"[47] Nick Ripstrazone describes her as a lapsed Catholic: "not merely distanced from the institutional church, but open to an idiosyncratic theology, a set of beliefs

---

[43] Even in *Paradise*, the closing book in Morrison's trilogy with *Beloved* and *Jazz*, a new beginning for the New World is signaled, as a mother, Piedade, and daughter, Consolata, wait, finally reunited, for a ship to come to shore, signaling yet another beginning. This ship holds passengers who are seeking healing, and the beach they approach is littered with signs of occupation. This is a New World that is already occupied and a group of pilgrims already fallen. Toni Morrison, *Paradise* (New York: Vintage Books, 2014), 318.
[44] Martha J. Cutter, "The Story Must Go on and on: The Fantastic, Narration, and Intertextuality in Toni Morrison's Beloved and Jazz," *African American Review* No. 34 (Spring 2000): 61-62.
[45] Ibid.
[46] Ibid.
[47] Linton Weeks, "Toni Morrison, Pulling Readers Deeper," *The Washington Post* (15 November 2003). https://www.washingtonpost.com/archive/lifestyle/2003/11/15/toni-morrison-pulling-readers-deeper-and-deeper/a9e3c7c9-3057-4d3e-b7fd-ebb9d771cd0c/.

of her own making."[48] And he also writes that she expresses a "paradoxical Catholicism." I would argue that this description characterizes the religiosity of many African American women, as I have written about in the lives of Alice Walker and Jan Willis, and, perhaps, of many Catholics, as Catholicism is a global religion with numerous intercultural expressions.

Catholicism, as Morrison jokingly reveals to Cornel West as they discuss *The Passion of the Christ,* is a material religion. In her statement about the Crucifix in contrast to the Protestant cross, she says to West, "Now, you know, I'm a Catholic, right, so we're used to images of blood and gore."[49] This materiality—seeing a body on the cross—is both Catholic and black. Charles H. Long, for example, explains that Paul Tillich argues that Jesus became "transparent" so that the believer could see God. What a person of any color sees, in contrast, is the unavoidable opacity of human suffering.[50]

Materiality pervades the Catholic Church of Morrison's 1940's youth--a materiality, perhaps, being lost or missing in Catholicism today. As Robert Orsi put it in an interview, "The general trajectory of the modern world is to deny divine presence as a physical reality in the mundane world of everyday life." Practices, like sewing sequins on a saint's gown, offer a powerful encounter with sacred presence, a material encounter that, he says, might trouble a post-Vatican II Catholic. These practices locate Catholics in a varied world and cosmos:

> In communities that practice religion, you have aunts, uncles, fathers, mothers, siblings, but these people very often live in networks that also include sacred figures or demons or ancestors or ghosts or spirits, and people are in very complicated and intense relationships with them.[51]

Morrison's pre-Vatican II Catholicism, exhibited in *Beloved* and her other works, are located in this kind of cosmos, one occupied by the living and the dead, the divine and the human, and the chthonic—what we call the demonic—as well.

---

[48] Ripatrazone, *Longing for an Absent God: Faith and Doubt*, 119.
[49] Toni Morrison and Cornel West, "'We Better Do Something'" Toni Morrison and Cornel West in Conversation," *The Nation*, May 6, 2004. https://www.thenation.com/article/archive/toni-morrison-cornel-west-politics/.
[50] Charles H. Long, *Significations: Signs, Symbols, and Images in the Interpretation of Religion* (Aurora, CO: The Davies Group, 1995)*,* 207.
[51] "Don't Trash Our Past: An Interview with Robert Orsi on Devotions," U. S. Catholic, October 25, 2011. https://uscatholic.org/articles/201110/dont-trash-our-past-an-interview-with-robert-orsi-on-devotions/.

The moments and rituals that Morrison creates in her novels signal her Catholic sense that reality is big, textured and complicated. She holds together the African and the American—as well as the African with the Greek and Roman, in her love of the classics--to lead to a sense that past is rich and that past, present and future are, as Beloved puts it, "is now/it is always now" (211), and that, through rememory, we experience that charged, translucent, and complex haunted present. She recognizes that Black life is at the intersection of the political, the social, and the cultural, and that, in these metanarratives, it seems that definitions "belong…to the definers—not the defined" (190). Morrison opens ritual pathways for her characters so they can talk back in their own language, whether storytelling or black music or naming. An example is when she tells Cornel West how she brought her understanding of the crucifixion into Gibson's film. For her, the crucifixion was a lynching: "This is an innocent and betrayed man who's being lynched. I didn't want to look away. I wanted to endure it."[52]

Morrison makes us endure it. Beloved, in this sense, is not only a character, but a catalytic process that demands and facilitates storytelling, as Caroline Rody puts it, of that which is almost impossible to tell, the innarrable, indescribable traumatic events of slavery:

> witnessing the murder, torture, or sale of family and friends; being whipped, chained, led with an iron bit in the mouth, and housed in an underground "box," being examined and catalogued in terms of "human" and "animal" characteristics, or forcibly "nursed" by white boys when one's breasts held milk for a baby.[53]

All these are, in the slave narrative, Morrison argues, the "proceedings too terrible to relate."[54] Morrison lifts the veil so that these things, as the quotation with which we began the ritual section says, can be released, thought, and felt.

---

[52] Morrison and West.

[53] Caroline Rody, "Toni Morrison's Beloved: History, 'Rememory,' and a 'Clamor for a Kiss,'" *American Literary History* No. 7 (Spring 1995): 99-100.

[54] Toni Morrison, "The Site of Memory," in *Inventing the Truth: The Art and Craft of Memoir*, 2nd Edition, ed. William Zinsser (Boston: New York: Houghton Mifflin, 1995), 91.

The conscientious reader takes this journey as well, entering the matrix of understandings that Morrison deploys. Morrison loved Greek tragedy,[55] and her work structures catharsis for the reader. This experience, in the American context of slavery, is painful and necessary. Tragedy shakes us profoundly even as we grasp its significance. In the work of the artist, like Morrison's, we are led to a moment in which something is made clear for us: we see "how it all hangs together."[56] Only in returning to the original sin of America, the original site of injury can we see "how it all hangs together, and atone and heal.

In *Beloved*, on which we have focused here, Morrison explores the unique nature of North American slavery and its violent aftermath. That terrain is that of the Black Catholic in America as one who is immersed in the ongoing struggle for equality, as this present historical moment shows us. The Church was part of these struggles, on both sides. Black Catholicism involves a practice that seeks justice, that works towards freedom and equality for African American peoples. And Toni Morrison's art, in its "breathtaking fusions of form and substance,"[57] is a moral fiction that generates a ritual mode in which, if we take it, we can as Paul D and Sethe are poised to do, put our stories next to each other's and, as Sixo says of the Thirty-Mile Woman, be friends of each other's minds, gathering "[t]he pieces [we are]… and [giving] them back… in all the right order" (272-73), generating moments that let us see, that help us to recover and face what is lost and, potentially, to make a new, more just and humane, world.

[55] See Tessa Roynon, *Toni Morrison and the Classical Tradition* (Oxford: Oxford University Press, 2013).

[56] See Eva Schaper, "Aristotle's Catharsis and Aesthetic Pleasure," *The Philosophical Quarterly* No. 18. (April 1968): 131-143.

[57] Laura Miller, "Toni Morrison Reshaped the Landscape of Literature," *Slate,* August 6, 2019). https://slate.com/culture/2019/08/toni-morrison-american-literature-faulkner-style.html.

CONTRIBUTORS

Rev Dr Mark Bosco, S.J., is Vice President for Mission and Ministry at Georgetown University, USA and a Professorial Lecturer in the Department of English. A native of St. Louis, Missouri, Fr. Bosco joined Georgetown after fourteen years at Loyola University, Chicago, where he was a tenured faculty member with a joint appointment in the Departments of Theology and English. He was also Director of Loyola's Hank Centre for Catholic Intellectual Heritage from 2012-2017. He has a particular research interest in religion and literature and has published widely in this field.
Email: mark.bosco@georgetown.edu

Dr Emilio Castaño is a lecturer in English at Shandong University, China. He has a research interest in Literature and Catholicism, especially 20th century Spanish drama and the revival of the *auto sacramentales* in Spanish theatre. He completed a doctorate in Spain and now works in China.
Email: telemilio@yahoo.es

Dr David Deavel is Assistant Professor, Catholic Studies at St. Thomas University, Minnesota, USA as well as editor of *Logos: A Journal of Catholic Thought and Culture* and co-director of the Terrence J. Murphy Institute of Catholic Thought, Law and Public Policy. He is co-editor of *Solzhenitsyn and American Culture* (Notre Dame, 2020) and has published widely in academic, public and popular journals. His research interests include: John Henry Newman, G. K. Chesterton, English Catholic Literary Revival Literature, Catholic Thought and Political Philosophy.
Email: DPDEAVEL@stthomas.edu

Dr Daniel Frampton is an independent scholar working in England. His research interests include English Catholic intellectual and artistic culture in the twentieth century, the Inklings, the Catholic literary revival, theology and modernism. Most recently, his written work has focused on the Catholic author G. K. Chesterton, the poet Roy Campbell and the artist Graham Sutherland, emphasizing in particular the theology of death and the interplay between lived Catholicism, mortality and the arts. He has published in various journals, including the *Chesterton Review* and *Logos: A Journal of Catholic Thought and Culture*; and contributed a chapter to the

first volume of *Literature and Catholicism in the 19th and 20th Centuries* (CSP, 2021).
Email: daniel.de.frampton@gmail.com

Rev Dr Michael Kirwan S J., Assistant Professor, School of Religion, Trinity College, Dublin, Ireland. He is the author of *Girard and Theology* (T&T Clark / Continuum, 2009), *Political Theology: a New Introduction* (Darton Longman & Todd, 2008) and *Discovering Girard (*Darton, Longman and Todd, 2004). His research interests include the French cultural theorist René Girard and the implications of his 'mimetic theory' of religion, culture and violence, contemporary political theology, the public role of religion, theology and literature and Jesuit spiritual reflection in a globalising world.
Email: kirwanm6@tcd.ie

Dr Carolyn Medine is Professor of Religion and Director of the Institute of African American Studies, University of Georgia, USA. Her research interests are in Arts, Literature, and Religion, particularly in Southern and African American women's religious experience. She has written extensively on Toni Morrison, Harper Lee, and others. Dr. Medine's research interests also include religion and politics, theory from the classical to the postmodern, and the intersection of classical and modern literature. She is a graduate of the University of Virginia and teaches courses on Religion and Literature, African American Religions and Literatures, Religious Theory and Thought, and Women's Spirituality and Writings.
Email: medine@uga.edu

Dr Michael Murphy is Director of the Hank Centre for Catholic Intellectual Heritage, Loyola University, Chicago. He earned his doctorate in Theology, Literature, and Philosophy from the Graduate Theological Union, Berkeley, an MA in English from San Francisco State University, and undergraduate degrees in English and Great Books from the University of San Francisco. His research interests are in Theology and Literature, Sacramental Theology, and the socio-political cultures of Catholicism; but he also writes about issues in eco-theology and social ethics. He is a National Endowment for the Humanities Fellow and his first book, *A Theology of Criticism* (Oxford), was named a "Distinguished Publication" in 2008 by the American Academy of Religion. His most recent academic piece is the theological introduction to Robert Hugh Benson's 1907 dystopian classic *Lord of the World* (Ave Maria, 2016).
Email: mmurphy23@luc.edu

Dr Terry Phillips, Liverpool Hope University, UK is an Honorary Senior Research Fellow. Her research interests are in the areas of Irish literature and conflict literature, in particular the literature of the First World War. She is the author of *Irish Literature and the First World War: Culture Identity and Memory* (Peter Lang, 2015). Other publications include 'The City of the Farset: Portrayals of Belfast in Three Novels by Glenn Patterson' in *Irish Urban Fictions* eds Beville and Flynn (Palgrave Macmillan, 2018) and 'Out on a Great Adventure: The Travels of Patrick MacGill' in *Voyages Between France and Ireland* eds Healy and Bastiat (Peter Lang, 2017). Email: PHILLIM@hope.ac.uk

Dr Adam Schwartz, Christendom College, USA is Professor of History at Christendom College. His chief research and teaching interests are in the Catholic literary revival and the Inklings. He has published widely in those fields, most notably in *The Third Spring: G. K. Chesterton, Graham Greene, Christopher Dawson, and David Jones* (The Catholic University of American Press, 2005).
Email: ajmschwartz@yahoo.com

Dr David Torevell is an Honorary Senior Research Fellow at Liverpool Hope University, UK and Visiting Professor at Mary Immaculate College, University of Limerick, Ireland. He taught in Catholic secondary schools before entering Higher Education in 1992. He was previously *Honorary Research Fellow* at Leeds Trinity University, UK. He is the author of *Losing the Sacred: Ritual, Modernity and Liturgical Reform* (Edinburgh: T&T Clark, 2000) and *Liturgy and the Beauty of the Unknown: Another Place* (Aldershot: Ashgate, 2007). He has edited many books and published numerous articles in international journals on a range of theological, philosophical and educational issues. His research interests include Catholic theology, theology and literature, theology and the arts, sport and religion and Catholic education.
Email: david.torevell@outlook.com